THE ASPEN IDEA

University of Oklahoma Press
Norman

THE
ASPEN
IDEA

by Sidney Hyman

with photographs by
FERENC BERKO

Library of Congress Cataloging in Publication Data

Hyman, Sidney.
  The Aspen idea.

  Includes index.
  1. Aspen Institute for Humanistic Studies.
I. Title.
L13.A643H95   061'.3   75-25133
ISBN 0-8061-1306-5

TO MY SONS
DAVID AND JOSHUA

PREFACE

The body of this book conforms to the general rule which commands a historian to call attention to his subject, and not to himself. That general rule, however, does not apply to a preface—a kind of surrogate court of equity—where the individual historian may use the confessional word "I" to explain why and how he undertook to do what he did.

Within the space of this preface, then, I want to comment on three points which may alert the reader to what he can expect. I want to comment on the conception of this book, the materials used, and how the original object changed in the months that passed between gestation and birth.

This book was conceived through a mating of two considerations. One was the impending twenty-fifth birthday of the Aspen Institute for Humanistic Studies. The other was de Tocqueville's classic observation about the American genius for private associations:

Americans of all ages, all conditions, and all dispositions constantly form associations. They have not only commercial and manufacturing companies, in which all take part, but associations of a thousand other kinds, religious, serious, futile, general or restricted, enormous or diminutive. The Americans make association to give entertainments, to found seminaries, to build inns, to construct churches, to diffuse books, to send missionaries to the Antipodes; in this manner they found hospitals, prisons, and schools. . . . Wherever at the head of some new undertaking you see the government in France, or a man of rank in England, in the United States you will be sure to find an association. . . .

Nothing, in my opinion, is more deserving of our attention than the intellectual and moral associations of America. The political and industrial associations of that country strike us forcibly; but the others elude our observation, or if we discover them, we understand them imperfectly because we have hardly ever seen anything of the kind.

As a private association, the Aspen Institute was not formed to give entertainments, to build inns, to send missionaries to the Antipodes, to found hospitals, prisons, and schools. It is deserving of attention precisely because, among the great variety of private associations, "we have hardly ever seen anything of the kind." So, since history, like music, can be written for "an occasion," the impending twenty-fifth birthday of the Aspen Institute seemed a proper occasion to study it and tell its story. In doing so, I proposed to focus on the individuals who founded and refounded the Institute, their motives, how they tried to bridge the gap between the ideal and the real, and the extent to which their actions had public consequences.

In a meeting of extremes, however, the material available for use in telling the story altered the character of my initial purpose. On the one side, the literary remains bearing on the early days of the Institute were sketchy in the extreme. Whether or not the founding generation expected the Institute to live beyond their own day, they did not "keep records" out of which one could reconstruct their experiences. The story of who did what, when, how, and why could only be pieced together from the fading memories of the surviving founders.

On the other side, however, the abundance of material dating from 1969, when the direction of the Institute passed fully into the hands of a refounding generation, far exceeded the limit for the initial purpose I had in view. Indeed, the original target date of publication, 1974—the anniversary year—could not be met, since in that same year four major new programs of the Institute were formally launched. In any case, the post–1969 material led to an irrepressible new conception of the book. It was to use the Aspen Institute as a proscenium arch framing a stage for a drama of ideas about sets of salient issues that now besiege societies the world over.

There are, of course, many other places where the problems of common humanity are examined or debated, or that inspire proposed responses in the realm of practical action. The process goes forward ceaselessly in universities, in government offices, in the press, in international agencies, in the great philanthropic foundations, in the churches, in the highest reaches of business and labor, and so on. Yet the nonbureaucratic nature of the Aspen Institute—its drive to cut through the barriers which specialists tend to raise around their enclaves of knowledge—provides a context in which the major concerns of our time can be more clearly seen and the debates over them listened to. With all this in mind, my revised purpose was to reconstruct some of the acts and scenes in the drama of ideas that unfolded on the Aspen stage.

Many difficulties of exposition still remain, but the book I have tried to write concerns the genesis of the Aspen idea and how it has evolved and expanded. I begin with the Aspen Institute in its infancy; look at the way the outside world was reflected in the unformed mirror of its mind; consider its first gestures; listen to the first words it utters; and notice its early struggles to endure. With all this set in place, the book then evolves into an analytical report of a significant segment of contemporary intellectual history.

One more thing remains to be said. I share the view of my friend Professor Richard W. B. Lewis of Yale, who observed in *The American Adam* that every maturing culture produces its own distinctive debate over the ideas that preoccupy it. The debate, in fact, can be said to *be* the culture, at least on its loftiest levels. It is so because a culture achieves identity not so much through the ascendancy of one particular set of convictions as through the emergence of its pairs of opposed terms, which, by their very opposition, carry a discourse forward. It is for the reader to judge the extent to which the Aspen Institute has carried such a discourse forward.

SIDNEY HYMAN

Chicago, Illinois
October 1, 1975

CONTENTS

ILLUSTRATIONS

PART I: **Pre-History**

1. THE LAW OF SURPRISE

I

A plan framed in the spring of 1948 by three men who lived in Chicago concerned a one-time event scheduled for three weeks in the summer of the next year. At that time, if all went well, an international convocation would be held in Aspen, Colorado, to celebrate the bicentennial of the birth of Johann Wolfgang von Goethe. No sequel was planned. The first law of life, however, is the law of surprise, and the writ of the law began to take hold in Aspen after the Goethe convocation was over.

One of the three Chicagoans was Guiseppe Antonio Borgese, professor emeritus of Italian literature in the University of Chicago, former professor of German literature in the University of Milan, editor of *Common Cause*, and son-in-law of Thomas Mann. The second, Robert M. Hutchins, had already served for nineteen years as president of the University of Chicago, and was still in the thick of his long battle to restructure American higher education. But since V–J Day, he had also been trying to arouse a world public to the imperatives of the Atomic Age that had been born in the University of Chicago's metallurgical laboratories.

Walter Paul Paepcke, the third figure among these Chicagoans, was the founder and head of the Container Corporation of America, a trustee of the University of Chicago, a trustee of the Chicago Orchestral Association, a trustee of the Art Institute of Chicago, and the main patron of the Chicago Institute of Design. Since 1945, he had also been engaged in converting snow into silver on the site of the old mining town of Aspen, Colorado.

When the plan for a Goethe celebration in Aspen was made known, skeptics compressed their reactions into taunting questions they both asked and answered. Among Americans in the mass, for example, how many had ever heard of Goethe? Probably not more than 5 per cent. How many could pronounce his name correctly? Most, no doubt, would pronounce it "Gouty" as in James Joyce's *Finnegan's Wake*, where the Triumvirate sitting on the throne of European literature were identified as Daunty, Shopkeeper, and Gouty.

More to the point, why should anyone alive attach any importance to the long-dead figure of Goethe? Half of his life (1749–1832) had been lived before the French Revolution. What could he possibly say that would have any meaning to mid-twentieth-century people who were being swept by an accelerating scientific and technological revolution, and who were simultaneously struggling to sort out the tangled legacies of World War II—social, economic, political, cultural, and military? In any case, why hold an international convocation in Aspen, a dot that could be found on the map only with the aid of a magnifying glass? If sentimentalists and antiquarians wished to salute Goethe's memory, let them lay a wreath before his bust in a library nook. Why invite "the world" to do so in a remote valley somewhere on the west slope of the Continental Divide?

Borgese, Hutchins, and Paepcke were not shaken by the thrust of these pointed questions. Their replies, however, were confined to the worth of the one event they had in view. None expected the Goethe convocation to be the prologue to the founding of a new institution on American soil. Much less could they imagine a future time when a succeeding generation, led by Robert O. Anderson and Joseph E. Slater, would create the structure for today's international Aspen Institute for Humanistic Studies—international in its governance, in the nature and scope of its programs, in the identity of the men and women who participate in its programs, in the creation of Aspen Institute Berlin, and in its partnerships with other institutions, private and public.

II

Genetic ideas are like seeds which travel invisibly on the wind and take root on soil far removed from their point of origin; the passing years alone can reveal what the days hide about their path and potentialities. So, too, in this case. It is only now that one can see the connections between aspects of the national and world picture in the spring of 1948, when the Goethe bicentennial was conceived and the events that followed—the bicentennial itself, the birth of the Aspen Institute, and the subsequent evolution in the Institute's form and work. The paramount object of this book is to tell that evolutionary story up to 1975.

In prologue to the main narrative, however, two things must be mentioned here. The first rises from the fact that the Aspen Institute today, despite its many current activities, can lay no claim to physical bigness. Placed alongside other institutions which have a high visibility on the national and international horizon, it is small scale in all of its measurable aspects—in its permanent staff, in its budget, in its brick-and-mortar plant. Why, then, should it attract the attention of a storyteller and of a reader? The full answer to the question will unfold in the following pages, but the nature of the answer can be conveyed through the device of contrast:

The Institute is not something like the business-oriented Committee for Economic Development, nor is it a degree-granting college or university. Yet through its Executive Seminars, it has significantly advanced the humanistic education of emergent or established business leaders—four thousand to date. At the same time, though it is not a degree-granting institution, the men and women who participate in the Institute's special conferences, in its Artists-and-Scholars-in-Residence programs, and in its seven on-going "thought leading to action" programs, could comprise among themselves a distinguished faculty for a major international institution of higher learning. One example will suffice. When Sir Alan Bullock retired as vice-chancellor of the University of Oxford, he declined an invitation to head the British Broadcasting Corporation, choosing instead to devote himself to the affairs of the Aspen Institute, of which he is both a trustee and a fellow.

The Aspen Institute is not an organization like the RAND Corporation or the Hudson Institute. That is to say, it is not a research center taking its bent from contracts with public agencies, national or international. The Aspen Institute defines its own tasks, and proceeds with them in its own way. Yet its work as an "early warning system"—in spotting emerging problems, in examining them from different perspectives, and in formulating alternative responses to them—has been increasingly valued by policy-makers and political executives in the United States government, in foreign governments, and in international agencies.

The Institute is not just a conference center offering its physical facilities to any random group of people in need of a meeting place. Nor is it like a foundation which grants funds in support of work done by others. Yet its own conferences and workshops, embracing participants from many different disciplines, have pinpointed cardinal problems of contemporary life that are, by nature, transnational, transregional, and transsocietal. Moreover, the innovative ways it has used funds from private and public sources to support its own ventures or joint ventures with other institutions suggest procedures that lend themselves to adaptation by financially hard-pressed agencies in the wide world of philanthropy.

Although the Aspen Institute has a headquarters in New York City, an identifiable physical home in Aspen, another in West Berlin, and still another in prospect in Hawaii, it is not territorially anchored to any tract of soil. Fully half of its work goes forward the year around in places other than Aspen—a fact vivified by the headquarters location of the directors of the Institute's seven "thought leading to action" programs. For example, while Washington, D.C., is the year-around base for the director of the program on The Environment and the Quality of Life, the director for the program on Communications and Society is based in Palo Alto, California. In the case of the program on Science, Technology, and Humanism, the director is based in Boulder, Colorado, while the one for the program on Justice, Society, and the Individual is based in New York City. At the same time, the director for the program on Education for a Changing Society is based in Boston, and the one for the program on International Affairs is in Princeton, New Jersey.

Each program brings its participants together throughout the year in order to advance the tasks at the immediate focus of attention. Many of the same participants then converge on Aspen itself during the summer months for highly concentrated work. Through this arrangement, the Institute—despite its geographical dispersion—conducts its operations in coherent fashion.

In a more fundamental sense, however, the Institute takes its unity from an idea and a commitment shared by the participants in its inner life, regardless of the city, nation, or continent where they otherwise make their home. The idea is, that any salient problem of contemporary human existence now shares a common frontier or merges with every other salient problem, and that any solutions framed for a particular problem must take into account its linkages to the rest. The commitment is to all the meanings packed into the strategic word "humanistic"—to search for ways in which "man," in Martin Buber's phrase, "can reach for the divine, not by reaching above the human, but by striving to become, in all that he does, more human."

Since the story to be told in these pages is in large part the story of "cultural pluralism"—since it deals with the interactions among diverse individuals, ideas, and institutions—it is haunted by a difficulty central to any cultural history: the difficulty of establishing direct cause-and-effect relationships. Not everything said, heard, or written has an extendible consequence. Not every gesture issuing from a statesman, a scientist, an educator, or man of letters has behind it the growing root for a new truth. How, then, is one to prove that because *this* conference was held, *this* paper was published, *this* person engaged another in an exchange of views, the direct consequences were thus and so? How is one to prove that *only* because things in immediate view intervened in the flow of life, subsequent events happened as they did?

In some instances—to be identified later—direct connections can be shown between what the Aspen Institute initiated and the events that followed in the public realm. But it must be admitted that in other instances such connections cannot be established in ways free of doubt. Mental and moral sensibilities, like the movements of time, work their effects slowly and quietly, with no clearly defined lines marking off stages that have been reached, with no thunderstorms or trumpets to announce either the onset of a new mental and moral order or the decay of a pre-existing one. Still, as one open spirit touches another and both touch a third, the future somehow enters into each, and all together add their force to the reshaping of the mental and moral life of an epoch. In this view, it can be claimed that the Aspen Institute nurtured and promoted the creative impulses of the human spirit. Its contributions to this process started with the Goethe bicentennial.

2. TRIPLE PLAY

I

In the idiom of baseball, it was a triple play. Professor Borgese first suggested to Robert M. Hutchins that the University of Chicago should bring leaders of thought from around the world to celebrate on the University of Chicago campus the bicentennial of Goethe's birth. To do so would be in line with a program initiated after V–J Day by Borgese and his colleague, Arnold Bergstrasser, in which University of Chicago professors were urged to accept teaching assignments at the Goethe University in Frankfurt in order to help revive German intellectual life. Hutchins, with his own interests in bringing Germany back into the world intellectual community, was intrigued by Borgese's proposal. More, he discussed the financial aspects of the matter with Walter Paepcke.

Paepcke was also receptive to the proposal, but modified it in two respects. The intellectual aspects of the celebration should go hand-in-hand with a music festival, and the affair should be held not in Chicago but in Aspen, Colorado, far away from any urban center. He would do what he could to cover part of the costs, but the main burden of raising the necessary money would fall to Hutchins, since the latter, as the head of a large privately endowed university, had much experience as a fund-raising "professional beggar."

II

Professor Borgese, who had come to the United States as an anti-Fascist refugee from Mussolini's Italy, joined the University of Chicago faculty in the mid-1930's. To the general reading public, he was best known for his book *Goliath*, which traced the rise of Italian Fascism in the cultural context of an Italy whose outlook had been shaped by an inherited cross-tension between the aims and values of Dante and those of Machiavelli. The book itself bore witness to the fact that he was no cloistered scholar but was very much of the political world. Yet his specifically scholarly pursuits were not confined to Italian thought and action alone. Formerly professor of German literature in the University of Milan, he had a consuming interest in the interplay of German culture in the north of Europe with that of Italy in the south, which led him to focus his attention on the titanic figure of Goethe—and to engage him in a protracted mystic conversation.

They had much to talk over in prewar years. They had even more to talk over in the aftermath of World War II, brought on by men who were the antithesis of everything Goethe was and did. Although Goethe spent most of his life in the tiny principality of Weimar—a town of six thousand—his world not only included all men of all continents, but also extended backward through recorded time and forward millions of years to the day when, as he thought in his more pessimistic moments, God might be required to smash His creation to bits as the only means of rejuvenating the human race. He was himself many things in the course of a long life which ended in 1832 when he was eighty-two, just six months after he finished the second part of *Faust*. In his youth, for example, he had experienced the Romantic sickness, and came to know it as something which brought him to the verge of suicide, despair, and madness. Yet unlike the suicidal Romantics who later gathered around an Adolph Hitler, Goethe's despair proved the force that eventually gave him such power of self-control— especially after his Italian journey in 1786–88, when he was directly exposed to the artistic and literary remains of the ancient classical ideal and fell in love with them.

The Romantic of the pre-Italian journey returned from it transformed. He ceased to be driven before the gales of *Sturm und Drang*, with their devils and witches and temptations. He banished all these from his being and surrounded himself instead with objective forces. "All eras in a state of decline and dissolution are subjective," he observed to Eckermann. "On the other hand, all progressive eras have an objective tendency. Our present time is retrograde, for it is subjective. . . . Every healthy effort, on the contrary, is directed from the inward to the outer world."

Freedom for Goethe was self-mastery; the object of organized society was freedom, and whatever liberated the spirit without giving us mastery over ourselves was destructive. "Let a man but declare himself free," said he, "straightaway he will feel himself limited. But let him be bold enough to declare himself limited, and he will experience a sense of freedom." This sense of limitation, however, did not imply for him a willful lapse into obscurantism. "Man," said he, "must cling to the belief that the incomprehensible is comprehensible. Else he would give up investigating." And again: "Man was not born to solve the problems of the universe, but rather to seek to lay bare the heart of the problem and then confine himself within the limits of what is amenable to understanding."

Besides being a poet, dramatist, and critic, Goethe was also Minister of State at the court of the Duke of Weimar. His personal life was full of deeply ironic sensual adventures. Yet in the public realm he was an able administrator who "balanced the budget" of the Duchy of Weimar and brought energy and foresight to his duties in connection with agriculture, horticulture, and mining— all vital to the welfare of the Duchy. These matters in turn led to his sustained preoccupation with the natural sciences. He worked out a scientific theory of colors and vision, discovered the intermaxillary bone in man, established an evolutionary outlook fully seventy years before Darwin, and was such a skilled geologist that he could describe in detail the topology of far-off sites he had never seen, such as Philadelphia or Boston.

Just as Goethe made all facets of his life a harmony of mind and body, of imagination and precept, of power and responsibility, his philosophy of life synthesized the natural sciences and humanistic studies. Undogmatic, religious in essence, related to the great heritage of Greek, Christian, and Renaissance thought, he looked to that humanistic heritage and to the sciences for the metaphors which illuminate the underlying unity of everything. "All things,"

11

said he, in an expression of his most basic conviction, "weave themselves into a whole."

Since Goethe placed his faith in the spirit of man, his first concern was with the means of enlightening, uplifting, and releasing that spirit. He was repelled by the rising industrial system of his day because it was anonymous, impersonal, and non-human. In Goethe's view, no man could be said to lead a human life who was caught in the economic machine, with no control over his own destiny, unable to identify the products of his own labor, with no opportunity to make the most of his individual self, and with no motive to make his thought intelligible to his neighbors.

To Goethe, the basis of the human community was communication. Decades before other people dreamed of the projects, he spoke of a Panama Canal, a Suez Canal, and a canal between the Rhine and the Danube, as the means by which the human community might expand and grow through communication. So, too, with Goethe's conception of a world literature. It would not be a tower of Babel, but would amount to the global circulation of anything that might ennoble mankind. What he wanted, said he, was "the union of groups of good mental standards which hitherto had little contact with each other, the recognition of one common purpose, the conviction of the necessity to keep informed about the current course of world events, in the real and the ideal sense." It was not necessary for everyone to agree with everyone else. "The question to ask," said Goethe, "is not whether we are perfectly agreed, but whether we are proceeding from a common basis of sentiment."

The monumental core of Goethe's literary work and the crowning achievement into which he poured all his genius was *Faust*, a drama of human destiny. The first part reflected his concern with the daemonic forces he saw at work in human lives and in human history. The second part reflected the distance he had traveled from the depths of his youthful despair. As in his own case, a calm optimism, a faith in man's divine ability to live a constructive personal and communal life, pervaded the second part, where he achieved a spiritual unity of Hellenic, medieval, and modern elements of civilization. The two parts, taken together, tell how Faust, in his unceasing search for the essence of existence, despairs of knowledge. He seeks the help of the incarnation of evil, concludes his pact with Satan, pursues his goal through passion and action, and traverses the entire universe from Heaven to Hell and back to Heaven again. As the embodiment of the eternal striving, failure, and redemption of man, he attains in the end the vision of a Moses when he sees a Promised Land in which he hopes to live with a free people on a free soil.

So much is packed into *Faust* that it was not until the third decade of the twentieth century that interpretations of the work began to appear which commended themselves to scholars. And among these, Professor Borgese's was widely acknowledged to be one of the most impressive.

Professor Borgese knew that it would be false to say that all things brought together under the proper name "Goethe" squared at every point with the concerns of men in the years immediately after World War II. Some were anachronistic, and to insist that they were not would be to corrupt the integrity of words themselves. Yet he was convinced that the main bent of Goethe's life and work—and his spirit above all—contained meanings as fresh and contemporary as any headline in the morning newspaper. In place of despair, Goethe offered hope. In place of violence, he offered self-discipline. In place of reactionary dogmas, he offered a vision of human progress. In place of obscurantism, he offered sustained inquiry. In place of fragmentation of effort, he offered a concert of hands. In place of man as a tool of production, he offered a vision of man as an end in himself. In place of huddled totalitarian conformity, he offered creative diversity. In place of walls and moats raised to isolate one mind from the next, he offered an open road to communion among human beings.

On all these grounds, Borgese made his approach to Hutchins. The two men had worked closely not only in arranging the contacts between the University of Chicago and the Goethe University in Frankfurt, but also in connection with the Committee to Frame a World Constitution. Borgese reminded Hutchins that

1949 would be the bicentennial of Goethe's birth, and that however much scholars elsewhere disagreed on other Germanic things, they agreed on the transnational genius of Goethe. Hence, to further the work of bringing Germany back into the world intellectual community, the University of Chicago should be the scene of a world-wide convocation of scholars and men of letters gathered not for antiquarian or for sentimental purposes on the occasion of the Goethe bicentennial, but to use Goethe's life and work as points of departure for analytical discussions about the state of the contemporary world and the human condition in it.

III

Robert M. Hutchins, at the age of eighteen, had dropped out of Oberlin College to volunteer for service in the American army during World War I. He was stationed in Italy, and the only book he had in his barracks bag was the first volume of the Witkowski edition of *Faust*. "I memorized long passages while I was on guard duty," he later recalled, "reciting the language of the enemy while in the midst of my sleeping compatriots."

After the war, he entered Yale as a transfer student, graduated from its college as the Class Orator, continued on in the Law School, and became the youngest dean in its history. Then, in 1929, at the age of thirty, he became "the boy president" of the University of Chicago. In the years after that, his name cropped up in press speculations as a possible appointee to high government posts or as a possible party candidate for the presidency or vice-presidency of the United States. Hutchins' interests in public affairs were deep and found expression in various ways. Yet he dismissed all speculations about political prospects by saying: "The only post that would interest me would be the Papacy. If elected to it, I would call myself 'Blasphemous the First.' "

He never accepted any of the major government posts offered him. Yet he appeared to be "Blasphemous the First" to some members of his own faculty and to most American educators in the 1930's and 1940's. The reasons lay in his searching and prophetic criticism of the structure of American higher education and his efforts to make the University of Chicago the place to initiate and test the revolutionary changes which he felt were imperative. "What we need," said he, "are more educated B.A.'s and fewer ignorant Ph.D's." The strong resistance he met in pressing his proposals for educational reform led him to say pointedly on one occasion that "every advance in education is made over the dead bodies of 10,000 resisting professors." On another occasion, he rephrased the thought, saying that "it is harder to change a curriculum than it is to move a cemetery."

In his time as president of the university (and as chancellor after a 1947 reorganization), his principal coworker was Professor Mortimer Adler. Other important sources of faculty support included Richard P. McKeon, dean of the humanities, and Clarence Faust and F. Champion Ward, each in his time dean of the college. Hutchins' collaboration with Adler, however, was the closest of all, and the most enduring in many different and difficult projects up to the present hour.

This is not the place to fully reconstruct the Hutchins-Adler critique of American higher education and their prescriptions for reform. But the general nature of their views must be mentioned, first, because of their effect on Walter Paepcke and Robert O. Anderson as founder and refounder of the Aspen Institute; and second, because the critique anticipated many of the problems in education which the Institute would re-examine.

In the Hutchins-Adler analysis, American institutions of higher learning suffered from at least four major vices. First, colleges were viewed as places to which adolescents—many of whom had already wasted the last two years spent in high school—could be consigned for four more years until they reached an age when it was safe to release them on the work-a-day world. Next, under the prevailing elective system, students could be certified as graduates of a college—and hence qualified for gainful employment—on the basis of having passed course examinations which tested nothing more than the extent to which they had memorized scatter-pattern facts. The third vice was a premature emphasis on vocational specialization which produced graduates who could talk only to their fellow specialists and were incapable of talking coherently with the rest of the community about common problems. Fourth, colleges created new courses and new departments with every turn in the news, with every change in the winds of public opinion, with every benefactor who was ready to write a check if programs were initiated which conformed with his special crotchets. All four vices acted and reacted on each other in ways which made the college a bric-a-brac place.

The Hutchins-Adler prescription for reform viewed the learning process as a lifelong enterprise. It pictured a liberal arts college which would begin when students ordinarily entered the junior year in high school and would terminate in a Bachelor of Arts degree four years later. The award of that degree would merely signify competence in the liberal arts of reading, writing, speaking, listening, watching, measuring, and calculating. Discipline in these arts would be cultivated through the use of various subject materials. But the immediate object would be to make the student not *learned,* but capable of *learning* what is to be learned about any subject matter. The larger objective would be to provide our democratic society with a body of citizens who would know how to communicate with each other in comprehensible ways.

Qualified graduates from such a four-year college would then proceed to the university level of higher education. The university itself would be held together and derive its internal unity from metaphysics—meaning the science of first principles and ultimate causes. It would not provide specialized training in the professions. That kind of training would be relegated to outlying institutions offering such practical experience as the professions themselves could not or would not give. The university would have one purpose only—to expound lucidly the nature of the world and the nature of man.

Beyond the different stages of formal schooling would lie the world of informal education for which there is no definite course of study, no institutions, no teachers, and for which there is an immeasurable goal never fully achieved—the acquirement of as much understanding, insight, and wisdom as the individual is capable of. Just as a muscle atrophies and dies unless it is exercised, the mind that ceases to go on learning atrophies and dies. The best formal education one could obtain would be almost worthless if it were regarded only as the completion of an education instead of as preparatory for a lifetime of adult learning.

Hutchins failed to achieve all aspects of his prescription for reform at the University of Chicago itself. But, in close collaboration with men like Adler, he managed over the years to alter the character of the education offered in the college. Moreover, in the conviction that good teaching in the college was co-equal in importance to good research in the graduate departments and professional schools, whenever possible he joined with Mortimer Adler in teaching a two-year "Great Books" course to a select group of undergraduates. No student ever took that course simply because it came at a convenient hour or because it was a "snap" way to accumulate credits toward graduation. The course was sometimes given in the late afternoon and sometimes at night. To hold his own under a barrage of questions, a student would spend a week in a close reading and rereading of the particular book to be discussed in a two-hour session. No academic trusses— "ponies," predigested summaries of a classic, notes borrowed from someone in a preceding class—were of use to a participant. The student must stand on his own, must be open to a direct, personal encounter with the original texts before him, must converse with their authors even as the authors "talk back" to each other over the ages.

Not all students were equal to the demands made on them. Some dropped out. But those who stayed the full route took away from a study of the Great Books what often became the invisible hand that shaped the order of values, judgments, and personal commitments in their mature years. Among the students who were seminar participants in the last half of the 1930's, what has just been said was true of Mrs. Katherine Graham, now the publisher of the *Washington Post*. It was true of Charles Percy, now the United States senator from Illinois. It was also true of

17

Robert O. Anderson—whose figure will loom very large in the narrative to follow.

Hutchins' vital interest in the quality of "continuing education" beyond the bounds of formal schooling was expressed in many ways. Beginning in 1931, he saw in the news media of radio broadcasting and talking motion pictures instruments for mass education, not just for mass entertainment. So he set out to make the University of Chicago the national leader in educational broadcasting and in educational talking motion pictures, and he achieved that goal after he induced William Benton—a master of communications—to join the university as a vice-president. To the same end—continuing adult education—he worked closely with Benton in giving the University of Chicago a major stake in the acquisition of the *Encyclopaedia Britannica* and in radically upgrading its quality. Again to the same end, he joined Mortimer Adler in teaching what was known as "The Fat Man's Seminar," based on the Great Books and offered to interested University of Chicago trustees and to leading Chicago businessmen and their wives. Walter Paepcke and his wife Elizabeth were among the regular participants. So was Meyer Kestenbaum, president of Hart, Schaffner and Marx, who in later years would "moderate" the first offering of the Aspen Institute's Executive Seminar.

The needs of the Fat Man's Seminar for readily accessible texts led directly to a Hutchins-Adler-Benton collaboration in a vast two-pronged publishing venture. One prong entailed the publication of a fifty-four volume set of the *Great Books of the Western World*. The second, associated prong, entrusted to Adler directly, had no parallel in the intellectual history of Western man. This was the preparation of a *Syntopticon* indexing references to 102 Great Ideas—from "Angel" to "World"—which recurred in the Great Books. A reader in college, after college, or who never went to college could find in the *Syntopticon* a guide to the debates about perennial human issues which engaged the authors represented in the Great Books over the centuries.

But increasingly after the end of World War II, Hutchins'

attention was focused on the shape of the newborn Atomic Age and the overriding question of man's capacity to survive a new war. At the first session of the United Nations Atomic Energy Commission, Bernard Baruch had introduced an American plan for the control of atomic energy by saying, "We are here to make a choice between the quick and the dead." Months of debate followed, without agreement on the terms of international control. The choice being made seemed to favor death partly because no nation would yield its rights of sovereignty to an international agency, but mainly because the Cold War polarized the world into rival camps led by the United States and the Soviet Union.

Thus, in 1947, American ships—propelled by the Truman Doctrine—began to carry food, bullets, and advisers to Greece and Turkey. Later, when a Communist coup pulled Czechoslovakia behind the Iron Curtain, five nations established the Western European Union in the Brussels Defense Pact of March, 1948. The next month, on the eve of the elections in Italy and France, where strong Communist forces were in the field, the American Congress voted funds for the Marshall Plan, partly to help Western Europeans rebuild their war-shattered economies and partly to give them something worth defending against internal subversion. Two months later, in June, Congress approved the Vandenberg Resolution, which sanctioned informal American collaboration with the Western European Union and also advocated American co-operation with regional defense associations. The stage was thus set for the development in 1949 of the North Atlantic Treaty Organization, with the United States as its commander-in-chief.

Diplomats, meanwhile, continued to hold Big Four conferences, ostensibly to ease the tensions that could explode in war. Yet each conference seemed only to bring the lighted match closer to the exposed fuse. Three years previously, right after Hiroshima, a Committee to Frame a World Constitution had been formed at the University of Chicago under the chairmanship of Robert M. Hutchins. As a forum for discussion, the committee had also launched a monthly magazine, *Common Cause*, of which

Professor Borgese was the editor. In a public statement preceding the March, 1948, publication of a draft world constitution, Hutchins had said among other things:

> There are two propositions about the atomic bomb that are worth remembering. There is no secret. There is no defense. Since there is no secret, other nations will have the bomb almost any day. Since there is no defense, we cannot use the bomb after our monopoly ends to kill other people without being killed ourselves. . . .
>
> One *good* world requires more than the sacrifice of ancient prejudices. It requires the formulation and adoption of common principles and common ideals. It requires that this be done on a world-wide basis. A world organization cannot be held together simply by fear. Not transportation but communication lies at the foundation of any durable community. By communication, I do not refer to the *means* of communication, but to a common understanding of what is communicated. . . . If peace through intimidation and peace through purchase are failing and in the nature of things are bound to fail, we might try peace through justice. . . . If we will grant that what we want is peace, and that justice is the only way to peace, then we may begin dimly to perceive both the outlines of a policy for the present and the constitutional foundations of a future world order.

Yet while Hutchins defined "communication as a common understanding of what is communicated," that precondition for a world order seemed more remote than ever in the spring of 1948. Censorship in some form prevailed among half the members of the United Nations. Quotas and exchange regulations impeded the free movement of films, pictures, books, and periodicals. Half the world seemed to be subdivided into principalities of controlled thought—as was shown in the line-up of mutually hostile forces at the United Nations Conference on Freedom of Information held in Geneva in March and April, 1948. Every effort to lower barriers so that people could express themselves and communicate freely with other people was stopped by the counter-battery fire of Cold War polemics.

Hutchins' profound concern over these developments was at the forefront of his thoughts in the spring of 1948 when Professor Borgese proposed to him that the University of Chicago should organize a worldwide convocation to commemorate the bicentenary of Goethe's birth. He could see many merits in Borgese's proposal. The celebration would revive in an hour of great need the idea of a free world literature long associated with the figure of Goethe. It could breathe fresh life into the efforts that had marked Hutchins' educational purpose as head of the University of Chicago—to achieve, as Goethe did in his own time, a unifying synthesis about man and his world.

There was, however, a third element in the proposal which was even more compelling. Hutchins knew that central to all the other causes for the Cold War—which threatened to change into a shooting war—was a struggle over the destiny of a divided Germany. He also knew that American economic and military aid would not of themselves insure Germany—or at least Western Germany—a healthy future. To insure such a future, the intellectual life of Germany, which the Nazis had ruined, would have to be revived and restored to the honored place it once held in the community of Western thought.

It could not be revived and restored merely by denazification proceedings or by war-crimes trials. In the long run, the West could not do without Germany nor Germany without the West. Yet the deep wounds of the war years complicated the task of bringing reflective minds in both areas back into the channels for cultural co-operation. The task of revival and reunion needed a model to serve as a bridge between what was best in the pre-Nazi German past and the best that was hoped for in Germany's future. Goethe, in Hutchins' view, was the best of all available models. On this principal ground, Hutchins agreed with Borgese that there must be an American bicentenary celebration of Goethe's birth, and that scholars and men of letters from around the world must share in it. He would talk over the proposal with Walter Paepcke.

IV

Walter Paepcke, a "Hapsburg handsome" man, made no pretense of having started life from scratch as an upward-bound Horatio Alger. He was the son of Hermann Paepcke, a scholar and music lover as well as an impressive Chicago businessman. The elder Paepcke migrated to Chicago in 1871 from Bismarck's Prussia. The Great Chicago Fire left much of the town in ashes, and the need for reconstruction drew Hermann Paepcke into the lumber business. Thus, with an initial investment of $8,000, he built the Chicago Mill and Lumber Company which was described in 1909 as "the largest lumber and box organization in the country." But his drive to succeed in business went hand-in-hand with a drive to make the Paepcke home in Chicago an oasis of culture and a constant stimulus to intellectual growth. It was in character for him to insist that nine months of school each year were not enough for the development of a young man, and he saw to it that his son, Walter, born in 1896, kept at his studies during the summer months.

Walter Paepcke received a classical-style education at the Chicago Latin School and then went on to Yale, where, in imitation of his father's dual interests, he combined a study of German literature with a study of economic subjects which were meant to prepare him for a career in business. He was graduated from Yale in 1917, Phi Beta Kappa, served for a year in the navy during World War I, and then returned to Chicago, where he worked as an assistant to the treasurer of the family-owned Chicago Mill and Lumber Company. During the war years when wood supplies were scarce, the elder Paepcke had built a paper mill in Chicago to manufacture paper containers. This was meant to be no more than a sideline venture until box wood would again be available in ample supply. Young Walter Paepcke, however, saw matters differently. In his view, that venture pointed toward a giant new industry, and he began to develop it in 1922 when he took over the management of his father's business—and its multimillion debts to banks.

But he was not "all business." As a man who could recite by heart whole sections of Goethe's *Faust*—and whose knowledge of classical music could make him a strong candidate for an appointment as program director for a major symphony orchestra—he entered into the cultural life of the University of Chicago community, where scholarship, art, and music were more prized than the financial rewards sought by most successful businessmen.

Years earlier, as a child, he had met Elizabeth Nitze, the beautiful blonde, blue-eyed daughter of Professor William A. Nitze, one of America's most distinguished teachers of Romance languages. It was not a case of love at first sight. A photograph exists, showing the two when children, obviously thrown together by their parents, standing next to each other, but with backs turned and faces wrinkled in mutual disdain. Love came later. Walter Paepcke and Elizabeth Nitze were married in 1922, and from that time forward stood together in mutual support. She would contribute much to Walter Paepcke's eventual work as a bridge builder between business leadership and the liberal arts.

In 1926, four years after Paepcke took over the management of the family business, he laid the foundation for a new enterprise when he acquired the Philadelphia Paper Manufacturing Company and merged it with the paperboard division of the family-owned Chicago Mill and Lumber Company. When a New York banker asked what he meant to call the new venture, he said it would be called the Container Corporation of America. The banker's eyebrows tilted upward, and he asked if the name didn't take in too much territory for a small start. Should not the new venture be called the Container Corporation of Chicago or the Container Corporation of the Midwest? "No," said Paepcke, in much the same spirit that he would show when he called a relatively small cultural adventure "The Aspen Institute for Humanistic Studies," "I plan to have the company grow to a size where it will fit its big name." It did grow to a point at which, by 1948, it was one of the largest producers of containers in the country.

This did not, however, make Paepcke himself a new member of the "big rich." A substantial part of his earnings had gone to pay off the heavy debts carried over from his father's enterprises, his stock holdings in the Container Corporation itself were relatively small, and his current income was represented in the main by his $100,000 a year salary from the firm. But of the many factors which accounted for the growth of the Container Corporation, perhaps the most telling stemmed from a truth Paepcke once voiced: "The man has yet to be born who says, 'I want to own 20,000 boxes before I die.' Nor has the housewife been born who will say 'I won't buy anything that isn't packed by the Container Corporation of America.'" Paepcke, therefore, set out to sell service, not cartons. "The basic purpose of a container," he said, "is to identify the product—to sell the steak instead of the sizzle." To him, design and elegance were central to the success of his enterprise. He deliberately located the main design laboratory in the middle of a plant floor, where the artists would confront production realities, and he also saw to it that designers worked closely with customers, delving into the psychology and philosophy of marketing.

His interest in design extended beyond the immediate concerns of his own company. When the Nazis closed down the *Bauhaus* in Germany, many of the members came to the United States, where they founded, with Paepcke's help, the New *Bauhaus* in Chicago. The enterprise floundered, however, when the managers of the school, hoping to increase their financial resources, speculated in the stock market with school funds, only to be ambushed by the sharp break in the stock market incident to the recession of 1937–38. Paepcke rescued the school from bankruptcy, put it on a new basis under the new name of the Chicago Institute of Design, and kept it alive until after the war, when it was taken over by the Illinois Institute of Technology.

In all that he touched, Paepcke preached the gospel of elegance in design. "Elegance," said he, "doesn't mean expensive. It just means the best possible taste." On the advice of Egbert Jacobson, the art director for the Container Corporation, Paepcke applied to his affairs the novel Germanic idea of the "designed corporate image." Everything concerning a corporation was cast in a distinctive style, beginning with the trade-mark and stationery and extending to advertising, office designs, architecture, and so on.

Further, instead of pressing the "hard sell" approach, Paepcke reasoned that if the Container Corporation published a series of advertisements in which modern design was the common denominator and in which the text of an idea was limited to only a few words, the reader would have something interesting to look at and to associate with the Container Corporation. At the same time, the techniques of the modern artists would identify the enterprise with current developments in applied graphic arts, which were becoming increasingly important to packaging.

In 1937 he began a series of twelve black-and-white designs by the great Paris artist, A. M. Cassandre. During the next few years, the names of artists such as Herbert Bayer, Toni Zepf, Fernand Leger, Jean Cörlu, and Leo Lionni all appeared on advertisements, each of which made a simple, brief statement about the company. Later, during the war years, the Container Corporation brought out the United Nations series and, following that, the State series, in a similar format. These were advertisements in full color which introduced many new artists. They included William de Kooning, Ben Shahn, Ruffino Tamayo, Jean Varda, Paul Rand, Henry Moore, Miguel Covarrubias and Mario Carreno for the United Nations series, and Stuart Davis, Morris Graves, Mark Tobey, Lester Beall, Charles Howard, Hazzard Durfee, Bernard Perlin, and Karl Knaths for the State series. Illustration completely dominated layout, and mention of packaging was held to a minimum. Yet these advertisements helped establish the company as the best known in the industry, made it a magnet for talented young men and women in search of a congenial place to work, and, no less significantly, attracted increased numbers of investors in its stocks.

About a year before the State series ended, Paepcke began to think about what to do next. He concluded that his company's advertising should serve a public interest as well as his own, and that this was all the more important in the postwar period when concepts central to a "good society" were being distorted or eclipsed by the nation's preoccupation with material and physical security. The ideas he wished to present were fairly clear in his mind, but there remained the question of statement and authorship.

By this time, Paepcke had been for many years a member of the Great Books seminar offered to Chicago business leaders. He was also by now a trustee of the University of Chicago and one of its representatives on the board of directors of the Encyclopaedia Britannica Company. In the latter capacity, he had joined Hutchins, Adler, and William Benton in pushing through the decision to publish the *Great Books of the Western World* and its *Syntopticon*—at a time when the financial prospects for that work looked very dim to virtually everyone else. As he carefully followed Mortimer Adler's prodigious labors in bringing the *Syntopticon* closer to the point of publication, he found assembled in one place an index to many great statements of the ideas that were at the foundation of the Western tradition. Here, then, was a vast reservoir of material on which he could draw for use by his own company in its advertising campaign, while at the same time focusing public attention on the moral, philosophical, and political ideas contained in the Great Books.

In the spring of 1948, when discussions were under way that would eventually lead to the Container Corporation's series of advertisements based on the "Great Ideas of Western Man," Paepcke was approached by Hutchins concerning the proposed Goethe bicentennial celebration. Paepcke, an admiring student of Goethe and of the German tradition of arts and letters, shared Hutchins' interest in reintegrating Germany into the world intellectual community. But in the course of the discussions between the two men, Paepcke urged that the proposed bicentennial celebration should include a music festival, since Goethe was the inspirational source of a great literature of *lieder*, orchestral compositions, and operas. He also urged that the affair be staged not at the University of Chicago, but in the close-to-nature, intimate setting of Aspen, Colorado. His motives in the latter matter were linked to his gestating plans to develop Aspen beyond its newly emergent role as a winter sports resort.

3. SILVER INTO SNOW
AND BACK AGAIN

I

Walter Paepcke's wife, Elizabeth, "discovered" Aspen on a winter day in 1938. She had a houseful of guests on the Paepcke ranch near Larkspur, Colorado, and was faced by the problem of frozen water pipes that had burst. So, to divert her guests from the domestic catastrophe, she organized an expedition to explore the long, beautiful ski slopes of Aspen, which were then undeveloped. The visitors were charmed with the Alpine splendor of this pocket in the Rockies, ringed by mountains rising from eight thousand to over fourteen thousand feet on the western slope of the Continental Divide two hundred miles west of Denver. Elizabeth Paepcke never forgot the place.

The possibilities of developing the area into a ski resort had been seen as far back as 1922 when a Department of the Interior representative convened a meeting of the remaining inhabitants of Aspen and urged that they join in constructing a ski lift. "We don't want a ski lift here," the answer came. "We want another silver boom." Later, in the early 1930's, when most of Aspen's three hundred residents were on relief, a modest ski tow was built by the W.P.A. on the theory that it would help the local economy by attracting skiers to Aspen. One of the few who came, partly to organize the Western Division of the United States Ski Patrol, was Walter Orr Roberts. He was then a young solar astronomer on the Harvard faculty, but he lived and worked in Climax, Colorado, where a unique solar observatory was under construction. More will be said about him later on.

The concussion of the bombs dropped on Pearl Harbor momentarily shattered any hopes that Aspen could be transformed into a winter sports resort. Many ardent promoters of the hope went to war, and some did not survive it. Promised capital was withdrawn. Aspen itself was almost forgotten under its mantle of snow until the U.S. Army decided to train the Tenth Mountain Division at Camp Hale, Pando, Colorado. The troops stationed in the camp included a large proportion of the most accomplished American skiers and instructors, who were generally foreign-born or graduates of Ivy League colleges. Many of these, on week end leaves, enjoyed a busman's holiday by testing themselves on Aspen's ski slopes.

One of the self-testers was Friedl Pfeifer, an Austrian by birth, former head of the ski school at Sun Valley, who had been assigned to Camp Hale in 1943. After he was introduced to Aspen on a week end, his enchantment with the place took practical form. He went to the Aspen town council, and, speaking with a strong accent, projected an exciting future. "I am coming back after the war," said he, "and this town's going to be my home. I want to start a ski school here, and I'll give the local children free lessons so that we can develop a real skiing community. People will be interested in expanding commercial possibilities, and we'll get enough money to build more adequate tows and lifts. The war won't last forever."

Pfeifer did come back in 1945 and, along with some other survivors of the Tenth Mountain Division, canvassed possible sources of capital for launching a proposed Aspen Skiing Corporation. That is where Walter Paepcke entered the picture.

II

Gasoline was rationed up to the end of World War II. By the spring of 1945, however, Elizabeth Paepcke had saved enough coupons to travel by car to a vacation spot she had long had in mind for her husband and herself. The spot was Aspen.

The Aspen the Paepckes reached on Memorial Day was not quite a ghost town such as dotted the slopes and valleys and river beds of Colorado and other parts of the Rocky Mountains. It still had several hundred inhabitants, among whom one could find descendants of the original founders. Most maintained themselves in the region around Aspen as cowboys and by cattle breeding, and potato production. The town itself could claim the honor of being the birthplace of a child who in the third grade was known as "Rough House Ross," but who gained a different kind of celebrity in later life as Harold Ross, the creator and editor of *The New Yorker*.

Aspen, however, had long ago lost its economic and cultural vitality. People still spoke of how a Mr. Bionis "migrated" out of hard times by putting three sticks of dynamite under his stocking cap with a fuse long enough to give him time to empty a jug of wine. In fact, Aspen could not even support an undertaker. When Tom Sardy came to the town hoping to practice as an undertaker along with his duties at the Aspen Lumber and Supply Company, which he founded—he went for days with gross sales under twenty-five cents since no one except Mr. Bionis needed his services.

Aspen owed its birth to a political event in Washington, the 1878 Sherman Silver Purchase Act, requiring the Treasury Department to buy a certain amount of silver bullion each month and to coin it into silver dollars. Previously in Colorado the search for gold lay behind the expansion of local mining. With the Sherman Silver Purchase Act, however, the search for silver became equally important. The effects were visible in the swift growth of Leadville following an 1878 discovery that the carbonate ores of the area had rich silver linings. Within two years, more than thirty silver mines were being worked on Fryer's Hill, and the population of Leadville reached 15,000, making it the second largest city in the state. It was a wide-open town around the clock. Perhaps half of the inhabitants were in the business; the other half were the transients, the newcomers, the lategoers, the card sharps, the cutthroats, the prospectors, miners, common laborers, capitalists, curious visitors, men in search of hard liquor and soft women—and the rag-tag and bob-tail of humanity who follow whatever leads anywhere. The prospectors prospected, the miners

mined, the laborers labored, and as one wave of people moved out
—dead or alive—another wave moved in.

In 1879, however, when it appeared that all promising claims
in and around Leadville had been picked up, small parties of prospectors made the difficult trek over the Continental Divide and
into Ute territory to see what they could find. In and around the
mountain ranges ringing the present city of Aspen, they found
marked traces of silver ore. After that, the story of Aspen to 1893
is in part the story of how its earliest inhabitants—William Hopkins, Philip W. Pratt, Smith Steele, Charles F. Bennett, Henry
Tourtelotte, Henry S. Gillespie, H. P. Cowenhoven, and his son-
in-law D. R. C. Brown—survived Indian raids, hard winter
weather, and wretched communications.

As Henry L. Stein, a long-time "new" resident of Aspen has
recalled, "The actual prospectors are mostly forgotten since the
typical activity was for the man who made a discovery to sell out
to a man or to a group who had the capital to exploit the mining."
Eastern capital was brought in by D. Clarke Wheeler, by David H.
Hyman, a young Cincinnati attorney, and by Jerome B. Wheeler
(no relationship to D. Clarke), who was the founder-president of
H. R. Macy and Company in New York City. With Jerome B.
Wheeler on the local scene, it was the beginning of the end of the
time when silver ore mining was a personal venture depending on
a strong back, a strong stomach, a pickaxe, and a shovel.
He set the style for big-time mining operations which raised Aspen
into a plane apart from the hit-or-miss operations in other areas.
Proper planning, exploration, and careful record-keeping became
the order of the day, as did the most advanced kind of mining technology. Steam drills were brought in; standards of safety and sani-
tation were set unusually high; vast tunneling projects were
pressed along with projects which were part of a life-support system for the burgeoning town.

Jerome B. Wheeler did not confine his attention to the mines
he owned outright or, as in the case of the fabulous Mollie Gibson,
in partnership with David H. Hyman. In addition to being a
rancher, he built Aspen's first smelter at the junction of the Roar-

ing Fork and Castle Creek; he began a reduction works; he acquired and opened up marble quarries and coal and iron mines; he established a bank, and so on. Other men were no less active. Cowenhaven and Brown formed the Castle Creek Water Company; and Brown organized the Aspen Electric Company which later merged with the former to become the Roaring Fork Water, Light and Power Company. With the arrival of electric power, Aspen became the first town in Colorado to have electric street lights, and electric power made possible the construction of electric tramways —an obvious forerunner of ski chairlifts—to carry silver ore down the mountains.

It soon became apparent that J. B. Wheeler's smelter, built in 1884, was not large enough to digest an ever increasing cascade of silver ore from the Gillespie mines in Ashcroft and the Highlands, from Tourtelotte Park, from the Mollie Gibson, from the Smuggler mines, and from other rich mines bearing names such as Emma, Little Lotti, Kitty B., Jenny Lind, Minni Moore, Keno Gulch, and Grand Duke. Much of this silver cascade had to be shipped out by pack train and wagon to distant smelters at exorbitant costs, if there were enough mules and jacks on hand to meet a producer's needs.

When the transportation problem was solved with the coming of two railroads—the first the Denver and Rio Grande—and the second the Colorado Midland—the sky seemed to be the limit to Aspen's growth. The boom that followed was accelerated still further in 1890 when the Congress approved and President Benjamin Harrison signed the new Sherman Silver Purchase Act, which doubled the size of the government's annual purchases of silver under the 1878 law. By 1892, Aspen had grown to about 12,000 population, and its annual silver-ore production was worth about $10 million. Everyone in town was prosperous, including the girls in twenty-five sporting houses, forty-three saloons, and many dance halls. Among its other features, Aspen had two elegant public structures, both the work of Jerome B. Wheeler. One was the Wheeler Opera House, built at a cost of $90,000, where townspeople could see and hear the leading actors, singers, and instrumentalists of the day who toured the "Silver Circuit." The other was the Jerome Hotel, built at a cost of $120,000.

The civic tone of Aspen was set by the silver kings whose capital and tastes came from the East, and who settled for nothing short of what they thought was the finest in the American version of the Victorian Age. They built their homes on "Bullion Row," now Hallam Street. They laid out a racetrack on the flats to the west of Hallam Lake, played polo on it, and traded fortunes in bets on the results of a trotter race. Some of the wives of the silver barons took empty trunks to Paris or New York to buy the latest and finest in fashions and jewels for later display at the grand balls held in the Jerome Hotel or at the operas staged in the Wheeler Opera House. All this and more could be afforded by a town that produced, in a seven-year period, silver ore valued in late-nine-teenth-century dollars at $112 million—or perhaps five times that sum in present-day values. But the bonanza ended as swiftly as it began. In April, 1893, against the background of an alarming drop in the Treasury's gold reserves, President Grover Cleveland called a special session of Congress to repeal the Sherman Silver Purchase Act. A protracted legislative struggle followed, but a repeal was voted on October 30, 1893, amid the spread of economic woes that blanketed the nation from the Atlantic to the Pacific.

The small core of Aspenites who remained after the disaster of 1893 looked to D. R. C. Brown and his diversified enterprises to alleviate the stricken economy of the town. They found work in lumber mills, ranches, water, light, and power works, with the railroads, and in the offices of the county seat. In 1912 two raging fires gutted the Jerome B. Wheeler Opera House. The citizens took it hard, since the event marked the almost total loss of the great days they had known. The Jerome Hotel, however, still stood. So did many of the lovely Victorian homes that had survived the vandalism of less sensitive citizens. Only about a dozen public buildings remained in the ghostly company of things which, like silver wine goblets in a museum showcase, served as sweet-sad reminders of what life was like in Aspen in its glory days. But the small core of families that remained, flanked around the central figure of Judge William Shaw, who served for forty-five years on the bench, kept Aspen from becoming a ghost town after the manner of its neighbors.

Mining did not entirely disappear from Aspen. It was carried on from one decade to the next under the auspices of two families. One was the Willoughbys—F. D. Willoughby and later his sons Fred and Frank—who operated the Midnight Mining Company and the Little Annie Mine. The other was the Herron Brothers, whose mining interests—covering lead and zinc as well as silver—included the Smuggler-Durant, Silver King, and Lone Pine mines.

III

When Walter Paepcke saw Aspen for the first time on Memorial Day, 1945, the only mortal visible out-of-doors was a drunk, and he was half-dead. The town contained one dirty restaurant, while the Hotel Jerome, where the Paepckes stayed, had been reduced to a refreshment stand. Lawrence Elisha, the owner of the hotel, was an amiable gentleman who managed his affairs on the interesting economic theory that plenty of hot water, clean linen, and fifty cents a night would insure a prosperous bar. The bar itself offered as its stable drink a concoction appropriately called "crud"—four parts bourbon and one part milk.

Elsewhere in Aspen, most of the Victorian houses were empty, their eaves dripping forlornly with jigsaw lace. In those still inhabited, there were relics of the past—hunks of glittering minerals and primeval crystals, heavy iron-barreled guns that had shot buffalo, skis that had seen hard use, not for sport but for getting about from mine to mine. But the breathtaking scenery caught Paepcke's imagination. With his eye for design, he also saw through the decay of the dilapidated houses, barns, and chicken coops to the possibility of restoring the Victorian grace of the community. The beauty of the natural world around the valley of Aspen suggested to him that here was a place where he could fulfill his long-held hope of creating an American counterpart to the Salzburg musical festival.

As it happened, his introduction to Aspen on Memorial Day coincided with the near approach of his wife's birthday, and on his second morning in Aspen he informed Elizabeth that for a gift he had bought her one of the finest Victorian homes. The news brought tears to her eyes, but not of joy. She had come to Aspen merely to enjoy the scenery, but was now burdened with another place to manage in addition to their other homes. Paepcke may have been dismayed by his wife's tears, but he was not deterred by them. He presently acquired Pioneer Park, a snug and proper little mansion under the cottonwoods—which had been abandoned years before by its Aspen owner under ambiguous circumstances. A bullet embedded in a staircase railing of the mansion, and still visible today, suggests an unspecified degree of murder.

Paepcke had cast his lot with Aspen. Soon he bought other houses for resale as vacation retreats to friends from the East. Aspen, however, still needed a viable economic base. With the help of Judge William Shaw, Paepcke in September, 1945, called a meeting of Aspen citizens in the Pitkin County Courthouse. Forty-five men showed up, plus three women, one of whom was Elizabeth Paepcke. Paepcke proceeded to lay out "fourteen points" for a "good life" in Aspen, combining work, play, and leisure—the last term being used in the Greek sense of "schooling." Municipal facilities—water supply, sewers, fire protection, and the like—all of which were in a primitive state, would of course, have to be modernized. But the economy of Aspen could be revived by adhering to a Swiss or Austrian Alpine model. There could be woodware made out of the native Aspen tree, jewelry out of native silver, clothes out of mountain wool, cheese and butter from the milk of local cattle. Aside from the economic revival all this would bring to languishing small shops and local crafts, Paepcke placed heavy stress on the cultural advantages that would accrue to Aspen in consequence of his "fourteen points."

The native Aspenites, however, did not take kindly to any of the points. They had no interest in being uplifted by an outsider, much less by one with a Germanic last name. They particularly resented his offer of a carload of house paint available at no cost to local citizens if they would spruce up their homes. Only one Aspenite availed himself of the offer. Paepcke, with his logical mind and strong drive toward any objective he set for himself, sometimes forgot that other people adhered to a logic of their own. He thus stumbled into a number of errors in community relations during the early months of what someone called his "Parnassus of the Deep Freeze." None of his errors were fatal, but they would be magnified in imagination and would be recalled later on whenever "town and gown" frictions complicated relations between the community and the Aspen Institute for Humanistic Studies. This would be true long after Paepcke, in a reversal of his initial manner, made it a point of policy quickly to remove the cause for any justified criticism directed at him.

While local Aspenites were left to mull over—or perhaps more precisely, to mutter over—the plans he had laid out, Paepcke joined forces with Friedl Pfeifer, so that any proposed summer attractions might be co-ordinated with ski activities in the winter. Two companies were formed. One, the Aspen Company, undertook to lease, modernize, refurnish, and operate the Jerome Hotel and to purchase some eighteen auxiliary real estate holdings. Walter Paepcke headed the first organization and owned 49 per cent of its stock. The second company, the Aspen Skiing Corporation, bought up old mining properties on Aspen Mountain or leased rights-of-way and planned the construction of up-to-date chairlifts to replace the old boat tow. George B. B. Berger, Jr., of Denver, headed this corporation; its largest stockholders besides Paepcke, who owned 12 per cent of the stock, were Edgar Hackney of New York, Robert Collins of Omaha and Paul H. Nitze (Mrs. Paepcke's brother), who by now was well into a distinguished public career that would see him become successively head of the State Department's Policy Planning Board, Assistant Secretary of Defense for International Affairs, and Secretary of the Navy.

Paepcke also interested personal friends, such as United Air Lines' William A. Patterson and hotelman Conrad Hilton, to invest in these projects up to $5,000 each. In a prospectus prepared for other investors, Paepcke wrote: "Definite plans are underway to provide opportunities for man's complete life—to earn a livelihood, to enjoy nature and physical recreation, and to have available facilities for education." To do this, Paepcke needed help from wealthy friends. He also needed and got helpful encouragement of another sort from long-time Aspenites Fred and Frank Willoughby, who had mining interests, storekeeper Mike Magnifico, Jerome owner Lawrence Elisha, and especially Judge William Shaw. They enjoyed the prospect of combining outdoor sports with indoor cultural events, of doing something unique in their uniquely endowed town and of restoring Aspen's luster.

IV

Above all, Paepcke needed the kind of help he got from Herbert Bayer, who was Austrian, had begun his professional career as an architect, but at the age of twenty-five was one of the youngest teachers of typography and graphic design in the *Bauhaus*. With the closing of the *Bauhaus* by Hitler, he had immigrated to the United States and settled in New York. Here he was presently contacted by Egbert Jacobson, art director of the Container Corporation of America, and was commissioned to produce a number of designs for the new-style advertising program of the corporation. Although Bayer subsequently produced some seven or eight designs in all, it was not until 1944 that he met the Paepckes. It had occurred to Paepcke that the artists who contributed designs to the corporation's advertising program comprised a "Who's Who" of the modern art world. Taken together, their work would provide a striking commentary on art and industry, while at the same time serving to enhance the reputation of the Container Corporation of America. The case called for the assembly of their work into a single show that would open at the Art Institute of Chicago, it would be sent on a grand tour of the country. Herbert Bayer was engaged to organize and design the show and to oversee the details of its prospective travels. The task brought him into direct contact with the Paepckes and thus into the web of their friendship.

Some time in the summer of 1945, when Bayer and his wife Joella were vacationing in Mexico, Walter Paepcke pelted them with messages urging them to come to Aspen, to buy a house for only $500, and to use it as a place to bring the children during summer vacations and during winter-time skiing. A train trip from New York to Aspen took two days, and since the Bayers had four children, they dismissed Paepcke's idea as not being worth serious consideration. On the other hand, Bayer was unhappy with his life in New York and wanted to settle somewhere else. His name and work were known in Europe, and there would be many outlets for his talents in the reconstruction of war-shattered European towns and industries. Europe, as a whole, however, struck Bayer at the time as being a pestilential charnel house. Mexico seemed a more promising place to settle.

En route there for another visit, this time in late December, 1945, the Bayers arranged to visit the Paepckes in Aspen between Christmas and New Year. Here Paepcke closed in on his objective. He revealed to Bayer that he had engaged a Chicago architect, Walter Frazier, to supervise the structural remodeling of some of the buildings which the Aspen Company had acquired. Although Frazier was knowledgeable in period architecture—he had previously built a Paepcke country house in Victorian style—he would not remain in Aspen after he had completed the specific projects he had undertaken. What Aspen needed was someone who would settle in the community, live there year around, and be the designer and planner-in-chief for the whole of its rehabilitation and development.

"You, Herbert," said Paepcke, "are the man for the job. You grew up in Austria. You know mountain villages, and are yourself a mountaineer. Combined with what you know about design, Aspen will provide you with a unique opportunity."

Bayer had had no previous personal experience in city planning, and had not been directly engaged in architecture since he was twenty-two. What he knew about city planning was confined to what he read about the subject in textbooks and professional journals. He could, however, satisfy himself on one point. Scarcely anyone else knew any more than he did about how to bring a near moribund community back to life, to modernize it from within, and at the same time to conserve and enhance the best of what was left from the inherited past. Bayer was intrigued by the prospective role which Paepcke invited him to play in helping to shape a better community. "I was," Bayer later remarked, "naïve at the time—but naïve ideas are sometimes very powerful."

Here was the place to settle. The terrain was beautiful, the climate wonderful, and all of Bayer's talents would find full play in the thousand and one things he could do or was expected to do for the Aspen Company. He recognized that as a former Austrian, he would be a "stranger in Egypt," cut off from all the people who knew him in New York and exposed in Aspen to a possible backlash of anti-German rancor. Moreover, although Paepcke offered Bayer a directorship of the Aspen Company, besides retaining him as a design consultant to the Container Corporation, his prospective income from these sources was scarcely magnificent. It would come to only one-sixth of what he had just been offered by a New York firm which had bid for his full-time services as a designer. Yet, on balance, he concluded that he could live a better and more challenging life in Aspen than in New York, and so he accepted Paepcke's proposal.

Briefly, after he had accepted Paepcke's proposal, Bayer joined him in a ride around Aspen in search of a possible house to buy. When he spotted one that appealed to him, he learned that it was not for sale. Paepcke owned it already. In some cases, all the latter had to do to acquire ownership rights was to redeem the house from the county by paying the unpaid taxes on the property. A particular house struck Bayer's fancy. It was known as the Four Seasons, and had been built by one of the old mining companies. "How much do you think it would cost?" Bayer asked Paepcke.

"Two thousand, five hundred dollars," came the reply.

"How do you know?"

"I just bought it."

"Well, then, why don't you resell it to me as a quick profit to yourself?"

Paepcke snorted his disinterest.

By the end of the third day of the introductory visit, Bayer became an Aspen property owner when he bought a house from Judge William Shaw, but not for a song. To the judge, property was like the law: It spoke from the past to the future. And as a man who dealt in "futures," he set the price of his home with an eye to its prospective value.

Bayer now returned to New York to tidy up his affairs there and then doubled back to the new life and work awaiting him as a director of the Aspen Company and its designer-in-chief. His immediate task was to modernize some eighteen houses belonging to the Aspen Company without doing violence to their Victorian style. Plumbing, heating, and electrical facilities were brought up to date; the interiors of the houses were furnished with Victorian objects collected from around the valley, while the faded exterior Victorian colors were replaced by a harmony of warm colors drawn from the Bayer palette, but leaning on Victorian tastes. The Jerome Hotel, which the Aspen Company leased from Lawrence Elisha, was similarly refurbished, by Elizabeth Paepcke (and Walter Frazier). At the same time, Bayer supervised the reconstruction in Victorian style of some twenty guest houses and a number of dormitories to house prospective skiers. To make these houses livable for paying guests, imagination, taste, and elbow grease were needed—and were forthcoming with the help of Joella Bayer, Herbert's wife. For extra measure, Bayer designed the brochures, posters, and other materials that would advertise Aspen to the outside world.

Meanwhile, there were fast-moving developments on other fronts. During the winter of 1945–46, Friedl Pfeifer and Frank Willoughby conducted prospective investors through Queen's Gulch over the ridge above Midnight Tunnel, where they could see Little Annie's Basin, then on, to Tourtelotte Park, and back to Aspen. The spectacle argued its own case, and by March, 1946, enough money was in the till that work could start on the world's "longest chairlift." Its construction kept pace with the construction of ski dormitories and the remodeling of pre-existing housing facilities, plus another detail. The renovated Jerome Hotel, which had previously offered easygoing credit at the bar and restaurant was changed in management from the charming services of Charles and Gaynor Bishop to the military precision of one Colonel Dutton. The Jerome Hotel would soon become known as "Fort Dutton," and a year-old bar bill had to be redeemed.

In late January, 1947, Colorado's Governor Lee Knous gave Elizabeth Robinson, daughter of Aspen's mayor, a ceremonial shove to start her on an ascent which opened the 15,000-foot ski tow. With six 14,000-foot peaks nearby and plenty of dry, powdery snow, Aspen at that moment began its evolution into a top winter sports playground in the United States. It would soon be the site for national ski meets (a judge at one of the first ever held was solar astronomer Walter Orr Roberts).

By the spring of 1948, Walter Paepcke had tied up all his personal capital in his various Aspen enterprises. Not that he risked one thread away from nakedness or one crust of bread away from starvation. The Aspen Ski Company alone during the winter sports season showed gross profits in excess of $3,000 daily, and all future projections of profits showed upward curves. For the time being, however, the profits went to pay off the costs of capital improvements estimated at one million dollars. More to the point, Aspen so far was known principally as a winter sports resort. True, Burl Ives had come to sing ballads in the still-charred Wheeler Opera House, but the event scarcely made Aspen what Paepcke wished it to be—the home of an American counterpart to the Salzburg musical festival. Nor was Aspen any other kind of cultural center. It seemed destined to be a secret hideout for people on the run from something else—artists, writers, and movie directors who wanted to get away from city life, wealthy sportsmen who wanted a fishing and hunting lodge, midwesterners who wanted a summer mountain cottage, eastern couples who wanted to try their hand at ranching, and ski-bums who wanted to start a business, any sort of business, to be close to Aspen's slopes.

Moreover, if Paepcke's hopes for a musical festival were still a case of hopes deferred, Herbert Bayer had ample cause to worry about his hopes for a unified development of Aspen. In 1946 at a meeting of the directors of the Aspen Company, he argued that if they acquired enough land to control the center of the town, they could indirectly influence the pattern of development on its periphery. To bring home to them the graphics of what he had in mind, he led the directors to an area south of the Jerome Hotel and across the street from the Wheeler Opera House where three city lots were available for purchase at the ludicrously small cost of $100 a lot. He proposed that the company purchase these lots as a nucleus, eventually buying all the remaining property up to the foot of Aspen Mountain, lying due south, whose ski runs led directly into the town.

Here, said he, was something that could not be found in any major ski resort in Europe. In Europe, skiers had to travel miles from their quarters in a resort town to reach the ski runs. In Aspen, all they had to do was to walk a few hundred yards. Moreover, Aspen had a major advantage over an American sporting center such as Sun Valley which was artificially built. It came to life only in the winter months and was dead in the summer. The Aspen Company, however, was not involved in building an artificial town. It was hooking onto an existing community—one, to be sure, near the bottom of the economic ladder, but nonetheless could and did have a life of its own in the summer as well as in the winter. All the planning of the Aspen Company, Bayer continued, should keep a schedule of year-round activities. But the immediate problem was to buy up all the land comprising the core of the town, to control its development, to set in place edifices and civic amenities that would serve human needs and yet set a standard of design from which other developers could take their cue.

The decision in the matter at issue depended on Paepcke's reaction to Bayer's proposal. "How much do you figure it would cost," he asked, "to buy the core tract?" The answer was an estimated $150,000. "Well," said Paepcke, "we don't have that kind of money." Nor did he.

With no one else in a position to offer resistance, the door was left open for the invasion of Aspen by real estate speculators and entrepreneurs with get-rich-quick schemes common to resort towns. When Bayer urged the Aspen City Council to take measures that would preserve Aspen's natural beauty, he was resented for his alleged high-handed interference with the normal course of buying and selling in the local community. The people who lived in Aspen could do what they pleased; it was not for an outsider to tell them what to do. Bayer could console himself with the thought that he had at least been instrumental with Fred Glidden in getting the council to bar all Neon signs in Aspen— and years later to develop a small area in the center of the town where no vehicular traffic was permitted. His larger consolation awaited Paepcke's purchase of 120 acres known as Aspen Meadows, an area that once included the racetrack where the old silver barons had gambled on trotting horses. Bounded on the west by the Roaring Fork River, on the north by Red Mountain, on the east by Hallam Lake, and on the south by the built-up section of Aspen, this secluded island of flat land within Aspen's municipal domain would be the future campus of the Aspen Institute. Here is where Herbert Bayer would leave his indelible mark on the terrain.

It was shortly after Paepcke's purchase of the 120 acres that he was approached by Hutchins with a proposal for a Goethe bicentennial celebration. Paepcke, as has been related, embraced the plan but argued against holding the convocation on the campus of the University of Chicago. If it were held in Aspen and were coupled with a music festival, said he, it would bring to Aspen world-renowned leaders in the world of scholarship and the fine arts, and would broadcast to the world in turn that Aspen meant to be the home of a major cultural center. Hutchins, with his interest in continuing education, agreed to Paepcke's proposal. So did Professor Borgese.

4. THE GOETHE BICENTENNIAL

I

A good idea without a plan of action is like a lever without a fulcrum, just as a plan of action with no clear end in view is like a fulcrum without a lever. In the case of the Goethe Bicentennial, many things had to be and were done to provide both.

The first step was to create a Goethe Bicentennial Foundation as a nonprofit American corporation. The legal matters were attended to by Glen A. Lloyd, a senior partner in a leading Chicago law firm, and chairman of the Board of Trustees of the University of Chicago. The next step was to recruit people to serve as officers and directors of the Foundation in accordance with certain clearly stated criteria. Together they must comprise a representative group of leaders in various fields of human endeavor. They must be sympathetic to the intellectual and cultural requirements of the world community. They must reflect the many facets of Goethe's own life as a poet, dramatist, novelist, historian, philosopher, critic, scientist, statesman, and administrator.

Former President Herbert Hoover agreed to serve as honorary chairman of the foundation, a gesture which helped emphasize the fact that its purpose transcended partisan political loyalties. The active chairmanship was assumed by Hutchins, energetically backstopped by the vice-chairman, Glen A. Lloyd. The choices of other officers and directors prefigured the kind of people—educators, scholars, political officials, publishers, artists, business executives, judges, and writers—who would eventually become the trustees of the Aspen Institute as well as those who would participate in its many-faceted lines of action. The identity of some would also foreshadow a salient trait of the Aspen Institute of the future—that it would be increasingly international in its

43

governance, perspectives, and programs. Thus the board of directors included two men who embodied different aspects of the German humanistic tradition. One was Thomas Mann, the Nobel laureate in literature, then residing in California. The other was Heinrich Bruening, the last of Germany's pre-Nazi leaders, who, after Adolph Hitler came to power, found asylum in the United States and joined the Harvard faculty.

While the board for the Goethe Bicentennial Foundation was being organized, other details clamored for attention. Where, for example, would public lectures and symposia be held in Aspen? The answer was the Wheeler Opera House, which the Aspen Company agreed to remodel under Herbert Bayer's supervision. But what about the music portions of the program? The stage and seating capacity of the Opera House were suitable only for chamber music. To provide a stage for a full orchestra, a tent "amphitheater" would have to be built on the flats of Aspen Meadows. To the costs of this project, must be added the larger costs of bringing to Aspen a major symphony orchestra and other performing artists for a Goethe-related music program. There would also be travel costs and honoraria for distinguished speakers brought in from all over the world. Where would the money come from?

It was clear that, regardless of any income from the sale of tickets to the concerts, the bicentennial would not be self-supporting. It was also clear that the total sum of money needed could not be estimated in advance since no one knew how many people would actually come to Aspen for the Goethe celebration. At Paepcke's urging, Hutchins searched for donations. It was not an easy task, considering, as Hutchins said half-seriously, that "99 per cent of the American population never heard of Goethe." Besides, any list of possible contributors was likely to be a carbon copy of the list of possible contributors to the pressing financial needs of the University of Chicago. Paepcke, however, airily waved to one side all questions involving a conflict of loyalties and badgered Hutchins to stick to the raising of funds for the Goethe bicentennial. As Hutchins later recalled:

44

He pursued me so relentlessly to raise money for the Goethe celebration that I told him he owed his success in life to his capacity to tire out the other fellow. I used to refer to him as my tiresome friend. I said he reminded me of Cecil Rhodes, who held that the story of the importunate widow was the best in the Bible. She prevailed not because of the justice of her cause but because of her importuning.

In the end, Hutchins managed to raise about half of the $250,000 the celebration cost over and above revenues from admissions to concerts. Paepcke, who was short of cash, would meet part of the deficit by mortgaging his Larkspur ranch. The remainder would be covered by contributions from personal friends and business associates.

II

By the early part of 1949 most of the structural aspects of the bicentennial celebration were completed. Paepcke, through his links with the world of art and architecture, engaged Eero Saarinen to design a massive tent at a cost of some $55,000 to house an orchestra and an audience of up to two thousand people. Through his connections with the world of music, he engaged the Minneapolis Symphony Orchestra under Dmitri Mitropoulos to be the mainstay of the musical aspects of the festival. Performing artists would include pianist Artur Rubinstein, cellist Gregor Piatigorsky, violinists Nathan Milstein and Erica Morini, and opera diva Dorothy Maynor. The total bill came to $110,000.

The format for the intellectual aspects of the bicentennial was largely Borgese's design. Colloquia, panel discussions, and addresses, all open to the public, dealt with the contemporary significance of Goethe from the standpoints of his work and personality and his relationship to a range of things—to the natural sciences and world literature, to humanity and the crisis of civilization, to ethics and politics, and to the unity of mankind. American participants included Borgese and Hutchins, anthropologist Robert Redfield, philosopher William Ernest Hocking, and dramatist Thornton Wilder. The international aspects of the convocation were apparent in participants who included Stephen

Spender from England; Charles J. Burckhart, an eminent Swiss statesman-historian, then Switzerland's Minister to France; Gerardus van der Leew, professor of theology in the University of Groningen and Netherland's Minister of Education, Arts, and Science in 1945–46; Barker Fairley, head of the Department of German in the University of Toronto and a world-renowned authority on Goethe's life and poetry; Halvadan Khot, Norway's most eminent historian and its Foreign Minister from 1935–41; Jean Canu of France; Elio Gianturco of Italy; and Ernest Robert Curtius, professor of romance languages in the University of Bonn, Germany. Martin Buber of Israel was invited to attend, but, being unable to make the trip, prepared an address that was read in his absence.

Although all these persons together comprised the heart within the heart of the intellectual aspects of the Goethe bicentennial, they were augmented by two more figures whose physical presence in Aspen imparted an ineffable electric excitement to the Goethe celebration. One was José Ortega y Gasset, the Spanish philosopher and humanist who was credited with being the best voice of Spanish thought and expression in the first half of the twentieth century. The other was Albert Schweitzer.

Ortega y Gasset, when serving as a professor of metaphysics in the University of Madrid, had shared the deep preoccupation of his generation with the political problems of Spain, and in the years before World War I, had founded three periodicals which were forums for discussions of political issues—to the extent that such discussions were permitted under the monarchy. At the same time, he also founded the League for Political Education, and he continued to be politically active in Spain in the years after World War I. His book *The Revolt of the Masses*, published in 1930 and later translated into many languages, made an essential contribution to the consciousness of the age, while his later volume, *The Mission of the University*, was a valuable addition to modern thought on the function and purpose of academic education.

In 1931, as a member of the Cortese, he helped draft a constitution for the new Spanish Republic, and he founded the Group at the Service of the Republic, in the hope that it could help the governmental institutions of the republic meet the challenges of Spanish society. That hope was shattered in 1936 when Spanish Moroccan troops, under the command of General Francisco Franco, invaded Spain. In the ensuing civil war, Ortega left Spain and went into voluntary exile for nine years between 1936 and 1945, part of which he spent in Europe and part in Argentina. In 1948, acting from a new base in Portugal, he founded the Institute of the Humanities in Madrid. His coming to Aspen for the Goethe bicentennial was his first visit to the United States.

The presence of Albert Schweitzer in Aspen as the principal speaker at the Goethe bicentennial—his first and only trip to the United States—needs a longer explanation. Schweitzer's life had many points of comparison with Goethe's. Like Goethe, he became famous at an early age, thirty, for his books interpreting the Bible, for his genius as an organist which won him accolades as the leading authority on the music of Bach, for his famed biography of Bach, and for his stature as a professor in the University of Strasbourg, where, over a century before, young Goethe had studied law. His intellectual life, like that of Goethe's, was centered on a search for ultimate truths in a complex, changing world; and if Goethe spent forty-four years in ministering to the material needs of his fellow men in Weimar, Schweitzer by 1949 had spent thirty-six years at his jungle hospital at Lambarene ministering to natives, many of them suffering from leprosy.

As is generally true of all figures larger than life, Schweitzer's true worth was attacked and praised in extravagant terms. At one extreme, he was called a bad doctor who arbitrarily threw modern medicines into the Ogowe River and who ran a hospital so filthy as to be unbelievable. It was also claimed that his hard work and self-sacrifice were really part of his search for publicity and power —or were his form of psychic escape from a Europe which disappointed him. At the other extreme, he was canonized as a saint or as God's vice-regent on earth. The two extremes denied him his right to his own fallible humanity and thus obscured the significance of what he actually achieved as a person in the face of massive difficulties.

The maneuvers which brought Schweitzer to Aspen have since passed into legend. Glen A. Lloyd, the vice-chairman of the Goethe Bicentennial Foundation, had contributed $5,000 as an honorarium for Schweitzer if he agreed to speak at the convocation. When Schweitzer declined a cabled offer from Chicago, Lloyd, Paepcke, and Hutchins met to decide what to do next. At one point in the dispirited discussions, someone suggested that their approach to Schweitzer had been wrong. He was more likely to respond favorably if the Goethe Bicentennial Foundation offered to give $5,000 in French francs, not to him personally, but to support the work of his hospital at Lambarene. A cable sent off in line with the new approach was quickly answered by Schweitzer's acceptance.

Even so, Schweitzer might not have come to the Goethe celebration if he had had an accurate grasp of American geography. The hospital atlas at Lambarene contained no references to Aspen, Colorado, and *Le Bon Docteur* assumed that the place must be a suburb of Chicago. Chicago was the point of origin of the cables he had received, as well as the subsequent correspondence which led to an understanding that he would deliver a lecture at the University of Chicago before proceeding to the site of the Goethe convocation. It is not hard to imagine his feelings when he reached Chicago, gave his lecture at the university, and was escorted to a train for another thousand-mile journey to a destination with an altitude of eight thousand feet. He would later confess his mistake in geography and add: *"Aspen ist zu nach an den Himmel gebaut"* —Aspen was built too close to Heaven and was not good for his health.

The word that Schweitzer would participate in the Goethe convocation helped rivet national and international press attention on what was unfolding in Aspen. But he was by no means the whole of the event, much less the source of the testament that would animate the Aspen Institute of the future. The first draft of

Walter P. Paepcke, Aspen Institute founder, and his wife, Elizabeth, during a concert intermission at the Goethe Bicentennial Convocation.

Aspen about 1949, looking north from Ajax Mountain. The Wheeler O
House (left) and Hotel Jerome (slightly behind and to the right) were the

he town. These landmarks were built at the turn of the century. *Courtesy icia Millington*

The "main event" of the Goethe Convocation was Dr. Albert Schweitzer's speech, delivered in German and French. Thornton Wilder provided a paragraph-by-paragraph translation.

Robert M. Hutchins chatting with William Ernst Hocking in the Amphitheater before the opening speech at the Goethe Bicentennial.

Thornton Wilder (right) with Professor Antonio Giuseppe Borgese, one of the founders of the Aspen Institute.

At Herbert Bayer's studio, José Ortega y Gasset converses with the Bauhaus artist-designer. Bayer has been for over twenty-five years responsible for much of what is best in Aspen.

55

Walter Paepcke and Adlai Stevenson.

It was in Aspen that the first photo conference in the United States was h
This group picture of the panelists, taken in the lobby of the Hotel Jero
shows, left to right: back row, Herbert Bayer, Eliot Porter, Joella Bayer, M
Paul Vanderbilt, Connie Steele, John Morris, Ferenc Berko, Laura Gilpin, F

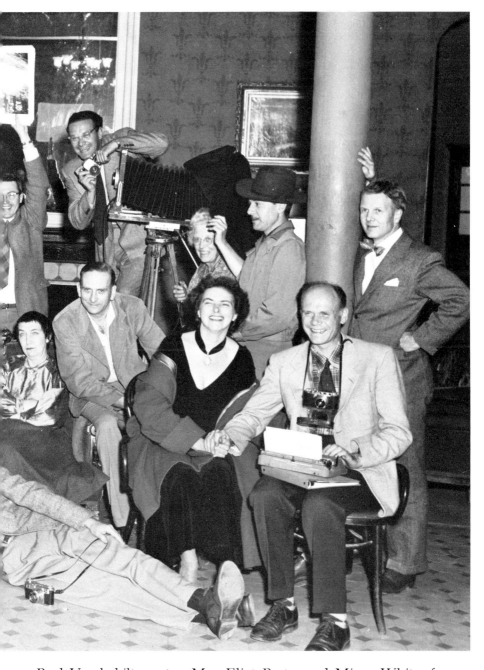

eser, Paul Vanderbilt; center, Mrs. Eliot Porter and Minor White; fore-
ound, Millie Kaeser, Ansel Adams, Dorothea Lange, Walter Paepcke, Bere-
ce Abbot, Frederick Sommer, Nancy and Beaumont Newhall; on floor, Will
onnell, Wayne Miller. *Photograph by Robert C. Bishop*

Aspen Institute Buildings and Amphitheater.

Robert W. Craig, assistant to President Walter P. Paepcke and executive director of the Aspen Institute.

Mortimer Adler, Executive Seminar moderator and active member of the Institute since its founding.

Robert O. Anderson, chairman and trustee, previously president of the Aspen Institute.

Alvin C. Eurich, president, Aspen Institute, 1964–67.

William E. Stevenson, president, Aspen Institute, 1967–69.

J. E. Slater, president of the Aspen Institute since 1969.

Jean Monnet, recipient of the Aspen Statesman-Humanist Award.

Willy Brandt (left), recipient of the Aspen Statesman-Humanist
Award, with J. E. Slater (center) and Robert O. Anderson.

Aristides Doxiades, recipient of the Aspen Award in the
Humanities.

Gilberto Freyre, recipient of the Aspen Award in the
Humanities.   71

Martha Graham, recipient of the Aspen Award in the
Humanities.

Benjamin Britten, recipient of the Aspen Award in the
Humanities.   73

Edmund Wilson, recipient of the Aspen Award in the
Humanities.

Wesley S. Melahn, Aspen Institute business manager.

Shepard Stone, director of Aspen Institute Berlin.

John Hunt, vice-president, Aspen Institute for Humanistic Studies.

75

PROGRAM DIRECTORS

Douglass Cater, Communi-
cations and Society.

Harlan Cleveland, Inter-
national Affairs.

Francis Keppel, Education
for a Changing Society.

Robert B. McKay, Justice,
Society, and the Individual.

Walter Orr Roberts,
Science, Technology, and
Humanism.

Thomas W. Wilson, Jr.,
Environment and the
Quality of Life.

Waldemar A. Nielsen,
Pluralism and the
Commonweal.

77

Annual Aspen Institute International Board of Trustees meeting,
July 3–4, 1973, with Institute Fellows.

Institute Program Planning Committee meeting, June, 1975.

A major element in the Aspen idea has been the music. Here Dmitri Mitropoulos is seen with Nathan Milstein and Gregor Piatigorski.

that testament was the statement which Hutchins and Borgese jointly prepared and which the directors of the Goethe Bicentennial Foundation released at the start of the convocation. The text read in part:

The difficulty of our time is a difficulty of the human spirit. We have to abandon the illusion, which some of our ancestors were able to cherish, that our difficulty is primarily political, economic, technological or educational. The social order has been rearranged, and old evils appear under new names. Literacy has flourished, and taste has been debased. Goods have been produced and distributed in untold quantities and blown up in untold quantities. Things seem to be bigger; they do not seem to be better. We are at last face to face with the fact that our difficulty is a difficulty of the human spirit. . . .

If Goethe's particular time has any relevance to our difficulty, it is only that his time bridged the ancient and the modern worlds, enabling him to stand where he stood and comprehend them both. If his place has any relevance, it is only that Germany is the bloody battleground which we all feel, however vaguely, however variously, must be planted again if the difficulty of the human spirit is to be surmounted.

We are gathered here to search out in ourselves the depths of the spirit that sustained the optimism of Goethe. . . . We call his spirit universal man, transcending the partial, the provincial and the passing. . . . The symptomatic difficulties of nationalism, classism and racism and the symptomatic phenomena of technology and industrialism were real and intelligible to him not in the old world he was born in, but in the new one he died in. The man who spoke of the level where "national hatred disappears and one stands above the nations" spoke to 1949. . . .

. . . If man is somehow one and if the world is somehow one, it is not too soon to wonder what it is that unifies both man and the world. World organization will be human community or it will not be at all. And the great society, fully, even distractedly, conscious of its divergences and distinctions, will not become the human community until it finds the common spirit that is man. We try here to undeceive and fortify ourselves. We turn here to Goethe and search him, the better to turn to and search ourselves, and cry More Light! More Light!

III

The twenty-day Goethe convocation began on June 27, 1949, with more than two thousand people who came to Aspen from all over the world. Most of the featured participants were lodged in the Wheeler Hotel, but whenever possible were accommodated in the homes of individuals closely associated with the Aspen Company. Ortega, for example, was the guest of Herbert Bayer for the duration of the convocation. Among the visitors there was some grumbling at first over living conditions. While a fleet of buses conveyed visitors from the center of the town to the tent where concerts were held, Aspen at the time had few paved streets or sidewalks, and after a rainfall, it took a high order of skill to navigate a clean passage between mudholes. Further, since there was room in the Jerome Hotel for only a fraction of the crowd that more than doubled Aspen's population, most persons were housed in the dormitories used by winter skiers or in the long-closed homes which the Aspen Company had converted into adequate, but far from luxurious, guest houses, or wherever else a roof and wash basin could be found in the Aspen valley.

Yet the grumbling stopped when it was discovered that the informal living arrangements made for a free interchange of ideas in an easy and pleasant way. Distinguished speakers did not retire to cloisters where they talked only to each other; they were close at hand and could be engaged in spontaneous discussions under a tree, in the course of a walk, over a cup of coffee or a midnight drink. As would be true of the Aspen Institute in later years, the new perceptions that might be suddenly earned during an informal encounter—along with new friendships—were often more important in their long-range effects than the sparks struck in a formal lecture. Evelyn Ames, of Cold Spring Harbor, Long Island, described the effect on her at the time, and the words she used would be echoed by statements of participants in the Aspen Institute of the future. "At such altitudes," she wrote, "everything was a little sharper, in clearer focus, a little nearer the sky. Here there was no superficially cosmopolitan gathering, no arbitrary elite, but the most surprising and heady brew of Europe and the New World, of Weimar and the corner drugstore, of Goethe and cowboy boots."

Dr. Schweitzer and his wife were not due to arrive in Aspen

until the convocation had been under way for several days, but
their schedule was upset when a rockslide on the Denver and Rio
Grande caused their train to detour via the Royal Gorge. (On this
train trip, incidentally, a woman came up to Dr. Schweitzer and
said: "Oh, Dr. Einstein, I am so interested in your book on
Relativity. I have it with me. Would you mind inscribing it?" He
complied by writing in the fly-leaf: "Albert Einstein, by his good
friend Albert Schweitzer.") When the wayfarers from Lambarene
finally reached Glenwood in the small hours of the night, they
were met by Walter Paepcke, who convoyed them to their beds in
the Paepcke guest cottage, the former stable at Pioneer Park—an
arrangement which inspired the comment that the Paepckes had
bedded a saint in their manger. When good-nights were being said
and the Schweitzers asked what time breakfast would be served,
they were told that it would be at eight o'clock sharp. Mrs. Paepcke
had not as yet met her distinguished guests, but the next morning,
at 7:45, it was not Schweitzer's organ music that put an end to her
slumbers. She has since recalled:

I was awakened by a spine-chilling yell which made me leap from
my bed and my sleep. In the bathroom Walter Paepcke stood, very red
and very naked, in six inches of water—water which was bubbling up
from the drain of the shower bath, spilling out of the washstand and
toilet bowl and rapidly filling the tub. "Don't stand there! Do something!" As I was, nylon nightgown, wild hair, bare feet, and what was
worse that mark of vanity on my forehead—a square of court-plaster
called a "frownie"—I darted out of the room, by the front door, through
the living room to the kitchen, where I seized mop, bucket, and sponge.
I gave the horrified maids orders to find and turn off the plumbing
connections, and then streaked back the way I had come.

At that moment our Victorian clock chimed 8:00. The front door
opened. There stood the great man himself, just as he had been described to me: shaggy mane of grey hair, amused brown eyes, immense
drooping mustache, the black folded tie, old-fashioned long coat—and
on his arm an elderly lady in gray and garnets who looked like a pale
moth. "*Denouement.*" I stared at the doctor.

"Oh," I cried, "our plumbing has backed up, there is water all over
the floor, and I have to rescue my husband from the bathroom."

"I see," said Dr. Schweitzer slowly, as he looked me over from tousled hair to bare feet and mop. "I see," he repeated. "Mrs. Schweitzer and I are just in time to witness the second flood (*die zweit Welt-flut*)."

Dr. Schweitzer gave two lectures in the orange and beige tent designed by Eero Saarinen. The first lecture, in French, was translated by his old friend, Dr. Emory Ross. The second, in German, was translated by Thornton Wilder, who discovered to his embarrassment that he began by translating a eulogy to himself. On both days, Schweitzer stood with folded hands, hardly moving, speaking in a surprisingly high and childlike voice. He wore his usual long, black coat and high, stiff, winged collar. But instead of looking pontifical, he gave the illusion of frailty and extreme vulnerability. It was hard to believe that this man with his bare hands had hewn a hospital out of a disease-infested jungle.

People who were in the audience later confessed that they were so overcome by the aura of his personality that they could scarcely pay attention to his words. Norman Cousins, editor of the *Saturday Review*, came close to the heart of the matter when he said that the most important aspect of Schweitzer's presence in Aspen was "the simple pragmatic fact that he was *there*." Later, however, the published text of Schweitzer's remarks contained a passage which served in its own way as a directional signal to the Aspen Institute of the future:

> The domain assigned to human reason, Goethe says, is that of work and action. Being active, reason rarely risks going astray. But what is duty? Goethe replies: "What the day demands." So, too, it is for us to open our eyes, to realize our immediate duties, and to carry them out. In doing this we become able to see what tasks still remain to be done.

July 16 was the closing day of the convocation. Robert M. Hutchins, the last speaker on the program, ventured to draw together in a single overarching statement the threads of thought that had run through the formal remarks of the other speakers and through the many informal discussions that had engrossed many members of the audience. In developing his theme— "Goethe and World Unity"—he argued that a world catastrophe was inevitable if "the tribal self-adoration" which goes under the name of patriotism continues unchecked and if mankind's expanding knowledge is not turned toward achievement instead of "trivialization, and a Coney Island." Hutchins observed:

If it is possible to apply atomic energy to peacetime purposes, then we shall have more vacant time. Atomic energy therefore confronts mankind with this dreadful choice. If we have war, we shall be blown to bits; if we have peace, we shall be bored to death. There is no military way by which we can avoid being blown to bits. There is no mechanical way by which we can hope to avoid being bored to death. Since there is no defense against the atomic bombs, that tribal adoration which is the current definition of patriotism is worse than silly; it is suicidal. Since the mechanical means of escaping from boredom that we have already employed have induced a universal passivity, we may be said to be sinking into a coma from which even the most fantastic mechanical means, like television and the comic book, can no longer arouse us.

Hutchins went on to observe that our rapidly expanding knowledge was attained by specialization and experiment. But the success of specialization led to specialism, a state of mind that favored technical training at the expense of liberal culture and stopped communication between the scholar and the scholar, between the scholar and the layman, between man and man. Worse, said Hutchins, the greatest menace to our civilization was the menace of the uneducated expert. He won respect because he was an expert. His advice was hearkened to in fields in which he was not expert because of his eminence in the field, necessarily narrow, in which he was expert. Yet he knew nothing of other fields and nothing of the relation of his field to the rest.

Further, because of a double assertion—first, that only experimental knowledge can have validity, and second, that there can be no normative knowledge since the matter cannot be obtained by experiment—the social sciences and the law had lost their ethical basis. They had become descriptive or statistical, usually centering around the idea that society is the organization of power and the law is what the agents of organized power will do. "At the same time," said Hutchins, "the rising power of the enormous, mysterious, bureaucratic state and of the equally enormous, mysterious bureaucratic industrial corporation has removed the control over the life of the individual to such distant, inaccessible points that we may with some justice relapse into a general cynicism, apathy, and triviality." It was necessary, therefore, to recognize the special characteristics of our place and time and proceed in the hope that through reflection and good will, we could liberate ourselves from the dreary and terrifying dilemma confronting modern man. "The triumphs of specialization were such that we ought not to abandon them if we could. But was there any reason why the specialist should be an uneducated man, ignorant of everything except what he specifically requires?" Hutchins concluded by saying:

There is no reason why, if we want to, we cannot use the incredible means of communication that science and technology have given us to promote the unity of mankind. We know now that mere improvement in the mechanics of transportation and communication cannot give us one world. . . . [They] can merely heighten our fears of a universal explosion ignited by bringing the sparks of greed and ambition too close together. One bad world, moreover, is worse than many; for in many worlds there is at least the chance that men of good will can escape, like Wilhelm Meister's pilgrims, from one world to another.

In one good Goethean world the means of communication and transportation would be used not to send bombs, spies, propaganda, and messengers of misguided self-interest from one country to another, but to exchange students, professors, ideas, and books and to develop a supranational community founded on the humanity of the whole human race. The essence of the Civilization of the Dialogue is communication, The Civilization of the Dialogue presupposes mutual respect and understanding; it does not presuppose agreement. . . . In *Wilhelm Meister*, there is a speech which, it seems to me, is appropriately addressed to this assembly on this great occasion: "Since we came together so miraculously, let us not lead a trivial life; let us together become active in a noble manner! . . . Let us make a league for this. . . ."

It is not too much to hope that the connections formed here in the past weeks by people from all over the world may be continued and strengthened and that through meetings, correspondence, and publication, communication among men of good will may be established and may spread to other individuals and other groups everywhere, perhaps even to those behind the Iron Curtain. Let us take heart in remembering that the Lord promised to save the city of Sodom if ten good men could be found in it.

The tasks awaiting the "ten good men" turned on the proposition that our knowledge had come to exceed our capacity to use it for good. The solution was not to reduce our knowledge or to halt the progress of science, but to make our moral stamina equal to it, since the problem of preserving our civilization was a moral problem. "Our difficulty was not in getting more knowledge and more goods, but to do the right thing with them when we get them." And on this central point, the perspective which informed Hutchins' summation of the Goethe bicentennial celebration, would also inform the perspective of the Aspen Institute.

IV

Financially, the Goethe bicentennial celebration wound up with a deficit of $150,000 that was covered in ways already indicated. The musical portion of the festival, however, was a sweeping success. Because of a great and unsatisfied demand for seats at the concerts, the whole program was repeated after the formal end of the convocation. Better yet, so many musicians were enchanted by the physical setting of Aspen and with audience reactions that they volunteered to return to Aspen the next year if a music festival was held—and if they could bring some of their students along. Here, so it seemed to the musicians, magical things not foreseen and not planned in advance happened anyway. An emblematic case in point, which the musicians relished, concerned a nameless Texan who, when roaring over Independence Pass in a rush to get to a concert on time, found the way blocked by an ancient jalopy lumbering up in the opposite direction. Since passing was impossible, the Texan got out, bought the jalopy, and with the aid of the former owner, pushed it over a cliff. The former owner, now bereft of transportation, got into the Texan's car and rode back with him to be his guest at the concert.

Newspaper reporters and music critics from the nation's major newspapers who were present at the festival helped broadcast the news to the outer world that Aspen was something more than a place for skiing. It was an emergent new cultural center, a fact that was semaphored in the captions over representative press reports:

U. S. CULTURE MOVES WEST
WHEN IT'S TIME TO THINK IN THE ROCKIES
BRAIN SPA

In Hutchins' terms, the Goethe bicentennial was also a marked success in "adult education." Men and women from diverse walks of life had come together not only to listen to what eminent scholars had to say, but also to communicate with them and with each other about a great range of common concerns. It was something he had long struggled to bring about in the context of a great university. Now here it was, suddenly, an authentic community of discourse. Could it be recreated and kept alive in some form once the convocation was over? The same point was raised by many other people who shared in the experiences of the convocation, and they signed a "petition" to Hutchins, asking that he take the lead in the search for an affirmative answer to the question.

Clarence Faust has recalled that when a group of the signers met with Hutchins and Paepcke for a discussion about Aspen's post-convocation future, Paepcke revealed that he had been toying with the idea of creating in Aspen "something like a university" but with none of the depressing aspects of university life. It would be a place with no degrees, no examinations, no football teams, no problems with alumni, no faculty committees, no squalid infighting over faculty tenure and promotions.

"No tenure and promotions?" asked a skeptic wise in the ways of academic life. "Who would come?"

"Young scholars," said Paepcke, "who want a chance to pursue their natural interests without worrying about what they would need to get ahead in the academic pecking order. They would be joined by retired scholars who had spent their life in academic housekeeping chores, and who would grab at a last chance to be scholars."

"Well," asked another skeptic, "what would you do about a library? You can't have a great university without a library, and the building of a great library is a work of generations."

Paepcke parried the challenge by turning to Mortimer Adler, who was standing nearby. "Mortimer," he asked, "how many Great Books are there?" The discussions ended in laughter.

"Form," said Goethe, "creates substance." And the form of what was to be done after the end of the convocation was visible only with respect to two matters. First, Aspen could be the home of an annual summer music festival and perhaps of a music school —considering the number of established musicians who said they would like to bring some of their students to Aspen for summertime instruction. To this end, Paepcke said his Aspen Company would buy from the Goethe Bicentennial Foundation the $55,000 tent which Eero Saarinen had designed and built. The tent would continue to serve as the "amphitheater" for summertime concerts, while music students would be lodged in the ski dormitories which would otherwise be empty in the summer.

Secondly, Paepcke's concern over ways to use the accommodations of the Aspen Company in the period after the end of the winter sports season but before the start of the summer inspired a Bayer-Paepcke plan for an Aspen Conference on Design to be held in the spring of 1950. The two men checked their ideas with Egbert Jacobson, director of design for the Container Corporation of America. He, in turn, agreed that there was at that time no event and no one place where artists, publishers, architects, engineers, manufacturers, and other business executives from around the nation could come together and seriously discuss the many-faceted aspects of design. A conference on design held in Aspen could fill not only this vacuum in communications, but also the empty housing facilities of the Aspen Company during the spring season. With Jacobson in the lead, steps were taken to bring such a conference into being.

But what else could be done?

After the main participants in the Goethe bicentennial had left Aspen, it occurred to Paepcke that José Ortega y Gasset—who was now back in Europe—might have some thoughts on the subject. So, in a letter to Ortega, he enclosed a copy of the "petition" that had been submitted to Hutchins, and after alluding to it, went on to say something else. He had in mind, said he, the creation in Aspen of "something like a university." Perhaps the Spanish philosopher "would laugh at the idea," but in any case, Paepcke would welcome his candid reaction.

PART II: The Founding Years

5. MIDWIVES TO A BIRTH

Ortega responded to Paepcke's communication with a ten-page single-spaced letter which reached Paepcke in late October, 1949. The text gave form to many inchoate things that were in the air, suggested the name for what would become the Aspen Institute for Humanistic Studies, and anticipated some of the structural features the Institute would eventually incorporate.

Ortega stated straight off that he would "not laugh at the idea" that had been sketched in "unless it be in the sense that all joy carries a smile on one's lips." But while he "unreservedly applauded" Paepcke's "appetite" for the proposed university, Ortega urged him for the time being to lay aside the term "university." The term, said he, had many connotations, and its use would serve only to obscure what Paepcke was reaching for. Once the term was laid aside and attention was focused on its nuclear meaning—"advanced studies" or "*Hochschule*" education—it would be possible to be more precise "in defining the *new* undertaking for a most *novel* institution."

Bearing this in mind, Ortega continued:

> I see in your initiative a magnificent possibility for creating something completely new, which is needed in America nowadays and may gradually attract, as regards both students and professors, some of the best intellectual and moral forces of your country. . . . There is in America an extremely unbalanced state as regards education in favor of the naturalistic (not humanistic), physical, biological, and technical education.

Ortega then went on to propose the creation at Aspen of a "High School [*Hochschule*] of Humanities." "By humanities," said he, "I have in mind not only the traditional humanities which

93

are summed up in the study of Greece and Rome, but all those matters which are concerned with specifically human facts, including—and even most principally—current human problems." The proposed High School of Humanities should not for the moment be a research center. Its educational mission should be to promote *"a total synthesis of human life,"* to make *"a single* discipline" of the physical and biological sciences and the humanities. The synthesis to be achieved, would be made "on the basis of *a library with very few but masterly chosen volumes."* This scarcity would not carry with it a sense of privation, of deficiency, but on the contrary would have a deliberately positive sense. "For the aim would be to teach how to read, how to *really absorb* an important book," and to apply to the reading "the principles of concentration and synthesis."

In coming to the specifically educational aspects of the proposed High School for the Humanities, Ortega observed that certain innovations were both possible and desirable:

> We all need a measure of physical comforts so that the human individual, free from material hindrances, can devote himself to being a man; that is to say, allow his inner self to live intensely and give himself fully to thinking, imagining, loving, and feeling. Man is "inwardness." Now we could call a certain amount of comfort excess as long as it does not produce this effect and if man instead gives himself over to comfort instead of to himself. I think I can be understood if I say that in my opinion the American *handles too many objects.* The circle of his personal life is too much taken up by implements, devices, gadgets. During my trip to the States I had the impression that the American runs the risk of getting lost in objects, of living *on* and *in* objects. For it is not only a question of handling and taking care of them, but of worrying excessively about them, desiring them, getting excited about them, being obsessed with their production and acquisition, sacrificing for their sake too much of oneself, of one's excitement, imagination, attention, energy. If this fear which I mention had any semblance of truth, we would find ourselves faced with a case of excessive comfort against which we had better react.

On this ground, Ortega argued that the proposed new school should "provide very few conveniences as long as that discomfort does not result in a shortage of their working capacity and joy."

Of a piece with this, the first and second educational principles of the new school should be "Spartanism" and "elegance." By "Spartanism," he meant not only austerity and temperance, but energy, continuity of effort, endurance, and the elegance the Greeks associated with "Doricism" or Sparta. "Elegance," said he, "must penetrate, influence a man's entire life, from his gestures and ways of talking, through his way of dressing, through the way he uses language, carries on a conversation, speaks in public—and so on to the most intimate side of *moral* and intellectual actions."

To the "normal curriculum" of the proposed new school, Ortega suggested that there be added a modest number of public lectures which would bring together five or six persons of the highest intellectual rank. If their meeting was to be significant, it was essential that they be roughly equal mentally. "Never mind," said he, "if one of them thinks A and the other B. Their meeting will be fruitful if their opposed views A and B are held at the same level." The theme of such courses, lectures, and colloquies "must be extremely vivid, deeply human, and should offer a great incentive to the general public even if they must be treated with a thorough-going scientific rigor." Students would gain much by simply observing the models of conduct presented by such speakers. Conversely, "elegant people" who found themselves immersed in a high intellectual and moral milieu would feel charged "with a new and exquisite electricity," with a heightened sense of responsibility for what they said and did, and would lose their "partly justified horror of pedagogy."

"The idea then," said Ortega in conclusion, is to

create in the Aspen summer a "world." A "world" however, is not a fortuitous gathering of individuals. It is a living together *informed* by unity. To that end, it may help if individuals attend courses and lectures, concerts, and festivals—as was the case at the Goethe Bicentennial, with its musical counterpart. Such unity, however, will not crystalize unless there is a permanent instrument of general collective life in Aspen.

Hence the most urgent need in Aspen is a place that can hold about one thousand people and where these people can move freely, spend their time comfortably, have their meals, have tea, have their drinks, in short, see one another all together many times a day. This would be the place for their collective existence, of co-existing for practically all the visitors to Aspen. The premises need not, nor should they have more than a single ground floor, with walls and ceilings of the least costly architecture. I do not think it should be difficult to obtain good restaurant facilities, etc. The grounds of the premises must be terraced so that everyone can see each other within the enormous space. I know you will smile, but I have good reason to believe that this humble physical detail is *vital* to the project which these pages briefly suggest.

Paepcke was in Chicago when he received Ortega's letter, written in Spanish. Within hours after he read an English translation of the text, he telephoned Mortimer Adler and invited him to lunch. When the two men met, Paepcke did most of the talking. The Goethe convocation, said he, had been a great success. But the more he thought about the matter, the more he thought that it was a waste of money to maintain Aspen only as a winter ski resort. To do so would be to leave the resources of the place unused for the other half of the year. While he meant for Aspen to be the home of a summertime music festival—and to that end, would form an Aspen music association and possibly an affiliated Aspen music school—he was concerned about the intellectual side of the summertime program. "Why not," said he to Adler, "offer in Aspen a summertime version of the 'Fat Man's Seminar in the Great Books?' " Adler has since recalled that he confined his reply to a single word—yes, whereupon he thanked Paepcke for the lunch and thought no more about what had been discussed.

II

In April of 1950 on the eve of the first Aspen Conference on Design, a telephone exchange in Chicago between Walter Paepcke and Mortimer Adler went something like this:

Paepcke: "I am going to Aspen with Pussy [an affectionate nickname for Elizabeth Paepcke] for a conference on design which Herbert Bayer and I have put together. Why don't you come out with us so that we can work on the schedule?"

Adler: "What schedule?"

Paepcke: "The schedule for the seminar in Aspen."

Adler: "What seminar?"

Paepcke: "The one we discussed last fall. The Great Books seminar. Remember, you said yes?"

Adler: "Yes, what?"

Paepcke: "Yes, it was a great idea to have one like it in Aspen."

Adler at the time was absorbed in the final round of work in connection with the fifty-four-volume set of the *Great Books of the Western World,* and with its indispensable two-volume *Syntopicon.* He nonetheless agreed to go to Aspen. Here, in a week end of work, he designed the format for a reading list of Great Books that would be tried out in the coming summer. He also compiled a provisional list of notable figures who might participate in the public discussions of the texts, and whose "starred" names might attract audiences to what was said.

Two matters of a legal nature were now attended to by Paepcke. At his request, Glen A. Lloyd drew up and registered with the appropriate Colorado authorities a charter for a not-for-profit corporation to be known as the Aspen Institute for Humanistic Studies. Concurrently, he presented an impressive roster of trustees, many of whom had been prominently associated with the Goethe convocation either as officers and directors of the Goethe Bicentennial Foundation or as featured speakers. In addition to Albert Schweitzer, who agreed to serve as an honorary trustee, those who had been associated with the Goethe bicentennial included Paepcke, Hutchins, Lloyd, Thornton Wilder, José Ortega y Gasset, James Laughlin, Robert L. Stearns, and W. Lee Knous. The last two—Stearns, president of the University of Colorado, and Knous, who had moved from the governorship of Colorado to the federal bench—provided symbolic links between the Aspen Institute and the state of Colorado. Another trustee, John Herron, of a mining family in Aspen, symbolically linked the Institute with the local community. Yet another of the original trustees, Clarence Faust, had been among the leaders of the Great Books

movement at the University of Chicago, but was now at the forefront of foundation work in support of education. The remaining
trustees, like those just mentioned, were drawn from the worlds
of education, business, and government. They included the Rev-
erend John J. Cavanaugh, Abram Leon Sachar, John Erskine, Carl-
ton Sprague Smith, Albert C. Jacons, General William H. Gill,
Harold Pabst, William Trumbull, Walter Walker, and Allan R.
Phipps.

A public statement issued in the name of these trustees, described the purpose of the newly formed Institute as follows:

Education, according to Whitehead, should hold before us and
sustain a "vision of greatness," the greatness of the human spirit and of
the worlds of man. To this educational objective, the Aspen Institute
for Humanistic Studies is dedicated. The essence of its humanistic
ideal is the affirmation of man's dignity, not simply as a political credo,
but through the contemplation of the noblest works of man—in the
creation of beauty and in the attainment of truth.

At the midpoint of the twentieth century, when men's lives are
dominated more than ever by science, men need the elevation and
liberation of a sound humanism. In a world which almost worships
science and technology, we must rediscover the moral and spiritual
truths which will enable men to control science and all its machinery.

To help launch the 1950 trial run of the Great Books Seminar, Adler recruited the support of Reinhold Niebuhr, Clarence
Faust, William Gorman, Robert M. Hutchins, Lawrence Kimpton,[1] Karl Menninger, Alexander Meiklejohn, Meredith Willson,
Yves Simon, Clare Booth Luce, Olin Downs, and others. They
were to continue the "search for greatness" through colloquia on
man and his institutions, the fundamental ideals that provide the
good life and the relation of the "search for greatness" to contemporary American conditions. The public meeting place chosen
for the enterprise was the Wheeler Opera House, with Mortimer
Adler giving the first lecture on the morning of July 2, 1950.

Since the Institute was to be dedicated to humanistic studies

---

[1] Hutchins had by this time left the University of Chicago to become the
vice-president of the newly formed Ford Foundation; Lawrence Kimpton had been
chosen his successor as chancellor of the University of Chicago.

—to the study of man and of human values in relation to all aspects of human life—it seemed appropriate for Adler to choose the nature of man as his theme. The central thesis he advanced was that man differs from all other animals and everything else on earth, not in degree, but in kind; that man has certain species—specific properties not possessed at all or in any degree by other animals, such as speech and conceptual thought. Man, certainly, is the only animal on earth who can consciously think about the extinction of his own species. Everything else in the human scene —every aspect of the human environment—may change, but man's specific nature is an unchanging constant and will remain so as long as the human race endures as a species. A quarter of a century later, Adler would look again at this theme.

Although the interior of the Wheeler Opera House had been refurbished under Herbert Bayer's direction, in the absence of paved streets outside, the route to the Opera House led through a sea of mud after a rain or through clouds of dust when the sun was shining. The same was true of the seminars initially held inside the Opera House. Here, as Adler and his collaborators readily agreed, the meaning of the word "seminar" when applied to the discussions of the Great Books was as muddy and dusty as Aspen's streets.

One of the reasons was a mismatch between the structure of Adler's reading list and the nature of his Aspen audience. The structure assumed a situation similar to a classroom at the University of Chicago or to the Fat Man's Seminar in "downtown" Chicago. In either of the latter contexts, the continuity of the participants enabled Adler to move back and forth among the themes of successive books and to weave them into a tapestry of understanding. In Aspen, however, the people who came for the first summer offering of the Great Books programs comprised a floating population. Some stayed one week, some two, some three, making it impossible to treat the material so that ideas would be as strands on a loom. Discussions tended to be confined to the frame of just one book each week.

For another thing, few members of the audience had read the

book under discussion. Hence they were either reduced to passive eavesdroppers on what was said or, when they spoke up, could not cogently challenge a discussion leader or be challenged in turn. The mismatch extended to the discussion leaders themselves. Depending on the book to be analyzed in a given week, the discussion leaders were four "panelists" chosen by Adler. As they sat on the stage of the Wheeler Opera House and talked among themselves, their individual performances could be dazzling. Yet they were only that—performances, as in a spectator sport. They did not make a seminar in which the roles of the teachers and the taught are interchangeable.

A saving suggestion was at hand, however, and its source was Henry Luce, Jr., the creator and head of the Time, Inc., publishing empire. Luce, Yale '19, had a natural interest in the business career of Paepcke, Yale '17, since the Container Corporation regularly placed handsome advertisements in the pages of *Time, Life,* or *Fortune.* He had also been drawn into the affairs of the University of Chicago through his friendships with Hutchins and William Benton, both graduates of Yale in 1920 and both coming, as Luce did, from missionary families. Thus he had served as a member of the American Policy Commission; formed at the University of Chicago in 1940 on the initiative of Paul Hoffman, a university trustee, and of Benton, a university vice-president, the commission was the forerunner of the Hoffman-Benton-led Committee for Economic Development. Luce was also a director of the University of Chicago-affiliated Encyclopedia Britannica Company, and again, he had financed the Commission on a Free Press which had headquarters at the university.

In the summer of 1950, Luce spent three weeks in Aspen, where his wife, Clare Booth Luce, was to participate in a Great Books seminar. He happened to be in the audience on the night when she shared the stage of the Wheeler Opera House with Adler, William Gorman, and Elizabeth Paepcke for a discussion of Pascal's *Pensées.* Luce was fascinated by the turns and twists of what he heard, but as an experienced and very successful consumer-minded publisher, he was also troubled by the profile of the people who comprised his fellow listeners. They were personally attractive, but were they the best audience for what was being offered on the stage?

After the seminar, when the participants went to the Paepcke home for refreshments, Henry Luce delivered a *Pensée* of his own. "It was a wonderful evening in the Opera House," said he, "and I enjoyed myself thoroughly. Yet, in what you are offering, you are guilty of a great oversight. Your audience is now made up of students, schoolteachers, lawyers, and the like. But what about the forgotten man in the cultural life of our society? What about the great, unwashed American businessman? Get the American businessman to come to Aspen, to share and experience directly what I saw occur here tonight. He is the man you want, because he is the man who needs you the most."

The *Pensée* led to a swirl of excited talk back and forth that extended well into the night. It was recognized that the postwar Committee for Economic Development was doing important work in getting businessmen to devote time, effort, energy, and money to the task of clarifying their own minds and those of their fellow citizens about the major alternatives of national *economic* policy for a free society. But the need was for something that went beyond the limits of economics—or even beyond the Fat Man's Seminar in the Great Books which Hutchins and Adler had conducted for many years in Chicago. The need was for business leaders to sit at the same table with leaders in the world of letters, theology, government, labor, and science to discuss a broad range of fundamental problems of contemporary society and Western civilization. The governing maxim for saving a nation's soil— "start with the hilltop and not the river bottom"—applied as well to saving a nation's soul: "Start with the men on top." American business executives had shown the world how to use men in order to make things great, but it was now imperative that they should try harder to make great men, starting with their own lives as citizens.

By the time everyone was bedded down for the night, it was agreed that the Aspen Institute would offer a program in the summer of 1951 to be known as the Aspen Executive Seminar. Many decisions on vital details still had to be made. They included the method for recruiting business executives, the number of participants, the place where they would be quartered, the fees that would be charged, the length of a seminar, the choice of seminar leaders and special guests, and the design of an appropriate reading program combining the classics with significant contemporary works of particular interest to established or potential heads of corporations.

The design, as worked out for the summer of 1951, did not stand in one place forever, after the manner of a painted soldier in a battle canvas. It underwent many experimental changes in the passing years, including, after 1969, an infusion of texts from Asian classical sources to supplement those which stemmed from Judea, Greece, and Rome. Indeed, the Executive Seminar itself would take on new meaning after 1969 when Joseph E. Slater, who had been chosen by Robert O. Anderson to be the president of the Aspen Institute, gave the Institute new programmatic directions. Yet for all the changes—including increases in fees which never caught up with costs—the Executive Seminar itself would remain a cornerstone of the Aspen Institute from 1951 to the present.

It would remain so, despite recurrent financial crises, recurrent doubts about the survival powers of the Institute, recurrent internal strains, and recurrent "town and gown" tensions, some of which now seem comical but which were full of rancor when they occurred. To Paepcke's logical mind, for example, Aspen's flourishing real estate industry and revived commercial enterprises owed much to the existence of the Institute and the people it attracted to its music festivals, music school, and Executive Seminars. It seemed reasonable to him, therefore, that 5 per cent of the gross receipts of every business in Aspen should go as a tax-deductible source of support to the Aspen Institute. But his public proposal to that effect outraged all local entrepreneurs, and his idea, which was meant to generate additional income for the businesses, quickly failed. So, too, did his plan of furnishing his Hotel Jerome guests with special tickets that would place them ahead of the line at the ski lift, thus encouraging guests to stay at the hotel, the increased profits to go to support the Aspen Institute. So, too, his idea of leasing the banks of the local creeks so that his guests could enjoy private trout fishing. All these publicly aired proposals did violence to local notions about the rights of squatter sovereignty, leading to outcries against Paepcke personally.

Paepcke, in turn, had his own grievances against the community, and the frictions between the two eventually came to a head in 1954. The circumstances, as recalled by Henry L. Stein, were these. A group of sporting types—this was before golf or tennis was available in Aspen—decided to form a roping club, requiring ten acres with a fenced arena for calf pens. On Sundays one would compete with his friends and show off his best horse. But with this installation, why not build bleachers and put on a regular Aspen-type rodeo? In a few days the proposal became the center of what the Denver papers called a "Music versus Manure" controversy which shook the earth from Independence Pass to the Frying Pan River. The reasons are best told directly in Stein's own words:

You see, Mr. Paepcke took a dim view of the $12,000 so readily available for a rodeo but never offered by the community in support of his Music Festival and Institute program. He literally fulminated with anger and forbade by decree the community from having a rodeo, stating that the summertime audience in Aspen was *his* captive audience and that they were not to be exposed to common rodeo entertainment. He further proclaimed, and he meant it, that if a rodeo were put on during the Festival season he would immediately withdraw all future music programs and close up the Institute and even foreclose on the Skiing Corporation. Well, the business community went into an uproar of fear and desperation. The rodeo types were stubborn about their rights and would not give an inch.

At the height of the controversy there occurred what Stein called "the most heroic confrontation in Aspen history." Herbert Bayer, whose bread and butter depended at the time on the Container Corporation of America, took his economic life in his hands by putting a simple truth squarely to Paepcke. "Walter," said he, "you have your Institute for Humanistic Studies. You preach and admire the humanities. Walter, now you *practice* them!" Paepcke thought this over for about forty seconds and said, "Herbert, you are right. We'll let them do as they please."

III

Before turning directly to the nature of the Executive Seminars, two institutional developments should be noted. From an intellectual standpoint, the first Aspen Conference on Design, held in the spring of 1950, was a success. The income from housing two hundred participants, however, did not cover the costs of the conference. So the deficits incurred at the time, as well as those incurred the next year, were met by subventions from Paepcke's Container Corporation of America. After that, the conference participants formed a dues-paying organization with its own board of directors and renamed themselves the International Design Conference. Spring meetings were held annually in Aspen— now for twenty-four consecutive years—and anyone familiar with what transpired at them could subsequently trace their ripple effects in many forms and places: in the graphic arts, in the design of consumer products, in engineering and architecture, in the curricula taught in schools of design, and in the creation of counterpart conferences on design in places such as New York. Moreover, an index of the themes of successive meetings reflected the steadily widening horizon of the directors. They were initially concerned only with the specifically technical or commercial aspects of design. As time went by, however, they raised their sights to include the interaction between design and a wide range of environmental forces—physical, social, economic, and cultural. As time went by also, the annual conferences regularly attracted about one thousand persons.

The second institutional development grew out of a proposal put to Paepcke and Egbert Jacobson in the summer of 1950 by Ferenc Berko, who had made his name in Europe as a photographer, had come to the United States after World War II to teach at the Chicago Institute of Design. With the rebirth of

Aspen, he settled in the place as its unofficial "photographer-in-residence"—a fortunate event for both himself and Aspen, since his lens was to chronicle the post–1945 history of Aspen and, as these pages show, of the Aspen Institute itself, starting with the Goethe bicentennial.

Paepcke proposed to Berko and Jacobson that Aspen would be an ideal place to hold a fall conference on photography. The whole of the surrounding region would then be ablaze with autumn colors; noted photographers could be invited to serve as panelists for the workshop session of the conference; and these facts, if properly publicized, would draw camera buffs to Aspen—thus making use of the ski dormitories before the winter season started. Berko had in mind a conference in the fall of 1951, so that the event could be properly publicized in the mass-circulation photography magazines—with their long lead time for publication. Paepcke, however, was impatient for action and insisted on a conference immediately after the end of the summer of 1950. The one that was quickly put together was judged a success from an artistic and pedagogic standpoint, but with only 150 people in attendance, it was a financial failure.

Paepcke balked at a second try, and there was none—though some of the participants in the pioneering venture in Aspen later made a financial success of the conferences on photography they organized elsewhere. It was left to Berko to make a different contribution of a durable nature to the Aspen Institute aside from his photographic history of the place. While at the Chicago Institute of Design, he had compiled a list of films which, taken together, comprised a graphic account of the evolution of the film in all its aspects. His list, along with explanatory notes, became the basis on which the Institute launched its program of Screen Classics—now the oldest continuous program of its kind in the United States.

6. THE EXECUTIVE SEMINAR

I

In Adler's design for the Executive Seminars, the point of departure and return were a set of "Aspen Readings," containing a sweep of tough thinking about social, economic, and political problems. Some of the thinking was done several thousand years ago, as in the case of selections from the Bible, from Plato, Aristotle, Sophocles, and Thucydides. Some was done in modern times, as in the case of selections from the Federalist papers, from Karl Marx, from Sigmund Freud, and, for that matter, from Senator Robert A. Taft. All dealt with ideas such as equality, liberty, justice, and property—ideas of central importance to an understanding of "democracy" and "capitalism" as well as of their opposites, "totalitarianism" and "communism."

In a sequence of sessions spread over twelve days, the readings were meant to open up in a fanlike fashion, to widen the arc of perceptions about the same four fundamental ideas, so that the participants could see and grasp more as each day's discussion built on those of the preceding days. At the same time, to avoid the bogus clarity where only one side of a case is seen, the readings for a given day would include conflicting views about major issues. Seminar participants would then be asked to formulate the terms of the conflict, to state where they stood with respect to the rival sides, and to defend their positions under challenge.

Although the premise of the readings and discussions assumed that the truth was *in principle* discoverable—else, why bother to seek it by means of an argument?—the seminars would teach no dogmas, but would encourage the participants to examine all dogmas, starting with their own. Further, the Executive Seminar would not provide businessmen with pat answers to the practical problems they faced, no more than it would try to preach them into "goodness." It recognized that though any two practical problems might have the same ingredients, they could be as different from each other as water and peroxide of hydrogen, which are composed of the same chemical elements but in different proportions. It also recognized that human beings could no more be preached into goodness than a car stalled in subzero weather could be started by a crack of a whip and a shout, "Giddiap!" The purpose of the Executive Seminar was to provide the thoughtful executive with a unique opportunity to look with fresh eyes at the routine of his own life, to test his own governing concepts in the light of the important utterances in the intellectual legacy of the West, to gain a certain critical distance from which he could get into better focus the dynamics of the society of which he was a part.

This was not only Adler's view but Paepcke's as well, and it was the *leitmotif* of the case he made to business executives whom he personally tried to recruit for the Aspen reading-discussion program. "It is not the aim of the Aspen Executive Seminars," he would say simply, "to make a better treasurer out of a treasurer, or a better credit manager out of a credit manager, or to show how an advertising vice-president can be more effective in promoting a product. The aim is to help American business leaders lift their sights above the possessions which possess them, to confront their own nature as human beings, to regain control over their own humanity by becoming more self-aware, more self-correcting, and hence more self-fulfilling."

The simple message, however, did not simplify the task of recruiting participants for the first Executive Seminar or for those following. Although the Committee for Economic Development was by now providing the American business community with carefully reasoned statements about socioeconomic issues, the greater part of that community still took its intellectual bearing from the frenetic utterances prepared by the entrenched staffs of the old-line business organizations such as the National Manufacturers Association and the United States Chamber of Commerce. As such, in the first years of the 1950's, many businessmen seemed at one extreme to subject themselves to a treatment not unlike that of hospital nurses who wake their patients in order to give them sleeping pills. At another extreme, they joined willy-nilly in the hysteria that threatened to shatter the foundations for rational order in the realm of American public life.

It is enough merely to recall the events of the time which fed the hysteria. The Russians had exploded an atomic bomb; the Communists were triumphant in China; President Truman had ordered work begun on the hydrogen bomb; Alger Hiss had been found guilty of perjury for having denied that he had passed State Department documents to Communists; Klaus Fuchs in Great Britain had confessed that as a worker on the atomic energy program in America, he had placed atomic secrets in the hands of agents of the Soviet Union; the Korean War was raging with no terminal point in sight; Senator Joseph McCarthy was on his rampage; and Senator Robert A. Taft, as part of his strategy to win the presidency in 1952 for the Republican party and himself, seized every opportunity to "rough up" the scene.

Most of the businessmen whom Paepcke recruited for the first Executive Seminars tended to be independent-minded heads of their own enterprises, whereas in later years an ever increasing proportion would be members of the managerial class holding or marked for leadership posts in their respective companies. But it would be wrong to imply that all the early participants were drawn to Aspen because of a sacerdotal search for the elusive Holy Grail of Truth. One of them, Gaylord Freeman, who became president of the First National Bank of Chicago and a trustee of the Aspen Institute, has recalled that some business executives came to Aspen because "they hoped to sell something" to Walter Paepcke and his Container Corporation of America. "I know this to be so," he ruefully added, "because that's how it was in my own case. I was sent to Aspen by my bank in order to persuade Walter to do something in connection with a business matter—only to be taken by surprise when the Executive Seminar sold itself to me. I've never been the same since then."

Another story of surprise is told by Irving Harris, a major figure in Chicago's financial world and a steadfast source of support for many worthy liberal causes and civic institutions in a range from public television to the Chicago Institute of Psychoanalysis. As a man of self-starting intellectual curiosity, Harris' involvement in the Great Books movement provided the bridge that brought him to Aspen for an early Executive Seminar. Here one day, a banker who was a fellow participant drew him aside during a picnic for a private exchange. "This whole program," said the banker in a blaze of anger, "is nothing more than a New Deal or Communist plot to undermine the free enterprise system. Look at the stuff we've been asked to read, and just listen to the outrageous things being said in the discussions!"

"That's odd," Harris replied. "I've read and I've listened. And do you know something? The effect has made me change my mind about some of my liberal articles of faith. They don't stand up under sharp cross-examination." Harris would later become a member of the Institute's Society of Fellows.

The seminars initially had a floating location in Aspen. They were sometimes held in the back yard of the Paepcke home, sometimes in the Four Seasons building, sometimes in the Jerome Hotel, and many times around the outdoor swimming pool of the hotel. The swimming pool, in fact, was the social hub of the Institute and the conversational setting where businessmen and musicians closed the gap between their respective worlds and freely exchanged views and experiences. A business executive who never before knew what an arpeggio was, or to whom a note was something due at the bank, could suddenly find himself drawn into an *ad hoc* seminar on the theories of music, on the structure of musical compositions, or on the development of Western music since the time of Pythagoras. Conversely, a musician to whom "art" meant only the "fine arts," could hear a businessman contend that in the conduct of his own affairs, he was daily concerned with the perennial issues of art—issues of sight and insight, form and substance, tradition and innovation, combination and proportion, continuity and discussion. A musician who was a partner in some such conversational encounters could be the composer Darius Milhaud or conductor Izler Solomon of the Indianapolis Symphony Orchestra, someone from the Juilliard String Quartet or a celebrated performing artist such as Isaac Stern.

If the area around the swimming pool was a surrogate for what Ortega y Gasset had in mind in his letter to Paepcke when he stressed the need for "premises formed by terraces so that everyone can see the others within its enormous space," another surrogate for the desired terraces was a bench outside the Jerome Hotel.

The bench was specially favored by Paepcke as a place where he could watch Aspen's life pass in review. Seated there, and generally shod in weather-beaten black shoes whose pointed toes made his feet look like rapiers, he would raise one of his feet to stop any passerby whom he thought *should* be interested in the Aspen Institute and should become directly associated with it. One of those he stopped was James H. Smith, Jr., who in 1949 had bought a ranch on the outskirts of Aspen. Smith's forebears were Yankee clipper-ship captains, and his own sea-roaming instincts found their first outlet in the major role he played in the development of the world-circling Pan American Airways. He would go on to become Assistant Secretary of the Navy for Air in the Eisenhower Administration, would work closely with Admiral Hyman Rickover in developing the nuclear-powered *Nautilus* submarine (and in dealing with the psychological problems that were bound to affect its crews), would preside over the birth of the Polaris missile, and over a great range of post–World War II naval aircraft. He would add to all this valuable services performed as the head of the United States foreign aid program until he resigned in 1959.

Smith, in a word, was used to thinking "big." As a man who could see far-off realities behind ideas which initially seemed to be as tenuous as cloth spun from dew drops and thistledown, he caught by contagion Paepcke's enthusiasm for the future development of the Aspen Institute. He signed up for an Executive Seminar, became an early trustee of the Institute, and eventually, a vice-chairman of its board of trustees.

II

Businessmen such as Freeman, Harris, and Smith were not the only individuals who, having been exposed to the early Executive Seminars, developed a lasting attachment to the Institute. This was true as well of some of the early moderators and special guests drawn from backgrounds other than business. Regardless of the route that brought them to the seminars and regardless of their changed personal circumstances as the years went by, they afterwards bound themselves and remained bound to the Institute. Two quickly drawn illustrations will suffice.

One involved the figure of William E. Stevenson. Stevenson was descended from Jonathan Edwards, the foremost theologian of American Puritanism. The family in more recent generations had close ties with the Princeton academic community. Stevenson's own father, for example, was president of the Princeton Theological Seminary. His brother, Ted, also educated at Princeton, became a medical missionary in the Far East—where he was made a Japanese prisoner in the immediate aftermath of Pearl Harbor. Stevenson himself, a Princeton graduate, won an Olympic gold medal in 1924 as a member of an American relay team. He went on to Oxford as a Rhodes Scholar and secured his legal training at Inner Temple, London. On returning home, he began the practice of law in John W. Davis' New York firm and founded his own law firm in 1931. Meanwhile, he married Eleanore Bumstead, whose nickname "Bumpy," was derived from her family name and not from the shape of her figure—which drew appreciative whistles. It was, in a sense, a marriage between "religion and science," since "Bumpy's" father was the head of the physics department at Yale, though her family stemmed from migrating New Englanders who settled in Illinois well before the Civil War —the same stock from which Adlai E. Stevenson descended.

After Pearl Harbor, William Stevenson took leave of his law

office, and volunteered for full-time war work with the Red Cross. He was sent to Great Britain in April, 1942, where he directed all operations of the American Red Cross, ably backstopped by "Bumpy," who arrived in the summer. He was flown to North Africa within days after the November, 1942, Anglo-American invasion, and "Bumpy" followed in the second convoy. In North Africa, Stevenson directed all aspects of American Red Cross operation from Morocco in the west to Tunisia in the east, while his wife was a source of sunlight to G.I.s at the front, in rest camps, in hospitals, and in staging areas.

The pair subsequently moved on to Italy, where they remained until the fall of 1944, when Stevenson, the former gold medal Olympic runner, was grounded by a leg injury. Upon his and "Bumpy's" reluctant return to the United States, Stevenson resumed the practice of law and kept at it for the next two years, but with an increasing restlessness which his wife shared. They had enjoyed working in tandem during their Red Cross assignment, and wanted to continue to work that way after the war. Education was a field in which this was possible, and the pair entered it when Stevenson accepted the presidency of Oberlin College in the fall of 1946. With a student body that tended to level out at around two thousand, many of whom worked for their keep, Oberlin stressed quality instead of quantity in the three parts of its institutional structure—the college of the liberal arts and sciences, the conservatory of music, and the graduate school of theology.

Robert M. Hutchins, who had been an Oberlin undergraduate for two years prior to World War I, not only was among Stevenson's circle of personal friends, but stood before his eyes as a model of excellence for a college president. He saw in Hutchins "the greatest figure in the twentieth-century history of American education." He also shared Hutchins' well-founded lament that just about the last thing college presidents are expected to do, or have an opportunity to do, "is to be the source of ideas about the educational process." The known link between Hutchins and the existence of the Aspen Institute was one of the reasons why

Stevenson welcomed an invitation to moderate an Aspen Executive Seminar in 1952. A second reason was the same one which explained why a number of university presidents, such as Harris Wafford of Bryn Mawr, readily accepted invitations to serve as moderators. The experience enabled them to refresh themselves from the bleak administrative chores of a college president and to know the pleasure of reading some Great Books in the company of mature men and women and of discussing ideas about ideas.

Subsequent to Stevenson's introduction to the Executive Seminar, his long association with the Aspen Institute saw him fill many different roles. For the moment, it is enough to say that he served as moderator for fourteen seminars, accepted a place on the Institute's board of trustees, bought a vacation home in Aspen in 1957 and thought of shuttling between it and his permanent Florida home after retiring in 1960 from fourteen years' service as president of Oberlin. He temporarily shelved the idea when he was asked to head an AID mission to the Middle East, but returned to Aspen at the conclusion of the mission, to be again drawn away from the place when he accepted an appointment as the United States ambassador to the Philippines. He returned to Aspen at the conclusion of his Philippine assignment in June, 1964, and in the next year moderated an Executive Seminar. Then, in the fall of 1967, he was prevailed upon to serve as president of the Aspen Institute and to conduct a "holding operation" until a "permanent" president could be found. The one found in the fall of 1969 turned out to be Joseph E. Slater.

The second illustrative case was that of Walter Orr Roberts, the solar astronomer. Much had happened to Roberts since he first skied the slopes of Aspen in 1940, and much would happen in the world of science because of him. Among other things, he would be a member of the Special Committee of the International Geophysical Year in Barcelona (1956) and Moscow (1958); member, Defense Science Board, U.S. Defense Department; Member, Solar Physics Subcommittee of the Space Science Steering Committee, National Aeronautics and Space Administration. But at no time did Roberts resemble the Greek astronomer

Thales who fell into a well while looking at the stars—a mishap which caused a Thracian maiden to say that Thales was so absorbed with heavenly things that he was blind to what lay before his feet.

Roberts was concerned with heavenly things mainly because of their effects on the whole of the earth below—climate, man, beasts, soil, water, crops, cultures, economies, social patterns, and political structures. The quality of his theoretical research would make him an internationally known "refounding father" of solar astronomy. But in a special sense of the term, he would also be a *political* scientist, always searching for ways in which the theoretical and applied sciences could promote the transnational cause of human welfare. He would press that search as president of the American Association for the Advancement of Science (1968), as a member of its Committee on Science in the Promotion of Human Welfare, as chairman of its Committee on the Public Understanding of Science, as a member of the Council of the American Academy of Arts and Sciences, as a member of the American Philosophical Society, as a member of the Committee of Consultants for the United Nations Stockholm Conference on the Environment, and, not least of all, as a beloved figure and vital intellectual force in the family of the Aspen Institute.

In the summer of 1949, when Roberts was the director of the new High Altitude Observatory at Climax, Colorado—a joint venture of Harvard and the University of Colorado—he was invited to the Goethe bicentennial convocation in Aspen. He was regretfully unable to attend, however, because of the press of a new project he had just initiated. He had long been troubled by the fact that the meteorological aspects of solar astronomy had been the victim of poor research work—so much so that other physical scientists tended to dismiss the general nature of the research done in this field, saying derisively that the *Farmer's Almanac*'s predictions about the weather were probably more reliable than any predictions by solar astronomers who studied "sun spots."

To redeem the study of solar astronomy from tradition-bound approaches, Roberts in 1948 made an M.I.T.–Harvard conference group the take-off point for a move to modernize the science of solar astronomy and to restructure its conditions for basic research. The next step was taken the following year when, as president of a commission of the International Astronomical Union, he assumed the leadership of a drive to standardize world-wide solar observational techniques. Later, to provide widely separated solar astronomers and meteorologists with communications channels indispensable to concerted research, Roberts became the president-founder of the Corporation for Atmospheric Research, a not-for-profit consortium of forty-nine universities having interests in solar astronomy.

His first direct contact with the Aspen Institute occurred in a roundabout way. He had regularly visited the White Sands Proving Grounds for the U.S. Department of Defense, and was drawn into the development of rockets mainly because of his interest in acquiring a better technical tool for solar observation. It was here, in early 1953, that he first met James H. Smith, Jr., the new Assistant Secretary for Air in the Eisenhower Administration and an enthusiast regarding the Aspen Institute. Smith, between rocket blasts, persuaded Roberts that the sun would still be there for study if he turned his back on it for a while and came to Aspen that summer to participate as a special guest in an Executive Seminar. He did come, and the seminar he attended had Mortimer Adler as a moderator.

By the end of the session, these two men had formed an intimate and durable friendship, and Roberts returned to the Executive Seminar again and again, either as a special guest or as a moderator. He often found himself in the role of the scientific adversary to Adler's philosophical humanism. Indeed, their clashing views once led to a celebrated debate they staged in Aspen on the concepts of "autonomous creation" and "infinity," remembered best for Adler's remark: "If we can say that a robin can think, then all of western jurisprudence falls." It was beneath either man to press a line of argument merely to score some vanity points in a game of one-upmanship. They became and remained close friends because each attached a high importance to the subjects they argued about, despite the differences in their respective positions.

Adler, for example, was persuaded by Roberts to make more room on the Aspen reading list for the reflections by contemporary scientists on the nature of science. One such work was *The Logic of Modern Physics*, by P. W. Bridgeman, a Nobel laureate in physics. To the surprise of the readers, Bridgeman made no omniscient claims for natural science. If he accepted its power, he also accepted its limits as a mode for discovering new knowledge. Since this left ample room for the humanist to pursue new knowledge by the use of philosophical methods, said Bridgeman, it followed that the iron line of division traditionally drawn between science and the humanities was false. The conclusion to that effect worked to enlarge the Institute's conception of what should be included under the heading of "humanistic studies." It also worked to tighten Roberts' personal bonds to the Institute.

III

It remains to be said that no Executive Seminar was an exact carbon copy of any other one. Each tended to have a character and destiny of its own, depending on the nature of the seminar leaders, the mix of the other participants, or the flow of current events which posed old issues in new forms. There were also times when special guests because of their prominence either wanted to do all the talking or awed the businessmen into silence. Either way, a seminar could be rescued from this peril only if the moderator was prepared to take strong measures, sometimes to the point of roughness. One time, for example, William E. Stevenson in his role as moderator drew the highly respected Judge Charles Wyzanski to the side before the start of the second morning of a seminar and explicitly asked that he not open his mouth until noon, so that businessmen would have a chance to speak. There was also the seminar at which Bishop James Pike, a special guest, ad-libbed long sermons while the businessmen around the table listened in reverent, stained-glass attitudes. This went on for some time until Stevenson, as moderator, posed a question, and with the sternness of his forebear Jonathan Edwards, quickly added: "Bishop Pike, could you limit your answer to two minutes?" The stained glass was shattered, but the life of the seminar was redeemed.

There were also times when seminars which could have degenerated into a shouting match were saved by the tactical wisdom of a single participant. So it was in the early 1950's, for example, when Jack Conway of the United Auto Workers and a key aide to Walter Reuther made his first appearance at an Executive Seminar. Labor-management relations at the time were still in an inflamed state; business executives as a group did not exhibit the social sophistication they would show in later years; and the executives at the seminar initially seemed to vie with each other in making known their hostility to everything Conway represented. Conway, a big, rawboned man, met their onslaughts with what Mark Twain once called "the serenity of a Christian holding four aces." When he spoke in response to their barbs, he spoke softly, succinctly, logically. And all the while he appeared to hold in mobile reserve an abundance of personal force which he saw no need to tap; if his purpose was to conquer, he would also spare.

As the discussions wore on—with time off for volley-ball games at which Conway, a superbly co-ordinated athlete, was the star—the initial hostility became an embarrassing memory. Stevenson, the moderator on the occasion, has since recalled that a point was reached "where Jack Conway took over the seminar, so that whenever I posed a question, the business executives wanted to know what Jack thought." Conway, in later years, regularly returned to the Executive Seminar in the role of a moderator. He is now the head of the Public Employees Union.

Successive "adversary" figures were drawn into the Executive Seminars. In the 1950's they came from the ranks of labor, as in the case of Jack Conway. In the 1960's they came from the ranks of the black community. By the end of the 1960's, coincident with the assumption of the Institute's presidency by Joseph E. Slater, student leaders were brought into the seminars to challenge the values of the business executives. Not everyone agreed with the wisdom of this last move. Slater was reminded that the seminars were meant for mature people, not for youngsters who scattered their passions at random on all sides of the world around them. Some of the student leaders, for their part, used the context of the seminars for displays of vulgarity and rudeness which conveyed no meaning except a deliberate intention to shock and to infuriate. Although several executives were provoked into leaving the seminars, it was Slater's view that they had denied themselves "a very interesting time"—that they should have welcomed the confrontations instead of being unhinged by them.

Today, the mix of participants in these seminars is richer than it was in previous years when Henry Luce, Jr., could with some justice refer to the "unwashed" American businessman as "the forgotten man in the cultural life" of the nation. In a typical seminar, business executives now comprise around 60 per cent of the participants. The remaining 40 per cent are drawn from other parts of society—judges, artists, political leaders, writers, rising young scholars, and so on. Although 70 per cent of the texts of the reading lists remain what they were in 1951, there has been a more conscious tilting of the list toward contemporary sources of thought, especially as it concerns international issues.

Still, for all this, participants in the Executive Seminars have tended to show the same pattern of responses, regardless of the year when they came to Aspen or the people who flanked them. In the opening sessions, for example, some businessmen tended to be restrained, wary, noncommittal, afraid to speak in an unfamiliar vocabulary lest they stammer and appear ridiculous in the eyes of their peers. Others tended to be unbuttoned, voluble, confident, seemingly certain that when they spoke, the gods in heaven would be edified. But as the days passed, both types found it increasingly difficult to adhere to their initial stance. The first could not evade questions when they were asked to explain themselves. The second could not speak and go unchallenged. Members of either group could be badly shaken, wounded in their pride of intellect, embarrassed by the exposure of their limited perceptions, angry on that account—and often all the more angry when their wives were present as onlookers. Most seminars, however, reached a moment where the crisis of self-esteem was passed and men began to speak their minds freely, often in salty ways.

Once, for example, the readings to be discussed put Aristotle's *Politics* and its thesis about "natural slaves" in opposition to the thesis about "economic slavery" advanced by Karl Marx in the *Communist Manifesto*. An East Coast banker, who was accustomed to making decisions and having them carried out, protested that the discussion up to that point had settled nothing. "I want to say where I stand, and I want to know where everybody else stands," he declared with white-lipped heat. "We talk and talk, and then jump on to something else, and we're always up in the air."

"Can't help that," replied a manufacturer from the Midwest. "We start on the ground at an altitude of eight thousand feet and take off from there. It's sure different at home. When I open my mouth in the plant, by God they listen. Here I find that someone just jumps down my throat."

At another seminar, for which the moderator was Barnaby C. Kenney, president of Brown University, the subject under discussion was Plato's *Republic* and the executives were giving Socrates the business. Summing up the feelings of many of his fifteen colleagues, one television executive said, "Socrates seems to have been a cunning fellow who used words in a slippery fashion. In fact, I can't see much difference between Socrates and those Sophists he's always criticizing." Across the table, Kenney puffed on the last half-inch of a cigarette and added a minor complaint of his own. "Well," said he with a mischievous smile, "there was one important difference. Unlike the Sophists, Socrates didn't accept any money for his teaching. This has had an unfortunate effect on the teaching profession ever since." "But that doesn't explain," said an investment banker, "why teachers can get emotional about abstract ideas." "*You* better than anyone else," said a steel manufacturer sitting across the table, "should know the reason why. You personally deal in the most abstract thing in the world—

money. And I don't have to remind you that people can get very emotional about money."

It was unlikely that the executives would enroll as Ph.D. candidates at the end of the two-week seminars. Yet many of those whose readings had been confined to stock tables had their appetites whetted for other things. "The seminars have opened windows in my mind that have been closed for a long time," said a vice-president of a New York advertising agency. "It may change back on Madison Avenue, but once you start thinking about some of these ideas, it's hard to stop." "I'll have to watch how I talk when I get back to the plant," a factory owner commented. "I don't know if I can get away there with some of the things I've said here." "Well, I'm spoiled for television and half of my neighbors," another member remarked. "Know what I want to go home and do? Talk!"

There was in all this a feeling of shared adventure, of having climbed a short distance up to the high mountains of the mind. On returning home, one executive was asked to write a report for the president of his company evaluating the seminar experiences. He ended by writing two reports instead of the one requested. The first went to the effect that he had enjoyed himself thoroughly, but couldn't see any benefit to the company from the money it had spent in sending him to the seminar. The second report, written just a few months later, was the reverse of the first. "Every day," said he, "I find that the subjects I discussed in an abstract way in Aspen have a direct bearing on the problems that flow across my desk."

7. ENTER ROBERT O. ANDERSON

I

The existence of the Aspen Institute and the various cultural programs it offered the public at large—concerts, lectures, film festivals, and so on—made Aspen an attractive place for people who wished to acquire or build a second home. The process radically enhanced the value of the property Paepcke owned outright or as a major shareholder in the Aspen Company. Paepcke, however, probably would have been better off financially if he had concentrated on the development of Aspen as a winter playground and a summer resort, without ever embarking on the creation of the Aspen Institute. This conjecture seems warranted because he drew heavily on his personal profits from his Aspen companies to cover the deficits of the Institute.

He also personally covered the costs of two capital improvements that were either indirectly or directly related to the affairs of the Aspen Institute. One was the construction of the Aspen airport on ranch property he owned on the outskirts of the town. Then he had the Institute charter Aspen Airways, which provided a schedule of daily flights from and to Denver. Aspen Airways, however, proved more of a costly toy than a business operation. Until it was sold to more experienced hands, it operated in the red and was kept airborne only by infusions of Paepcke's money.

The second capital improvement had a more immediate bearing on the needs of the Institute's Executive Seminar. Varying the location of the seminar from one day to the next had its charms. But it also had a negative side. For example, a delightful out-of-doors seminar could be disrupted by eavesdroppers, by a sudden rainstorm, or by street noises. On the other hand, one held indoors, whether in the Jerome Hotel or the Four Seasons, meant either cramped quarters or an oblong table where the seating arrangements made it hard for a seminar leader to draw all persons present into a discussion, or for the participants to see and speak directly to each other without straining their necks.

The problem seemed to defy improvised solutions, no matter how many were suggested and tested by Paepcke, Adler, and Herbert Bayer. The solution called for a building, specially designed and constructed for use by the seminars. Paepcke was intolerant of any long-range plans for the development of the Institute as a whole since he had good reason to be riven by doubts about its survival powers. Nonetheless, in August of 1952 a strategic plan which he and Clarence Faust devised in confidence and then revealed to a handful of well-placed intimates may have been instrumental in bringing matters to a head regarding a permanent structure.

It is enough to say that the plan detailed the steps whereby the Aspen Institute could be converted into a new kind of post-doctoral academy with feeder lines to the universities of Harvard, Princeton, Columbia, Stanford, Chicago, Virginia, Yale, and Notre Dame, and the colleges of Claremont and Santa Barbara. The scheme would subsequently be reincarnated in many forms, only to die and be revived in a new form and then die again. But it appears that the existence of the plan—with its implied need for some sort of brick-and-mortar headquarters for the proposed academy—prompted Paepcke to do something that would also serve the immediate needs of the Aspen Institute's Executive Seminar.

As noted previously, the Aspen Company, on Paepcke's initiative, had acquired one hundred acres of Aspen Meadows, bounded on the west by the Roaring Fork River, on the east by Hallam Lake, on the north by Red Mountain, and on the south by the built-up portions of Aspen proper. Now, on behalf of the Institute, Paepcke bought back some acres of this land from the Aspen Company and instructed Herbert Bayer, in collaboration with the architect Fritz Benedict, to design and supervise the construction of an Executive Seminar building on the site.

Although the project was, in Bayer's words, a "shoestring operation"—the cost was $52,000 (in 1953 dollars)—the tight budget forced him to live up to Ortega y Gasset's dictums about "Spartanism" and "elegance." What he built, after close consultation with Mortimer Adler who spoke from the standpoint of the user, was a hexagonal structure consisting of two large seminar rooms and several smaller offices. When it was completed in the summer of 1953, Adler, who moderated the first seminar held in the place, judged it to be a "perfect realization of the ideal of functional architecture and design" whose "utility has been achieved with no loss of delight to the eye."

Under the circumstances [Adler added] the only pains or discomforts suffered by anyone came, as they should come, from the intellectual difficulties of the subject matter and the effort to deal with it intelligently and intelligibly.

I do not mean to suggest that removing all the physical obstacles to good discussion guarantees the attainment of excellence in the hard task of carrying on a discussion. But it actually goes a long way toward making it easier and pleasanter to do. With the physical aspects of discussion so perfectly disposed, there is no need for all the antics and folderol of "group dynamics" to get and keep a discussion going. The leaders and the participants can devote all their wits and energies to the only thing that matters in discussion, which is having something relevant to say and saying it well.

Prior to 1953, Paepcke personally attended to most of the administrative details of the Aspen Institute. But in advance of the time when the seminar building would be ready for occupancy, he cast about for someone to share in the management of the Institute. He settled on Robert Craig, a former member of the K–2 expedition in Tibet, who had been drawn to Aspen partly because of his interest in skiing—though his many talents once led to his being included on *Life* magazine's list of America's one hundred most promising young men. Not long after Craig arrived in Aspen, he began to write a column for the local *Aspen Flyer,* and the column regularly attacked Paepcke on assorted grounds. Paepcke, in response, followed the practice of the British Crown, which appoints its critics to a committee, and the critics, as expected, soon deliver reverent speeches about King and Country on Empire Day. Paepcke thus hired Craig to set things right—but only in matters related to the Aspen Institute.

Craig, a shackling man of marked personal charm and abundant imagination, was not a tidy administrator. If he had been, he would have thrown up his hands in despair once he was initiated into the mysteries of the task he had assumed. Instead, his loose-jointed notions of administration enabled him to accept the naturalness of chaos when he tried, with the meager resources at his disposal, to make the Institute run smoothly. His office was the bellmaster's closet in the Jerome Hotel, and his support structure was one secretary, one typewriter, one mimeograph machine, and one telephone. With these he was expected to co-ordinate the affairs of the Institute.

When Paepcke was free from the immediate pressure of his many involvements elsewhere, he could talk all night long about his plans for the Institute, but as he was seldom free, few people could say precisely how this or that visible fragment of what he was trying to do meshed with all the invisible fragments he carried around in his mind. Even members of the Institute's board of trustees were generally left in the dark. Episodic meetings of the board were *pro forma* affairs held in the Chicago law office of Glen A. Lloyd. Minutes were thin and sometimes nonexistent, nor were any annual reports of the Institute ever issued in Paepcke's lifetime. The trustees apparently reached the pragmatic conclusion that since Paepcke seemed willing to cover the Institute's deficit, he should be left free to manage its affairs as he saw fit. Yet a point was finally reached when Paepcke himself doubted that he had a viable enterprise in the Aspen Institute. Indeed, the Institute might well have disintegrated had it not been for the fact that in September, 1953, Robert O. Anderson came to Aspen to fish in the streams which abound in the area.

II

One would most likely also be taken by surprise if he were later told that Anderson was, among other things, the chairman of the board of the Atlantic Richfield Oil Company, the foremost rancher in New Mexico, the owner of assorted mining and manufacturing companies, a former president of the Dallas Federal Reserve Bank, a director of the Chase National Bank, a director of the Columbia Broadcasting Company, president of the Lovelace Clinic, a director of the Museum of Modern Art, a painter and short story writer, a trustee of the University of Chicago, a trustee of the California Institute of Technology, a former chairman of the Business Committee on the Arts, the chairman of the Eisenhower Fellowship Committee—and a figure of central importance to the Aspen Institute and its network of affiliated institutions. The logistics of his movements on so many different fronts seem to warrant his wife's estimate that "Bob spends more time in an airplane than on the ground." Yet he is free of the pomp and buffers commonly associated with a maker and shaker—no entourage of harried secretaries, no truss of legal counsel, no wary vice-presidents, no public relations advisers who invent "personal images." He moves about with relaxed innersprings, and he does his own asking, seeing, listening, sifting, weighing, and judging.

The manner marked the way he first became interested in the Aspen Institute. In the fall of 1953 he had not reached the commanding economic position he would hold by the early 1960's, but he was financially and psychologically poised to do something about a promise he had made to himself when he was still a very young man, under the influence of his father.

His father, Hugo Anderson, a vice-president of the First National Bank of Chicago, believed that the education of his children was the most important investment he could ever make. As a result of this belief, he chose not to imitate other Chicago business leaders who acquired homes on Chicago's Gold Coast, starting north of the Loop and extending toward the Wisconsin line through a string of sanitized suburbs; instead, he moved his family into the University of Chicago community on the South Side of Chicago so that his children could be directly exposed to its richly varied intellectual life.

Young Bob Anderson received his secondary schooling in the university's laboratory school and then in its high school. Many of his classmates were the children of university professors, and competition for academic distinction was brisk. A classmate, however, has since recalled that "Bob moved through this intensely competitive setting with the interior balance of a youth who, as an infant, swallowed a gyroscope with his mother's milk." He stood near the top of his class in his studies, and he distinguished himself in athletics—where his competitive abilities as a freestyle swimmer seemed to anticipate his freestyle approach to larger tests in later life. At graduation, he was pleasantly surprised when he was singled out as the beneficiary of a windfall prize. This was the John Crerar Scholarship—a four-year university scholarship awarded a graduating senior in the University High School, without regard to financial need, but solely on the basis of demonstrated proficiency in the mechanical arts. Bob Anderson won the Crerar Scholarship in 1935 because of his skill in woodwork, and he entered the University of Chicago in the fall of that year.

He joined Psi Upsilon fraternity, among whose members were a number of athletes destined to make their mark in the world. One of these, Elmore Patterson, captain of the university's football team in 1935, eventually became president of the Morgan Guarantee Company in New York. Bob Anderson's outlook, however, seemed not to point toward a business career. He continued to participate in athletics and won his "C" as a member of the varsity swimming team—again in the freestyle event. His chief interests, however, were his studies in two fields. One was geology. The other was philosophy—or, more immediately, the hard discipline to which he was subjected as a student in the Hutchins-Adler seminar on the Great Books.

He had in view a possible career as a university professor, partly because he saw in it a chance to cultivate his own mind and partly because he associated human companionship with it. His model was a professor who lived next door to the Andersons on the University of Chicago campus. This was John U. Nef, a distinguished student of French history and culture whose intellectual interests, like those of Mortimer Adler, were too spacious to fit into any tight, specialized academic slot. With the support of Hutchins, Nef ventured to cut through all the subdivided enclaves of learning, which duplicated their own narrow focus in the Ph.D. degrees they granted. He created and was the first chairman of the Committee on Social Thought, whose members were drawn from within the university and external to it, but who had made their mark in different kinds of intellectual endeavor, in most cases without the benefit of a certifying Ph.D.[1]

As a youth who spent much time in the Nef home, Bob Anderson saw what a university professor's life ideally could be like. But as a youth with a feel for solid things—geology and the grain of wood—he also realized that Nef could move about as he pleased because he did not have to depend on his university salary for his keep. In this way, a plan and a promise took shape in the young Bob's mind. He would spend the years of his life up to the age of forty in securing his economic independence. If all went well, he would then enter the world of education through one avenue of approach or another, perhaps as a teacher, perhaps as an administrator of an educational institution.

Anderson was graduated from the University of Chicago in June, 1939, and was married in August to the beautiful Barbara Herrick Phelps, a university student whose openness to the world was reflected in her choice of the International House as a place of residence. Although the marriage meant a termination of Barbara's studies before she received her degree, she would return to that unfinished piece of business by enrolling more than three decades later as a student in the University of California at Los Angeles.

Subsequent to his graduation, Bob Anderson worked until December, 1941, in the Chicago office of a broker who dealt in oil leases. Then, armed with this brief business experience, and grubstaked by his father, he and Barbara headed for the American

---

[1] This remains true of the committee today. Not one of its leading members —novelist Saul Bellow, sociologist Edward Shils, classicist David Greene, or art critic Harold Rosenberg—holds the Ph.D. degree.

Southwest, where he embarked on high-risk ventures in the oil business. When an oil lease he acquired proved worthless, when a well he drilled proved dry, when an exploration for oil yielded nothing except exhaustion, he did not brood over what might have been or rail at any of his associates. He and they had run rational risks on the basis of available information, and if things didn't work out as he had wished, there must be another try somewhere else. He would extend the same outlook to ventures in the social sciences and the humanities, saying: "Ninety-five per cent of all experiments in the physical and biological sciences fail, but the 5 per cent that succeed make the preceding *instructive* failures worthwhile. Why, then, should we expect to succeed every time we experiment with something new and infinitely more complicated in the spheres of the humanities and the social sciences?"

By 1953, fourteen years after his graduation from the University of Chicago, the Hondo Oil Company he created—and presently merged with Atlantic Richfield—made Anderson an important "independent" in the exploration, production, refining, and marketing of oil. He was also involved in mining, milling, and general manufacturing enterprises, besides engaging in extensive cattle-raising and feeding operations. He was not yet forty years old. But with the active encouragement of his wife, who shared directly in the management of the ranching operations in New Mexico, he concluded that he had reached a point where he should consider anew the plan of life he had set for himself in his student days.

It was in such frame of mind that he came to Aspen in September, 1953. The number of fish he caught is not a matter of record, but what he saw in the place caught *him*—and ruined his fishing. Beforehand, he had heard only vaguely of the Aspen Institute for Humanistic Studies. Nor was he an intimate of Walter Paepcke, a man of a different generation, though they shared mutual friends. In Aspen the two apparently met by chance in front of the Hotel Jerome, after which Paepcke played a part not unlike a dedicated Christian missionary striving to save the soul of a pagan by converting him to the Gospel. He took Anderson to the newly constructed seminar building, revealed his plans to build lodge units nearby, showed him the facilities for the Music Festival and the Music School, identified some of the properties of the Aspen Company and the Aspen Ski Company, and urged Anderson to buy a home in the town and to interest himself in the future of the Aspen Institute.

While the older man was preaching his gospel, the younger one was adding up, in a different mental column, a set of pros and cons bearing on a problem often discussed in his family. The growing family of Anderson children were then attending school in rural New Mexico, and while they gained much from village life, their cultural growth was limited to local resources. To change the case for the better meant moving the children a great distance from home into an urban environment, something the parents were reluctant to do. Now, however, it occurred to Anderson that Aspen might provide the kind of solution which he and his wife had been groping for. Here might be a place where his children could enjoy during the summer months the benefits of a small village, yet have direct access to a cultural life ordinarily found only in a great metropolitan center. If so, he could partly duplicate in Aspen what his father had done a generation earlier by moving *his* children into the University of Chicago community.

As it happened, Herbert Bayer was building a new studio home for himself on Red Mountain and was offering his Aspen house for sale to the right buyer. Anderson looked at the house, did some more sums, but was noncommittal when he started the drive back to his home base in Roswell, New Mexico. At Independence Pass, however, he stopped at a roadside telephone and put in a call to Bayer. Was the house still for sale? It was. For how much? The price was stated. All right, he would buy it. And so the deed was done. Three months later, at Christmas time, 1953, Anderson brought his family to Aspen for their first introduction to their auxiliary home. It was at that time also that he accepted an invitation to become a trustee of the Aspen Institute.

8. THE SUCCESSION

I

Between 1954 and 1955, Paepcke could look across the country and derive satisfaction from the flattering way in which the external form of the Aspen Executive Seminar was being imitated in one place and another. But the quality of the Executive Seminar of the Aspen Institute continued to surpass the rest. In the person of Mortimer Adler, who shaped the intellectual content of the seminar, it had one of the "founding fathers" of the Great Books movement in the United States. In the cadre of seminar leaders Adler recruited were some of the most experienced and gifted teachers in the nation. These factors, coupled with the emotional pleasures of the music festival and the physical delights of the Aspen setting, acted as a magnet which drew to the Institute's Executive Seminar figures of the first rank in the realms of commerce and industry, government and the professions, the arts and sciences.

Still, the quality of the Aspen Institute was no guarantee of the Institute's power to survive. Rachel Carson in *The Edge of the Sea* spoke of "the tidal strip of the seashore between the mark of the high tide and low" as being "the cruel training ground where sea creatures learned to live on hostile land." In the case of the Aspen Institute, "the tidal strip of seashore" which held the key to its future fate seemed bounded by Paepcke's willingness to cover the financial deficits that were being incurred in every aspect of the Institute's operations, with the exception of some modest grants from several foundations. Precisely on that account, a crisis in late August, 1954, in the triangular relationship of the Aspen Institute, the Aspen Summer Music Festival, and the Aspen

Music School—a crisis which bore hard on Paepcke's spirit—threatened the life of the Institute itself.

As noted previously, Paepcke had endorsed and pledged his financial support for a proposal put to him by a group of musicians at the end of the Goethe bicentennial convocation in the summer of 1949. The musicians would happily come to Aspen every summer to play in the festival orchestra, provided they could combine orchestral work with the teaching of some of their gifted students whom they would bring to Aspen for the summer season. On the cornerstone of this understanding, Paepcke had carefully built a music festival orchestra comprised of instrumentalists who held leading chairs in the best symphony orchestras of the nation. In addition, the programmatic offerings featured individual performers such as Lauritz Melchior, the Paganini String Quartet, Helen Traubel, Igor Stravinsky, the Juilliard Quartet, Darius Milhaud, Uta Graf, Rudolph Firkuzny, Szymon Goldberg, Reginald Kell, Herta Glaz, Joseph Rosenstock, William Primrose, Nikolai and Joanna Graudan, and Brooks Smith, as well as other artists mentioned elsewhere in this book.

At the same time, after the manner in which a coral reef is formed from minute bodies of marine life, the agreement reached about teaching and playing led to the rise of an Aspen Music School housed in structures owned by the Aspen Company. As of June, 1954, the school had grown to some one hundred summertime students, with a faculty comprised mainly of instrumentalists who held chairs in the festival orchestra. The whole of the development, though unplanned, initially pleased all parties. It made sense to stress the link between teaching the individual performer and ensemble playing. It also made sense to have a school nearby if one wanted an enlightened audience for a musical festival. "You know," said a soloist, "music is a lonely art when you're off on a tour all winter, listening to nobody but yourself. Here in Aspen we have a rare chance to play with and for each other—as well as for interested students and other people who aren't spoiled."

Walter Paepcke had his own reasons to be initially delighted with the unplanned rise of the music school alongside the deliberate creation of the festival orchestra. "Walter," said Herbert Bayer, "had too much imagination to be satisfied merely to solve problems involving what he called 'the profanity of boxes.' He had strong aesthetic cravings, and he turned to design to satisfy them in the industrial world. That is why the support he gave to raising the standards of design wherever he could was not limited to the act of writing a patron's check so that others could work. It also entailed, for example, a direct, personal involvement in the affairs of the Chicago Institute for Design and the International Conference on Design. But in addition to design, his aesthetic cravings found their outlet in the intensity of his personal interests in the world of music."

But then came an explosion, the causes of which have since become the subject of several conflicting versions. Of the two leading versions, the first goes to the effect that the musicians who both played in the orchestra and taught in the music school could not simultaneously and satisfactorily serve the rival claims of their dual interests. When faced with the need to decide whether the music school or the orchestra rehearsal had a prior claim on their time, any choice they made led to inflamed tempers whose bile ate into the soul of the orchestra and engulfed Paepcke in the mutual rancors until his stomach could not stand the business any more.

The second leading version, which apparently seems closer to the truth, goes like this. Paepcke was dissatisfied with the way the director of the music school was managing the venture, and informed him that he would not be engaged to come back to Aspen for the 1955 season. The director kept this intelligence to himself, but proceeded to foment an anti-Paepcke movement among the musicians of both the school and the orchestra. They would be far better off, said he, if they organized themselves to function in an autonomous way, without being tied to Paepcke and his Institute. Why? Because Paepcke wanted to see more rotation among the musicians who came to Aspen, whereas the musicians who had been in on a good thing from the start wanted to keep the benefits of Aspen to themselves and to their small circle of friends.

No one is certain exactly what happened next. Apparently, however, when Paepcke learned of the palace revolution, his reaction was one of disgust, capped by a two-point *dictate* which he issued at the end of the summer concert season in late August, 1954. Point one: The Aspen Institute could not be counted on to sponsor a music festival in the summer of 1955. Point two: No one else could count on having access to the Institute's tent-covered "amphitheater" for staging concerts. A third point, though unstated, could be extrapolated from the logic of the preceding two: If the Institute severed its connections with the festival orchestra and the music school, the musicians would be without the housing facilities Paepcke or the Aspen Company had been providing.

If Paepcke meant only to whirl the kind of storm needed to clear a foul sky, the immediate result was more like a war of all against all. As musicians assailed musicians, and musicians and townspeople assailed Paepcke, it seemed that all that remained to be done was for the dead to bury the dead. The music festival and the music school were finished. Their dead hands might even pull the Aspen Institute itself into the grave with them, and Aspen itself might then contract into just another winter sports resort.

At the crest of the public commotion, however, Paepcke was approached by Cortlandt D. Barnes, Jr., and Nathan Fleming, two national patrons of music who lived in the East but maintained second homes in Aspen. They were speaking, they said, on behalf of a group of interested townspeople and musicians who had devised a plan, the main terms of which were these: If the Aspen Institute would no longer sponsor and financially support the festival orchestra and the music school, the group led by Barnes and Fleming was prepared to do so through a proposed new organization that would be called the Music Associates of Aspen. The new organization was not in a position to build the requisite facilities. It would still depend on the right of access to the facilities owned by the Aspen Institute or by the Aspen Company, but it would undertake to cover all the operating deficits incurred by the orchestra and school.

Paepcke accepted the proposal, pledged his support for it, and honored the pledge when the Music Associates were formed with a board of trustees independent of those who served on the Aspen Institute's board, though there was some overlapping in the membership of the two. For the summertime use of music school students, he made available to the Music Associates the Roaring Fork Ski Dormitory which the Aspen Company had built. For the use of the festival orchestra, he made available the tent-covered amphitheater, along with an array of instruments such as concert pianos that could not readily be transported by individual performers. The Music Associates picked up the rest of the pieces, forming themselves into a self-governing co-operative with the power to hire or fire directors, teachers, conductors, musicians—and to set their own salaries.

II

In the judgment of Robert O. Anderson, who with his wife had quietly helped to restore what had been shattered, the transition from the revolution of 1954 to the musical season of 1955 was "far smoother than anyone previously thought was possible." But it was Anderson's further judgment that Paepcke never really recovered from the trauma of the revolution. "It was my impression," he later explained, "that Walter's heart was centered more in the musical component of the Aspen Institute than in the Executive Seminar. In the case of the seminar, he was the source of indispensable support to Mortimer Adler, but Mortimer clearly was its creator and mainspring. To an even greater extent, however, Walter gave direction to all the musical aspects of the Institute. When the development of Aspen as a major center for music passed from his direct control into the hands of the Music Associates, he was in a position of a parent who sees a favorite child leave the family nest. I have reason to believe that the Institute itself never again seemed quite the same to him."

Outwardly, however, Paepcke bore himself as if not even the skin on his finger-tip had been scratched by a pin. He continued to expand the physical plant of the Institute and to plan its future development. At one point, for example, he hoped to make the Meadows campus of the Institute the site of an "architectural museum," consisting of twelve different types of medium-income homes, each to be designed and built by an architect chosen from among the world-wide leaders of the profession. Twelve such architects were in fact chosen and brought to Aspen so that they could conduct on-the-spot surveys of the project's physical setting. The surveys were followed by many sketches and much earnest talk, but despite the ferment, the architectural museum remained an idea floating in the astral void. Nothing came of it on the Aspen earth below.

Another plan, however, did materialize in 1955, though the costs were great. Paepcke had concluded that the Latin dictum, "a sound mind in a sound body," was an appropriate goal for American executives. President Dwight D. Eisenhower's heart attack during his first term of office had both dramatized the importance of the maxim and had led to a new spurt of national interest in physical fitness programs. Paepcke himself, in his business career, had seen corporations make enormous investments in the preparation of executives for posts of leadership, but when the executives reached what should have been the peak years of their productive abilities, all too many of them were disabled by heart attacks or other physical afflictions. With all this in mind, Paepcke conceived of an Aspen health center designed along the lines of a European spa. It would be a forward-looking project in preventive medicine or, in Paepcke's words, "health maintenance." It would seek to prevent illness by inducing basically healthy people to keep fit by a regimen of exercise and diet that would be individualized for each executive who came to the health center for a week-long stay.

To help Herbert Bayer draw plans for the envisioned health center, Paepcke reached out for highly qualified advisers and brought them to Aspen. One was a certain Dr. Stevenson, then the head of the athletic commission for the state of New York. Other advisers were the husband-and-wife team of Bruno and Erna Geba, Austrian physiotherapists, then residing in Canada, though they had previously been physiotherapists to the Shah of Iran. Subsequently, Paepcke persuaded the heart specialist Dr. Charles Houston, who had been on the K–2 expedition in Tibet, to accept the post of medical director for the center.

When the structure was completed and ready for use in 1955, its professional staff and facilities were judged to be among the very best in the nation. It got even better after the program for physical exercise was placed under the direction of Tage Pedersen, whose previous work as the head of all YMCAs in Denmark was much admired by directors of athletics elsewhere in Europe. It presently became clear, however, that Emerson overlooked the factor of timing when he asserted that if a man built a better mousetrap, a mass of people would beat a path through a forest to get at it. Paepcke's vision was premature. Most of the corporations he approached with arguments about the importance of a "health maintenance" program, replied that they already had the problem in hand by requiring their principal executives to submit to annual checkups at the hands of company doctors. As a result, very few executives beat a path to the Aspen Health Center; so few that Pedersen has since recalled that days would go by when the staff at the center did nothing except look at each other. Operating losses between 1955 and 1957 were in the neighborhood of $80,000 to $100,000 annually.

Paepcke, in confidential conversations with Mortimer Adler, often wondered how long he could or should continue to cover all the deficits incurred in the various operations linked to the Institute. One set of records after another showed that, from a financial standpoint, all the personal resources he had poured into the Institute seemed to yield little more than a harvest of dead leaves. Yet, here again, the outward impression he gave was that everything was progressing in grand style, in faithful obedience to his will. The impression beguiled even as experienced a journalist as William Harlan Hale, whose articles in *The Reporter* showed him to be a man whose eye regularly searched for the truth lying beneath surface appearances. Hale visited the Aspen Institute in

June, 1957, caught a glimpse of Paepcke in action, and recorded his impressions in *The Reporter*, saying in part:

Walter Paepcke, at a lean sixty-one, gives a striking impression of vigor and dash as he strides in jodhpurs and a sport shirt around the central pool of the community he recreated. Waiters snap to attention —the Hotel Jerome, once a miners' hangout of questionable repute, has now been refurbished as a prestige establishment on lease to one of Paepcke's enterprises in the valley. The board chairman approaches, brisk and aquiline, and then something surprising happens: he stops and bends in Continental fashion to kiss the hand of a lady guest. Paepcke is certainly one of the rare living corporation chiefs in America who do this.

All the things Hale saw at the Aspen Institute itself also seemed to be shot through with vigor and dash—the Tuesday Night lectures for the general public, the Executive Seminars, the festival orchestra, the students in the music school. Yet it was in that same summer of 1957 that Paepcke, who had recreated the community Hale described, concluded that he must loosen his personal grip on the Aspen Institute. It was a conclusion which went against the grain.

By nature, he clung to any object that had touched his life at any point, whether it was old clothes, old shoes, or the double roll-top desk which had belonged to his father. As for Aspen itself, the depth of his attachment to the place was brought home to Herbert Bayer following the day when the two men discussed the design and content of a summer folder for the Aspen Institute, the publication costs of which entailed but a small sum of money. On that same day the two men had participated in a meeting of the Container Corporation where a very large budget for a "world geographic atlas" had been approved in record time. Twenty-four hours later, Paepcke, in a holiday voice, said to Bayer, "Didn't it go well yesterday?" When the latter replied that he appreciated the unanimous decision that had been reached on the costly geographic atlas, Paepcke brushed the remark to one side. "Oh," said he, "I didn't mean *that*. I meant the Aspen folder."

A major but unstated reason why Paepcke decided to loosen his grip on the Aspen Institute had something to do with the fact that the music festival orchestra and the music school were now flourishing as autonomous institutions, not subject any longer to his personal sway. The stated reason, however, the one he gave Robert O. Anderson of the Institute's board of trustees, was compelling enough in itself. The Container Corporation of America, said Paepcke, was about to embark on an overseas expansion program in advance of the impending official birth of the European Common Market. Many problems were bound to arise in connection with that expansion. He must deal with them personally, and so would be unable to give the affairs of the Aspen Institute the close attention they needed. This did not mean that he wished to end his association with the Institute, but he had a suggestion to make. If Anderson would accept the presidency of the Institute, then Paepcke would step out of it and into the chairmanship of the Institute's board of trustees, once such a post was created.

There was more. "Maybe," said Paepcke, "we should face the fact that the Aspen Institute is not a viable operation with future in it." If that were the case and if Anderson agreed to serve as president, he might consider doing either of two things. The first would be to liquidate the Institute completely by selling the land it owned and the existing structures on it—the seminar building, the three chalets, and the health center—along with another building then under construction. This was the Aspen Meadows containing complete restaurant facilities, reading rooms, game rooms, bedrooms, terraces for outdoor dining, and an outdoor swimming pool. The second choice—which had often been discussed—would be to convert the existing facilities of the Aspen Institute into a college for about one hundred students. The many new colleges then being built across the nation entailed heavy investments in brick and mortar, but the proposed Aspen college might show how students could be provided with a basic education in the liberal arts at a reasonable cost. It could appeal particularly to students who wished to pursue a self-study program under a tutorial system based on the Oxford or Cambridge model.

The likelihood is that if a conventional man had been invited to assume the presidency of the Aspen Institute on the understanding that he might have to dissolve it, he would run to the nearest exit. Anderson, however, was a freestyle swimmer. The difficulties he saw in the Institute appealed to his nature, just as its humanistic aims conformed to his youthful hope that he might some day re-enter the world of learning once he had acquired financial independence. He had now acquired that. His time was his own, and he was free to use it as he wished—free, if he wished, to take his bearing from the fact that the words "leisure" and "school" stemmed from the same Greek root. His wife, Barbara, was of the same mind, down to the last syllable.

Anderson agreed to assume the presidency of the Aspen Institute, and the succession was formally ratified by the board of trustees, with Paepcke stepping into the newly-created post of chairman. The new arrangement by no means meant that a rainbow was permanently painted across the sky, promising an end to all storms forever in the affairs of the Institute. In the years ahead, there would be many disputes within the Institute over the content of its programs, some clashes of personality, some errors in the choice of staff members, many strains of a generational nature, many difficulties of a financial nature—and a bruising moment when Anderson had his fill of both Aspen and the Institute and seriously threatened to withdraw from both. In retrospect, however, it was Elizabeth Paepcke's publicly stated judgment in 1974 that "if Bob Anderson had not assumed the presidency of the Institute when he did, the whole of the enterprise might have been mortally afflicted" starting in 1957, when Walter Paepcke reduced his involvement in it, and ending with his death from cancer in the spring of 1960.

PART III: The Years of Transition

9. ORDER WITHIN CHANGE

It was easy to state the administrative problem Anderson faced as the new president of the Aspen Institute. He must bring a sense of order to the enterprise, but without subordinating its values of spontaneity and innovation to the rigidities of hierarchy, rules, specialization, and impersonality. The easy statement of the problem, however, did not also simplify the solution to it. Among the complications was the fact that though Paepcke had formally relinquished the executive leadership of the Institute, his role as a "founding father" pointed to the need to secure his personal consent before any proposed changes were put into effect.

This was all the more important because he alone knew how the different parts of the Institute were related to each other. Which of its parts bore solely on the affairs of the Institute, and which were linked with the development of Paepcke's economic interests in Aspen as represented, for example, by the Aspen Company and the Aspen Ski Company? If such links actually existed, should they be preserved? If not, where and how should they be cut? Anderson, fortunately, was mindful of Paepcke's sensibilities, and avoided any gesture which might appear to threaten his central place in the Aspen sun. In fact, few outsiders were even aware of the change in the executive leadership of the Institute. Yet he gingerly sorted out the parts of Paepcke's Aspen enterprises, focused on those which were directly related to the Institute, examined their worth, proposed that some be eliminated, and that the remainder should form a coherent ensemble where decisions reached in particular matters could be made in the light of the whole.

Anderson, from the beginning, was convinced that if the

Institute ever became the fiefdom of an individual or of an interest group, its life would be at the mercy of the changing fortunes and attitudes of the single sources underlying its existence. With this in mind, his first move as president of the Institute was to try to activate its dormant board of trustees. He was not entirely successful. A fully active board, but of a special kind, would have to await the period after 1969 when Joseph E. Slater became president of the Institute. But Anderson at least tried to keep the board members informed of emerging problems and to hold board meetings at regular intervals in a setting conducive to helpful policy discussions.

Out of this kind of "group diplomacy," for example, a decision was eventually reached to detach the money-losing Aspen Airways from the Aspen Institute, and to sell the airline to a private carrier competent to manage an airline. The Aspen Health Center was maintained, but its ambitious program requiring a very expensive medical staff was scaled down to the size of the demand. Thus, while Dr. Charles Houston moved on, Tage Pedersen remained as the director of the athletic program and soon took over all operations of the center on a lease basis. He made the place pay for itself by attracting Aspen residents, skiiers from the outside, as well as members of the United States Olympic ski teams of which he became the trainer. More to the point, whereas the health center had previously functioned at arm's length from the Executive Seminars, he impressed Anderson with the wisdom of bringing the two together by having tuition fees for the seminars cover without further cost the right to participate in the sensible exercise programs designed for the executives. Matters were so arranged, and the effects swiftly broke down the barriers among the executives and loosened them up for the discussions in the seminars themselves.

Pedersen designed his exercise drills in ways which avoided monotony, required equipment no more elaborate than a piece of rope, were a sure source of much laughter, but from a physiological standpoint would have been approved by an exacting professor of anatomy. He meant to inculcate in the executives something of the same sweaty satisfaction they knew when they took part as youths in athletic games—and so would have an inducement to continue with the exercises long after they left Aspen. So it was, for example, in the case of Adlai E. Stevenson. As a special guest at one of the Executive Seminars and a participant in the exercise program, he took Pedersen to one side to say in the utmost confidence: "You know, I get more out of *your* class than I do out of the discussion in the seminar room." Later, at leave-taking time, this same man, who had been showered with gifts from high and mighty sources, shyly asked for a gift which Pedersen was in a position to bestow. Could he take away from the health center one of the lengths of rope that were used in the stretching and skipping exercises? The gift was his.

In the course of restructuring the Aspen Institute, Anderson closely examined a range of other activities grouped under the managerial roof of the Meadows Corporation, and initiated a number of money-saving changes without loss on the side of quality. Still other matters were left as they were found. They included the Aspen Festival of Film Classics, the scheduling of Aspen Lectures open to the public, and the existing pattern of co-operation with the International Conference on Design, the Music Festival, and the Music School. At the same time, after much discussion about cost benefits, the Institute's Executive Seminars were put on a year-round basis in 1957 with the inauguration of a winter seminar series.

While Anderson moved to bring a new sense of order to the Institute, he was mindful of the need to preserve and cultivate what he believed was distinctive about its inner life. He reasoned that the Institute would cease to be "humanistic" if it strove to be big for bigness' sake. It must remain a small-scale operation, highly personalized, and largely informal. It must remain modest in its claims, and yet provide individuals with a forum not readily available elsewhere—a forum where they could cross disciplines in an open manner and could speak their minds freely. It must remain a place whose *institutional neutrality* would permit it to consider any topic however "controversial," and to bring to bear on it a great diversity of viewpoints, however heretical. It must help define the questions of public policy worth asking, must help clarify the range and implications of alternative answers to them, but the conclusions drawn by individuals who shared the work of clarification must in every case be their own.

In another direction, however, Anderson risked being misunderstood by some of the Institute's "first generation" leadership because of his stand on a particular point of policy. He was personally devoted to the Great Books movement, of which he was a University of Chicago product, and he would be one of its missionaries in the business community. But he did not want the Institute to be bound to that movement alone, like two mountain climbers tied together by the same rope. To do so would give the Institute a one-dimensional identity in the public mind. It must consider the possibility of undertaking special projects in order to enrich what it was already offering in the realm of leader education.

II

Walter Paepcke, for his part, continued to be active in the affairs of the Institute even after he was stricken with cancer. He had previously induced his friend John F. Merriam, the president of a western utility company who had a home in Aspen, to join the Institute's board of trustees; later, as Paepcke's death drew near, he brought Merriam onto the board of the Container Corporation so that he could be the link between it and the Aspen Institute. Meanwhile he had hoped that the music festival and the music school—his true loves—could somehow be brought back under the direct wing of the Institute. But the approaches made to the Aspen Music Associates were unrewarding. The latter preferred to preserve their autonomy as a self-governing co-operative. In support of their stand, they would soon be in a position to cite the judgment of the music critic for *The New York Times* who proclaimed the Aspen Music Festival "the finest summer offering in the United States, and the most adventuresome in its programmatic mix of new composition in a modern idiom along with those drawn from a traditional repertoire." They would also observe that the swift rise of the music school into an internationally renowned institution with eight hundred summertime students from around the world might have been hobbled if it had been indivisibly tied to the Aspen Institute, and had to scramble annually for a slice of the Institute's slim budget. As it was, the Music Associates collected funds from sources in Aspen and around the nation that would not have responded to the intellectual appeals of the Institute, and these funds covered operating deficits over and above the income accruing from tuition fees and paid admissions to the concerts.

Despite the decision of the Aspen Music Associates to preserve their institutional autonomy, Paepcke continued to yearn for a reunion. Even when death was close, his mind teemed with plans to bring his musical children back under their original parental roof. Thus he asked Herbert Bayer to draw plans for a permanent auditorium which would be the home of the Festival Orchestra in place of the circus tent amphitheater where concerts had been held since 1949. What he had in mind was an auditorium seating around 750 people and designed to give the audience a sense of intimacy without being aware of an empty balcony. The exterior walls should be built so that they could open to the outdoors, allowing for the accommodation of overflow audiences in the summer seasons and giving added spaciousness to the building itself.

The plans, however, never moved beyond the drawing board stage. After his death, it was realized—and by no one more clearly than by Bayer—that what the Institute needed was not the structure Paepcke had in mind. It needed an intimate hall with a seating capacity of around 350, suitable for lectures, for chamber music, and for the screening of films. The auditorium, moreover, should be incorporated into a structure containing a library, archives, conference rooms, administrative offices, and a communications center where reading materials and other documents could be prepared for use within the Institute or disseminated to a growing audience of leaders of opinion in America and around the world.

The trustees of the Aspen Institute commissioned Bayer to design an edifice along the lines just indicated, and it would bear the name of the Walter Paul Paepcke Memorial Auditorium. Construction began in 1961 with a ground-breaking ceremony at which Mortimer Adler was the principal speaker; the structure was ready for use the next year, and was formally dedicated in 1963 at a ceremony for which Arnold Toynbee gave the main address. In that same year, when the auditorium became available for chamber music concerts, the cause of music in Aspen was further advanced by Robert O. Anderson and his wife, Barbara. To provide students and teachers in the music school with something they never had before—a central place in Aspen which they could call their own —they gave the Aspen Music Associates the valuable Aspen property known as the Four Seasons and a spread of land around it for use as the music school's permanent home.

III

When Walter Paepcke died in the spring of 1960, the question was asked whether there could be any continuity in the life of the Aspen Institute itself. Robert O. Anderson, who by now had served for three years as president of the Institute, meant for the question to be answered in the affirmative. So did Elizabeth Paepcke and her brother, Paul H. Nitze, who had joined the Institute's board of trustees. Other members of the original board— Glen A. Lloyd, John F. Merriam, Harald Pabst, John Herron, and Robert L. Stearns—were also of that mind. So were the men who joined the board at different times in the years between 1951 and 1960. They included William E. Stevenson, president emeritus of Oberlin College; Louis T. Benezet, president of Colorado College; former United States Senator William Benton, chairman of the board of the Encyclopaedia Britannica Company; Gaylord A. Freeman, Jr., president of the First National Bank of Chicago; William Gomberg, professor of industry, Wharton School of Finance and Industry; Robert Ingersoll, president of the Borg-Warner Corporation (and a future U.S. Ambassador to Japan);

William Janss, president of the Janss Investment Company; George C. McGhee, president of McGhee Production Company, counselor to the U.S. Department of State and soon to be the U.S. Ambassador to Germany; Sir Leslie K. Munro of New Zealand, president of the United Nations General Assembly; James Hopkins Smith, Jr., who has been identified already in these pages; John V. Spachner, executive vice-president of the Container Corporation of America; George H. Watkins, vice-president of the Chicago firm of March and McLellan; and Byron White, president of the Social Science Foundation at Denver University, soon to be Deputy U.S. Attorney General and after that, a justice of the United States Supreme Court.

Few private institutions in the United States could lay claim to the range of talents, interests, and perspectives embodied in the roster of these distinguished names. Distinguished names, however, could not of themselves guarantee a future for the Aspen Institute. The answer to the question of whether the Institute could survive Paepcke's death surfaced in the course of successive tests starting in the early spring of 1960, when the first Executive Seminar of the year was held. The seminar was well attended by an impressive group of business leaders, with moderators and special guests such as Congressman Gerald Ford, then a rising star among the Republicans in the U.S. House of Representatives; Robert Amory, deputy director of the Central Intelligence Agency; Dr. Ernest Anderson of the Los Alamos Scientific Laboratories; Brian Urquhart, special assistant to the Secretary-General of the United Nations; Admiral Ellis Zacharias who had been the head of United States Naval Intelligence in the Pacific theater during the post–Pearl Harbor years of World War II.

Also in the early spring of 1960 there was a suggestion in the air that the Institute might emerge as a major conference center for organizations whose purposes were congruous with those the Institute set for itself. The annual International Design Conference had set the early precedent in the matter. But the precedent was modestly enlarged in the spring of 1960 when the Institute's facilities were used first by the International Pressman's

Union Liberal Arts Seminar for Management and Labor Executives, and then by the Third Annual International Emphysema Conference. In much the same way that a "breakthrough" in science is often only tangentially connected with the object of an original research project, the Emphysema Conference foreshadowed the multiple links that would be forged in due course between the Aspen Institute and the world of science and technology.

Still, despite these promising signs, it was recognized that the make-or-break test of the Institute's survival powers would be the series of Executive Seminars extending from June to mid-September. If these failed to draw an adequate number of corporate and paying individual participants, the Institute could be written off as a noble experiment in leader education that failed. Happily the seminars attracted 112 people, the largest registration in the Institute's history up to that time. Of greater importance than the head count was the quality of participants.[1] The kinetic energy they generated still crackled in the air when the Institute's board of trustees met after the 1960 Presidential election to discuss future policies in the light of recent experiences. Some members, citing the sparkle of the latest round of Executive Seminars, argued that the Institute now had a known and proven constituency, and hence should do nothing more than what it was doing. To do something more would be to spread the Institute thin, to smudge its clarity of line, and to imperil the spirit of fraternity which sprang up among business leaders who jointly wrestled with

[1] Among others, they included Charles Bohlen, the former U.S. Ambassador to the Soviet Union and soon to France; Supreme Court Justice William Brennan; John Burchard, dean of humanities and social sciences, Massachusetts Institute of Technology; Cass Canfield, publisher, Harper & Brothers; Sir Pierson Dixon, Great Britain's Ambassador to France; Lester B. Granger, executive director, National Urban League; Najeeb Halaby, head of the Federal Aeronautics Administration; O. A. Knight, president of the Oil, Chemical and Atomic Workers Union; Jacob Potosky, general president, Amalgamated Clothing Workers of America; Leonard Woodcock, vice-president, United Auto Workers; Dr. Walter Orr Roberts, chairman, University Corporation of Atmospheric Research; Sterling McMurrin, U.S. Commissioner of Education; Carey McWilliams, editor, *The Nation*; C. L. Sulzberger of *The New York Times*; Dr. Samuel Miller, dean, Harvard Divinity School; Major General Glen Martin, deputy director of Plan, U.S. Air Force; and Bayless Manning, Yale University Law School.

problems posed in classical form by texts drawn from the Great Books. One of the trustees who spoke forcefully for this view was William E. Stevenson, who had just retired as president of Oberlin College.

Anderson, however, spoke to an opposite effect, saying again, as he had on other occasions, that the Institute must expand its field of action beyond the framework of the Executive Seminars. But how should it expand? In what direction? As it happened, Walter Orr Roberts and Robert Craig had spent many hours together in Aspen and in Boulder, discussing the place of science in the Aspen Executive Program. They agreed that the seminars, since their inception, had enabled business leaders to enter into face-to-face discussions with major representatives of the American scientific community such as Enrico Fermi, Leo Szilard, Hans Bethe, Hermann Muller, Harrison Brown, Gerard Kuiper, Donald Hughes, George Kistiakovsky, and the scientists who had participated in the 1960 seminars. They also recognized that the problems of science and their historical development were raised in various assigned readings. All this was to the good. But it was not enough. The format of the seminars did not permit a sustained examination of the ever-widening breach between the humanities and the sciences and of the possibilities of synthesizing into a single culture what threatened to be a society divided into two rival cultures that could not speak to each other. Nor was the picture much different even in the case of major scientific organizations. At their annual meetings, many of these—the American Association for the Advancement of Science is but one example—had on their agenda a series of questions bearing on the relations between the sciences and the humanities. But the press of other business tended to limit the amount of time that could be devoted to these questions to a one-time, half-day seminar, and this scarcely made for depth of analysis.

Roberts and Craig conveyed their appraisal of the case to Anderson, and out of the further discussions which ensued, a proposal was formulated which the latter put to the trustees of the Aspen Institute. It called for a series of Institute-sponsored seminars that would systematically deal with two cardinal and interrelated issues. The first was the bearing the dynamics of science had on human welfare. The second was the need for science to initiate its own inquiries free from the exigencies of momentary pressures. "The public interest in, and understanding of science," said Anderson, "is not commensurate with the importance that science has attained in our social structure. We need to understand more clearly that what science contributes to the national purpose is measured by what it adds to the sum of *human knowledge*."

After much discussion back and forth, the trustees of the Aspen Institute endorsed the proposal for the special series of seminars which Anderson had advocated. In a follow-up, eminent scientists who had either participated in the Executive Seminars or served on the Institute's advisory board, endorsed an Institute application to the National Science Foundation for a grant whereby the Institute could present four one-week seminars every year for three years—the unifying theme being "The Public Understanding of the Role of Science in Society." The grant was made.

Meanwhile, in January, 1961, the inauguration of John F. Kennedy as President seemed to signal a revolutionary shift in the generations who became the center of authority in the United States and a hopeful shake-up in the nation's governing outlook, values, and purposes. In the aging figure of former President Dwight D. Eisenhower—supreme commander of the Allied invasion of Europe on D–Day, hero of V–E Day, Chief of Staff, supreme commander of NATO—one could see the eclipse of the old generation that had managed World War II and brought it to a successful conclusion. In the figure of John F. Kennedy—commander of a PT boat crew in the Pacific war, a hero survivor of the loss of the boat, a young congressman, a young senator, and the youngest man ever to win the White House in a direct election— one could see the ascendancy of the new generation that had made none of the great strategic decisions during the war, but rather bore the brunt of the front-line fighting. As a man still in his early forties, President Kennedy seemed to write large the national fact that the war had accelerated by half a generation the age at which men normally come to places of great power in American politics. Indeed, the national climate seemed charged with bright possibilities for all other young Americans. Simply to be young and an American was to live in a vibrant moral condition and to have a full-time career in translating into realities the new administration's campaign slogan: "Let's Get America Moving Again."

In this general atmosphere, the initial seminar on The Public Understanding of the Role of Science in Society was held in Aspen in October, 1961, and the event set the pattern for the rest of the series until 1965. The co-moderators were Walter Orr Roberts, then the director of the National Center for Atmospheric Research, and Robert S. Morrison, director of the Medical and Natural Sciences for the Rockefeller Foundation. In attendance were humanists, scientists, business leaders, university executives, labor leaders, clergymen, editors, and key governmental officials in both the civil and military order.[2]

The central question the seminar put to American leaders was this: How could the various facets of the scientific revolution be kept in balance with other activities vital to the American states and society? The question, in turn, subdivided into many particular questions. They included the extent of the schism between the humanities and the sciences in America, the problem of "Big Science" versus small-scale individual research, the increasing domination of government over science at large, the problems and responsibilities of research and development in the private sector,

---

[2] It is enough to mention a few representative figures. They included Major General William J. Ely, director of Army research; Dr. George Fister, president of the American Medical Association; Dr. Gill Hollingsworth, director of the Science Research Laboratory of the Boeing Airplane Company; Harrison Norton, president of the Institute for Defense Analysis; Loren Olsen, commissioner of the U.S. Atomic Energy Commission; Dr. Eugene Fubini, deputy director of research in the Department of Defense; Chancellor Chester M. Alter, of the University of Denver; Dr. Dael Wolfe, executive officer, American Association for the Advancement of Science; Donald B. Strauss, chairman, International Planned Parenthood Association; Ralph Bergmann, director of research, United Rubber, Cork, Linoleum, and Plastic Workers of America; Dr. Ralph C. M. Flynt, associate commissioner, U.S. Department of Education; and Walter Sullivan, science news editor of *The New York Times*.

the implications of defense research, and the stock-piling of scientists by defense-oriented corporations or in-house government research facilities, the political pressures brought upon basic research and experimentation, from both the private and the public sector, and the military and industrial exploitation of science for their own ends.

Emerson had once remarked that when old friends meet after a time of separation, they should greet each other by asking, "Has anything become clear to you since we were last together?" The continuity among some of the participants in the successive seminars, augmented by cadres of new participants, permitted the Emersonian question to be asked at regular intervals, leading to a progressive clarification of the subject matter under discussion. Moreover, the Aspen initiative helped stimulate many regional seminars in universities and among private organizations on the understanding of science by laymen, on the social and economic implications of the scientific revolution, on the relationship between science and government, and on the conflict or interplay between the sciences and the humanities. There was a further consequence. The discussions spreading outward from Aspen helped prepare the ground for the creation of the National Endowment for the Humanities (NEH) as a matching piece to the National Science Foundation. Two men who played major but different roles in the birth of the NEH—Barnaby C. Kenney, president of Brown University, and Thomas Watson, president of the International Business Machines Corporation—had long been intimately associated with the activities of the Aspen Institute.

IV

Coincident with the onset in 1961 of the science and society seminars, individual physicists who participated in the Institute's programs suggested to Craig that the Aspen setting offered a unique environment for concentrated work on problems of physics involving fundamental theoretical research. The kinds of problems they had in mind did not need experimental laboratories jampacked with steaming test tubes and electrical fireworks as featured in Boris Karloff films or in science fiction fantasies. The research would require little more than a blackboard and a piece of chalk by way of equipment, supplemented by the informed comments of such colleagues as one might wish to consult.

Craig was enthusiastic and passed the idea on to Anderson at a time when the Aspen Institute trustees were weighing alternative lines of future operations. In one direction, for example, they had considered anew and again laid aside the old idea of converting the Institute into a special kind of "free-standing" college. In another direction, they had advanced a proposal which would make the Institute an adjunct or western outpost of the University of Chicago. The necessary legal documents were drawn up, and their terms came within an ace of being approved by the trustees of the University of Chicago, only to be finally rejected. It was then that the trustees of the Aspen Institute favorably considered a proposal which recalled the 1952 "secret" plan for a post-doctoral academy that would be tied in with the Institute. In its new reincarnation, the plan contemplated the creation from within the Institute of a new Center for Advanced Individual Studies. Scholars from diverse fields would come to the center in order to pursue their individual research and to profit from the exchange of ideas across the disciplines of the humanities, the social sciences, and the natural sciences. The center would be open initially only during the summer months, but would eventually function around the year, attracting post-doctoral scholars who were either on sabbatical leaves of absence or had made other arrangements with their parent institutions.

All this, to repeat, was under serious consideration when the interests of the physicists who had been in Aspen came to the attention of Anderson and other trustees of the Aspen Institute. The latter now agreed that a division of physics readily fit into their concept for a Center for Advanced Individual Studies—as did a division for molecular biology, a division for theological studies, and a program of fellowships for resident writers, poets, and composers of music. The Aspen Institute lacked the means to initiate in a single stroke all such envisioned intellectual ventures. In fact, the center itself would never materialize in an institutionalized form. Yet most of the activities it was meant to oversee did come into being in Aspen, sometimes in a transfigured form and in a series of steps, starting in 1961.

At that time, Anderson invited a diverse group of American physicists to serve on an advisory committee to help plan a projected Aspen Institute for Theoretical Physics. As formed, the committee included Hans A. Bethe, chairman of the Department of Physics at Cornell University, and the recipient of the United States government's highest award for his contributions to the peaceful and military uses of atomic energy.[3] Other committee members included Julius Ashkin, chairman of the Department of Physics, Carnegie Institute of Technology; Henry Primakoff, chairman of the Department of Physics, University of Pennsylvania; Frederick Seitz, chairman of the Department of Physics, University of Illinois; Richard A. Ferrell, Department of Physics, University of Maryland; and M. L. Goldberger, Department of Physics, Princeton University. Men such as these were among those in the mind of the observer who, after contrasting many centuries of slow development in the natural sciences with the quantum jump in the pace and scope of the advances made since the 1930's, concluded that "90 per cent of all scientists are alive."

The negotiations between spokesmen for this committee and for the Aspen Institute produced a set of terms that were ratified by the two parent bodies. It was agreed, for example, that the Aspen Institute for Humanistic Studies would arrange to house the physicists and their families when they were in Aspen and would also absorb some of the overhead costs of the Institute for Theoretical Physics. But the scientists would depend for their upkeep on the summer salaries or fellowships provided by other sources. It was agreed, secondly, that unlike most summer institutes organized around an intensive program of lectures, the Insti-

[3] At the award ceremony, Dr. Bethe met the words of praise for his own work by saying that not atomic energy but "peace will be the greatest discovery of our time." A friendly critic contended in rejoinder that the remark was imprecise. It would be more precise to say that peace cannot be discovered. It has to be invented.

tute for Theoretical Physics would be a free-wheeling place where each physicist could do his work in a style that suited him best.

It was further agreed that the theoretical physicists would reserve a number of spaces in the new institute for those experimental physicists who might want to come to Aspen to plan new experiments or to analyze data from tests they had previously run in their home-base laboratories. The arrangement would enable the experimenters to benefit from the speculative constructs of the nearby theorists since "the most practical thing in the world is a good theory." The theorists, conversely, could benefit by testing their constructs against the empirical data possessed by the nearby experimenters. More, the same relationship would bring to the theorists the coverage of an insurance policy, whose ironic terms, applicable to any kind of serious intellectual endeavor, were first recognized by Thomas Huxley. Next to being right, said he, the best thing is to be clearly and absolutely wrong since in that case, "you are bound to have the extreme good fortune of knocking your head against a fact, and that sets you all straight again."

Finally, it was recognized that though the new institute would have no experimental laboratories, the physicists could not be expected to do all their work simply by sitting under an aspen tree. Even the legendary apple which fell on Newton's head when he was out-of-doors was preceded and succeeded by Newton's years of indoor study before he published his principles of mechanics. The physicists in Aspen, to no lesser degree, were in need of indoor offices, a library, and a seminar room. Part of the need was met when the Aspen Institute for Humanistic Studies made available to the physicists the use of land on the Institute's Aspen Meadows campus and commissioned Herbert Bayer to design and oversee the erection on it of a Physics Building. The other part was met by special grants from interested corporations and private foundations covering actual construction costs.

The Physics Building was completed and ready for use by mid-June, 1962, and its clients during the remainder of the summer were some forty-five American and foreign physicists from twenty-two major institutions of higher learning. They found, as did their counterparts every summer after that, that the Aspen Institute for Theoretical Physics was a place where a scientist was unencumbered by the distracting housekeeping demands of institutionalized academic life. He was free to walk alone with his private thoughts, free to participate in such seminars as might aid in individual research, free to enter into the circle of activities connected with the Aspen Institute for Humanistic Studies.

This is not to claim that Aspen itself was the source of the combustion which set the physicists afire with the ideas issuing from them. When it is often impossible to recall how a casual conversation began, how can one establish beyond doubt precisely where and when the spark of a new view of nature ignited a human mind? A particular kind of claim, however, can be made on the basis of naked-eye observation. It is that starting in the summer of 1962, Aspen attracted more and more physicists bent on sorting out and giving coherence to their ideas. The result was evident in the increasing number of scientific monographs on a great range of subjects that were completed in Aspen every summer and were readied for publication in scientific journals.

10. SEEDLINGS FOR THE FUTURE

I

Robert Craig, who continued to serve as the on-the-spot director of the Aspen Institute, was the source of many imaginative ideas about what the Institute should do. In other matters, he was guided by Anderson and by several of the other trustees, most notably Gaylord Freeman and John F. Merriam. There was not as yet a master plan for the growth of the Institute beyond the core Executive Seminars. Beginning in 1962–63, however, some suggestions of how the Institute might evolve could be deduced from two closely related events. One was the marked increase in the Institute's special conferences and projects devoted to both national and international issues. The other was the marked increase in the joint venture of variable length, sponsored by the Institute and an expanding range of co-operating agencies. Some of these wore the aspect of an immediate response to the challenge of immediate events, and some were either addressed to long-range matters or to the need to clarify a current stock of general ideas. Some led to discernible consequences, and some were merely absorbed in the atmosphere of the time.

There is room here for only a handful of illustrations.

The first illustration—an extraordinary interdisciplinary conference organized by Walter Orr Roberts and held at the Aspen Institute in the summer of 1962—prefigured the Institute's future role in promoting an informed national and international approach to environmental issues. The subject of the conference was "Climate in the 11th and 16th Centuries." A casual bystander might wonder why any living person should think it worthwhile to talk about weather conditions three or eight centuries before his own. Yet the subject entailed an inquiry into the ways sharp

159

climatic changes could affect the conditions for life on earth, no trifling matter. Its importance was recognized by the four major scientific organizations—the National Academy of Science, the National Research Council, the High Altitude Observatory, and the Air Force Cambridge Research Laboratory—which joined the Aspen Institute as co-sponsors of the conference. Its importance also accounted for the extraordinary mix of conference participants who met in Aspen under the chairmanship of Walter Orr Roberts. In their national identity, they came from Japan, Spain, England, Sweden, Denmark, and Iceland as well as the United States. In their professional identity, they included meteorologists, historians, anthropologists, botanists, biologists, and geographers.

The importance of the conference was further underscored by the year-long research work performed in different countries in anticipation of the meeting in Aspen and by the unusual nature of that research. In Iceland, for example, which once depended exclusively on home-grown food, teams of scientists studied the skeletons of children that had been moved from eleventh- and sixteenth-century graves and whose exact dates of birth and death were known. By means of this approach, they were able to construct a curve of nutrition in Iceland and relate the curve to changes in the local climate. Or again, an English scientist studied the records in the Town Hall of Nottingham of manorial estates for the periods between the eleventh and sixteenth centuries. From the entries stating the reasons why people who worked the land failed to achieve expected taxable yields—including broods of chickens—he extrapolated a picture of how climatic changes affected agriculture, an important by-product of the conference's main purpose.

The data collected by all modes of year-long scientific detective work pursued in widely separated places was brought to Aspen in the summer of 1962 and laid out on the floor of the Institute's seminar room for study and argument. Two results followed from the fact that the work of every participant in the conference became available to all the others. The first and more immediate result was the construction of a whole series of tables about climatic conditions, season by season, for two centuries—which are still widely referred to as the Aspen Climate Series. The second result, having a multiplier effect lasting for years, was the general impact the conference had in transforming the nature of climate research.

As was true of other events staged in Aspen, none of this made any headlines at the time. What is more, when some U.S. Air Force officials—civilian as well as military—belatedly learned that the Air Force Cambridge Research Laboratory had joined in sponsoring a conference on climate in the eleventh and sixteenth centuries, the danger of collective apoplexy in the Pentagon was averted only when Walter Orr Roberts and several of his colleagues put cooling hands on overheated foreheads and explained the importance of such studies to the Air Force. Yet the full defense of the conference would appear as the years went by. It would appear when the Aspen Institute, under Joseph E. Slater's direction, turned its attention to the "outer limits" of the life and death interplay between the factors of climate, food supply, and population growth in a world in which an estimated 1 billion people were undernourished and an estimated 200 million faced actual starvation.

A second item—which also prefigured the Aspen Institute's future involvement in environmental issues—was the series of summer institutes held in Aspen, cosponsored by the Aspen Institute, the National Science Foundation, and Colorado College. The first of the series, starting in June, 1962, was under the direction of two ecologists, Richard G. Beidleman of Colorado College and Robert Lewis of Aspen.

Rachel Carson through her book, *The Silent Spring*, had done much to raise the level of public consciousness about the dynamics of out-of-door living organisms viewed either from the standpoint of the single biotic community or as components in an overarching ecosystem. At the same time the public consciousness of the need to conserve open spaces as recreational areas for an expanding population found expression in the support mobilized for the so-called Wilderness Act submitted to Congress by the

Kennedy administration. The Aspen program in field biology, however, aimed at a "multiplier" principle in education. Thus it was expressly designed for high school teachers of biology—to advance their knowledge about collecting techniques, identification and measurement of environmental factors, census-taking and sampling, determination of indicators, and the preparation of field maps. In this way—through the accumulation of more reliable data by the use of perfected techniques—teachers and students alike could deduce significant ecological concepts from that data.

Teachers who participated in the Aspen summer institutes in field biology exhibited something more than an attractive sun tan when they returned to their high schools. They soon became the nuclei for similar programs in field biology organized at state and local levels. They were also at the forefront of a drive to enrich the field work portions of the high school biology curriculum through better co-operative planning between university biology departments, teachers' colleges, and state departments of education. The cumulative impact these efforts had on school children starting in the early 1960's may have helped prepare the ground for the leap in the intensity of the interest young people showed by the end of the decade in ecological and environmental issues.

II

Different classes of Aspen-based events, unfolding in the early 1960's, merit notice because of what they reveal about the Institute's early efforts to extend the meaning of "humanistic studies" beyond the traditional metes and bounds of academic humanists. The two illustrative cases, sketched below, stand for others that could be offered.

First, since the founding of the Institute, its film classics program—by 1963, the oldest in the United States—had brought to Aspen a wide range of distinguished foreign and American films and, in addition, sponsored public lectures on films of particular historic interest. But in the discussions of plans for 1963, Robert Murray, then the program director for the Aspen Institute, joined by Robert Craig, advanced the view that the Aspen Institute might be to the American motion picture what the British Film Institute and the *Cahiers du Cinema* were to their respective countries—the meeting ground on which the fragmented and competitive parts of Hollywood and its environs in the industry might compare values, exchange ideas, and ultimately improve their work.

The need for such a meeting ground was clearly indicated when one took into account two indivisible facts. First, the motion picture industry, perhaps more than any other industry, was sustained by a crucial but uneasy alliance between business and art. Second, both elements in the alliance were in trouble—the business element because it was being subjected to new economic pressures; the artistic element because the former mass audience for the film had become a fragmented audience, with different segments preferring different kinds of films.

The early trait of the Hollywood movie as the projection of dreams to an industrial society by industrial means had not been seriously challenged during almost a half-century of technological development to the end of World War II. Many talents and crafts were joined to make films for a mass audience that responded uncritically to the movies as an escape into dream, as a form of entertainment to be enjoyed several times a week, as a habit, as an anodyne for neurotic pain, as folk art and custom. There was no compelling reason for the movie industry to subject itself to searching self-examination. Its mass audience gave it a market for a standardized product—75 per cent of which was produced according to a "box office formula"—that could be duplicated and distributed like other industrial products.

After 1948, however, all the certitudes of Hollywood were undercut by four interacting factors. First, with the advent of television, the American public quickly became aware that they could remain comfortably at home and see without charge essentially the same bill of fare which occupied most of the screen time in their local theaters. Second, with the development of installment consumer credit, the American consumer discovered that the dollar he used to spend on the movies could serve him as a down payment on a broad spectrum of leisure-time activities—whether it was a trip, a power boat or sailboat, or power saws. Third, in 1950, the major companies—Paramount, MGM, and Twentieth-Century Fox—which had previously produced films in the assurance that no matter what they produced would be shown in the theater chains they owned, entered into a consent decree with the government in which they agreed to divorce themselves from their theater ownership and only produce and distribute motion pictures. They must henceforth take care to produce films which the newly liberated exhibitors might want to show. Finally, there were the realities of foreign production—government subsidies of film industries in foreign countries, film censorship in some sixty countries, lower production costs in foreign countries, and American tax laws which induced high-income actors, actresses, producers, and directors to settle abroad and make their films in foreign countries.

All these factors—and the discontents to which they gave rise—were ceaselessly discussed in Hollywood. But the discussions tended to be of an "in-house" kind, and as such were unaffected by the ideas and criticisms of interested outsiders. To provide a common meeting ground for all interested parties, the Aspen Institute took the initiative in organizing an Annual Aspen Film Conference, the first of which drew to Aspen in 1963 a volatile and articulate group of some one hundred people who were actively engaged in the motion picture industry as producers, directors, actors, and exhibitors, or who stood outside the industry proper but were keenly interested in the topic of the conferences, "The American Film—Its Makers and Its Audience."

The keynote address was given by literary critic Lionel Trilling. Many individuals in the Hollywood contingent attending the conference initially reacted with violent hostility to his remarks, and it is not difficult to understand why. He observed that even the friendliest of critics of the film such as James Agee and Robert Warshaw were always working for the day when the potentialities

164

of the medium would be realized, when films would be made that would have validities and powers equivalent to those to which we respond in the great traditional arts of fictional narrative and stage drama. But the day when the film would be *liberated* to realize its potentialities always remained in the future, and in this, its situation was unique.

In all the history of culture [said Trilling] there is no other example of an art coming to so high a point of technical and aesthetic development without gaining full autonomy—at the risk of being pretentious, I will say without gaining full spiritual autonomy. We are all aware of one reason—a chief reason—why this is so. No other art ever was an *industry* before it was an art.

Trilling admitted that new and intense efforts were being made under new economic conditions to "overcome the financial controls which have limited the artists of film in their right to say what they think ought to be said, to show what they think ought to be shown." There was also the hopeful fact that the cultural circumstances which kept the film in economic chains—namely, the efforts by financial interests to satisfy the tastes and preferences of large egalitarian populations—were undergoing a change. The taste of the American population was now more diversified and complex, so that certain segments who had new taste were in themselves sufficiently populous to support artistic activities of a very advanced kind. This revolution of taste was a very notable event in American culture, but, said Trilling, there was an unhappy underside to the same event. With the new acceptance of high and advanced art had come a new imperturbability to art, meaning that because nothing can shock our taste, nothing can disquiet our minds.

Despite the initial naked animosity which greeted remarks in this key, it was not long before the industry people were earnestly discussing specific points in Trilling's thesis. Soon, too, attitudes began to change. Industry representatives grew less defensive, outsiders less doctrinaire. At the end of the conference, the film makers called the affair unique in its approach to criticism of the corporate problem behind the finished motion picture, and unanimously agreed that the conference should be repeated the next year. And so it was.

"The Young American Film Maker and His Contemporaries" was selected as the 1964 theme, to provide the young film maker with a sounding board for his problems and aspirations, to expose the quality of his work to judgments by his own peers in other arts and professions, and by "older" people representing the industry and the audience. Skilled mediation was often necessary. The conference not only re-examined Trilling's question of whether the movies are an industry or an art, or perhaps a good deal of both; it also confronted members of "the Establishment" with a whole galaxy of young film makers who, in most instances, wanted to make it very clear that the ways of Hollywood were not their own.

The matters discussed at the Aspen Film Conferences later became the themes for debates carried on elsewhere in private forums or through the public media. The Motion Picture Association of America formally resolved to support the distribution of the best work of young, independent film makers. Mrs. Thomas Braden, an observer at the film conferences and co-chairman of the new National Cultural Center that was to be built as a memorial to John F. Kennedy, was instrumental in incorporating the film more firmly into the proposed activities of the center. A new awareness of experiments underway in film-making stimulated the showing of innovative films to interested audiences around the country. At the same time, when it was learned that the papers prepared for the conferences brought together into a single packet a treasury of perspectives and ideas about the American film not found elsewhere, the material was soon put to use as teaching aids in colleges which were responsive to student interests in film-making.

The successive Aspen Film Conferences appeared to deepen an understanding of the film, its makers, and its audience. But by 1965, they ran out of steam, or perhaps were overrun by the national turmoil occasioned by the Vietnamese conflict, and were allowed to lapse. Not, however, forever. At intervals after 1969, under the direction of Joseph E. Slater, the Aspen program of activities included periods set aside where innovative figures in the film-making industry, such as Peter Brooks, were brought to Aspen to exhibit their work and to conduct seminars on the experimental work going forward in their metier. Above all, the film—with its rapidly advancing technology as in television—became the subject of sustained inquiries by the Aspen Institute's major program on Communications and Society.

The second illustrative case showing how the Aspen Institute tried to extend the meaning of "humanistic studies," has its gravitational center in an area seemingly remote from the one just sketched. On the initiative of John F. Merriam, a trustee of the Aspen Institute and chairman of the Committee on Educational Development's (CED's) Subcommittee on Education, the two institutions agreed to co-sponsor for three successive years a special conference on aspects of economic education, starting with a 1963 conference on the kind of economic education provided by the nation's business schools.

Leaving a handful of exceptions out of account, economic education in these schools tended to lag far behind the pace of changes both in the business world and in the subject of economics itself. The case study method of instruction was the general rule— meaning that the schools taught "how to do it" instances of success or "how not to do it" instances of failure in business. The premises underlying the method were seldom stated explicitly. Yet it seemed to be assumed that the conduct of business proceeded from a fixed mechanistic set-up where an abstract "economic man," prompted solely by economic motives, behaved in the same way when placed in the same circumstances. Hence a business school student who mastered the cases which illustrated the "rules" of economic behavior would be prepared to master the problems awaiting him in the realm of applied economics.

There were, however, two obvious difficulties with this simplistic contention. First, man is not a creature governed solely by his measurable economic interests; he is also governed by his immeasurable convictions, his nostalgia, his will, and his passions. Second, his interests are not confined solely to a desire for pecuniary profit. They also include the desire for a sense of personal worth, for attention, for variety, for leisure, for independence, for security, for friendship, for social utility, for knowledge. Nor is the concept of interest confined to the bounds of a single person. Starting with the single person, it can move outward to become family interest, corporate interest, class interest, ethnic or cultural interest, national interest. The more it expands, the more the concept of interest moves beyond the province of "pure economics" and encroaches on the province of ethics and politics, and the more its underlying social philosophy must take into account not only the facts of utility but those of justice.

The careful economic theorist was not unmindful of any of this. Although he focused on efficiency in the use of means, whatever means were available and whatever ends were pursued, he did not confuse his pure abstractions of economic behavior, or the economic man, with the actual behavior of real men. He did not confuse a mode of analysis with a comprehensive social philosophy for an industrial society. He was aware that marketplace competition, in the psychological meaning, is a noneconomic interest; that applied economics in business life must try to take account of errors and motives such as prejudice, curiosity, and the various forms of human interplay which do not conform to the pattern of economic rationality; that the essential factor of wants—their propriety and how they are met through a system of distributive justice—cannot be assessed with the tools of economic analysis alone. They can be assessed only with the help of other disciplines such as philosophy, history, political science, ethics, sociology, psychology, cultural anthropology, and statistics. These supply the necessary data and interpretation which put content and definiteness into the economic theorists' highly abstract laws of economic choice and of marketplace phenomena.

Still, what the careful economic theorists knew about the limits of "pure economics"—and about the importance of the things lying beyond those limits—was seldom reflected in the curriculum of business schools. Even within the sphere of "pure economics," the curriculum seldom reflected the advances that were made in economics either through the perfection of mathematical tools or through the remarkable developments since 1940 in new fields which could be applied to the problems of organized economic complexity. Students in the business schools continued to be taught applied economics in ways which left them ill prepared after the mid-1940's to cope with the realities of an American business world that was being swept by winds of swift social, political, cultural, and technological change.

It was a world whose rapidly changing face eluded an identifying name until Daniel Bell, with his great gift for illumination, saw that its five salient features pointed to the coming of "the postindustrial society." One of its features—the economic sector—showed a change from a goods-producing to a service economy. The second—occupational distribution—showed a growing preeminence of the professional and technical class. The third—the axis on which social wheels go round—showed the growing centrality of theoretical knowledge as the source of innovation and of policy formulation for society. The fourth—future orientation or forecasting—showed an increasing dependence on the control of technology and on technological assessment. The fifth feature which absorbed all the others—decision-making—showed the creation of a new intellectual technology as a method for identifying and executing stategies for rational choice among variables.

Bell's thesis had obvious implications for the academic training of future businessmen; and as his thesis became known, it entered into the decision by the Aspen Institute and the CED to co-sponsor for three successive years special conferences on aspects of "economic education." The one held in 1963 brought together the deans of twenty-five leading schools of business in America, along with representatives of industry, the foundations, and the business press. Nothing like the encounter had ever occurred before in the history of American business and education. All the participants were challenged by the same question. Was it possible to reconstruct the curriculum of business schools so that their graduates would be armed with the tools of perception, research, analysis, and decision equal to the demands of a social, political, cultural, and economic world in flux?

It was not the purpose nor within the power of the conference to impose on the business schools by fiat any collective decision that was reached. Points of view could be clarified. Needs could be noted. Possible answers to the needs could be explored. But what happened afterward varied according to the attitudes of the deans, their faculties, their administrative superiors, and their patrons. In some cases such as the University of Chicago Business School, the Aspen discussions merely reinforced a move that was already under way to broaden the conceptual foundations for the curriculum and to bend it more on the side of theory. In other cases, one of the main difficulties in attempting to raise the level of the education offered was the fact that patrons whose support was essential had been brought up on substandard education and ascribed to it the success they had attained in the business world.

Events, however, were in the saddle. As a by-product of the Vietnamese conflict, a vocal segment of American youth would soon make the whole structure and ethos of the American business community—and the business schools with it—the object of polemical attacks. At the same time, the "post-industrial revolution," as Daniel defined it, continued to unfold in ways which increasingly cast into bold relief the decisive role of "intellectual technology" in social change, not only in the United States but around the world, not only with respect to the conduct of business but in all other realms of human activity.

After Joseph E. Slater became the president of the Aspen Institute, the Institute would respond to the challenge of the "post-industrial revolution" in many ways. For example, it would join with the International Congress for Cultural Freedom in sponsoring in Aspen an international conference on "The Role of the Intellectual." It would mount a series of special conferences on "The Educated Person." It would bring the challenge to the center of some of its "thought leading to action" programs and especially to its program on Science, Technology, and Humanism.

11. MOVEMENT
AND CONSOLIDATION

I

In the fall of 1963, Robert O. Anderson and a growing circle of people who had been drawn into the work of the Aspen Institute could derive some personal satisfaction from the contributions they had made over the years to an emergent national consensus which found its voice in two developments. One was the introduction of a bill in Congress authorizing the creation of a National Foundation for the Humanities and the Arts, a modest enterprise at the outset but potentially capable of attaining the stature of a matching piece to the National Science Foundation. The second was sounded at Amherst College on October 26, when poet Robert Frost was awarded an honorary degree and President John F. Kennedy, as the convocation speaker, gave voice to a vision central to the aspirations of awakened Americans and seemingly attainable within their own generation.

I look forward [said the President] to an America which will not be afraid of grace and beauty . . . an America which will reward achievement in the arts as we reward achievement in business and statecraft. I look forward to an America which will steadily raise the standards of artistic accomplishment and which will steadily enlarge cultural opportunities for all our citizens. And I look forward to an America which commands respect throughout the world not only for its strength but for its civilization as well.

In this same hour, the eve of President Kennedy's assassination, the Aspen Institute underwent a change of administration. Robert Craig, who had rendered devoted service to the Aspen Institute for a decade between 1953 and 1963, held the affection of all persons associated with the Institute, as well as their respect for his imaginative powers. Yet a point had been reached where his position invited a paraphrase of Dante's utterance as he reached for the mystic rose of Paradise: "Our vision is greater than my speech." So, too, Craig's vision for the programs of the Institute were greater than the reach of his power to mobilize outside funds for their support. The main source of funds continued to be Robert O. Anderson, who, at the same time, maintained a close but unobtrusive watch over the Institute, counseling and seeking counsel as he helped guide the evolution of its affairs. By the fall of 1963, however, Anderson's rapidly expanding personal involvement in the business world and in countless civic and philanthropic enterprises on many fronts imposed limits on the extent of the minute attention he could give to the day-to-day problems of the Institute. At the same time, if the Institute was to grow beyond its existing programs, the funds Anderson personally advanced every year must be supplemented by other sources.

Robert Craig, for his part, recognized that "circumstances alter cases," and, besides, he was eager to give more of his own time to his lively personal interest in writing, ranching, and politics. He submitted his resignation as executive director of the Aspen Institute, but agreed to stay on for a transitional period as an aide to his successor, and would then join the Institute's board of advisors. The search for a successor came to a head in the fall of 1963 when Alvin C. Eurich agreed to an arrangement whereby he would become the president of the Institute, a post Anderson had filled since 1957. Anderson in turn would become chairman of the Institute's board of trustees, a post that had been left vacant since Walter Paepcke's death.

Alvin C. Eurich was no newcomer to the Institute. He had closely followed its career since the time of its creation, and as a member of the Institute's board of advisors, he had been an unfailing source of constructive, far-seeing counsel. Though he had none of the external flair of a charismatic figure, as "a Diesel engine in pants," he had proved his hauling power when hitched to a train of very heavy freight. This made some people wonder why he would hitch himself to an enterprise such as the Aspen

Institute, a dwarf when placed alongside his other institutional experience.

Among other things, for example, he had been successively the executive vice-president of Stanford University, the acting president of Stanford, chairman of the Stanford Research Institute, and the first president of the State University of New York where he brought thirty-two state colleges together into a state university system. He then became vice-president and director of the Fund for the Advancement of Education, and from 1958 to 1963 served as the executive director of the Ford Foundation's Educational Program. All this, by itself, would make a full-time career. Yet, he was also a member of the Hoover Commission on the Reorganization of the Executive Branch of the Government, of President Truman's Commission on Higher Education, of President Kennedy's Task Force on Education; he was a consultant to the public affairs program of NASA, a consultant to the Surgeon General and to the Peace Corps. In addition, he remained in close touch with the business world by serving on the board of directors of the Penn Mutual Life Insurance Company, the Commercial Bank of North America, and the Prentice-Hall Publishing Company. On top of everything else, as if to forestall the danger that he might lapse into delinquency if he were allowed an idle moment, he conceived of the "current affairs" test published by *Time* magazine and helped design the questions put to readers. The same interest in journalism accounted for the initiative he would take in bringing to life *Atlas* magazine—by and with the financial backing of Robert O. Anderson.

In 1963, however, Eurich's experiences with the Ford Foundation's educational program apparently impressed him with the force of the distinction Beardsley Ruml drew after he left his position as dean of the social sciences in the University of Chicago to become the treasurer of Macy's. On being asked whether he saw any differences between his former life in education and his new life in business, Ruml answered: "What you want to do in education is very important, but you can't do it; what you want to do in business is unimportant, but you can do it." Eurich may have been frustrated by the many obstacles in his way when he tried through the Ford Foundation to initiate promising new educational programs. The Aspen Institute, on the other hand, precisely because it was small, flexible, and nonbureaucratic, may have appealed to him as an instrument more readily adaptable to innovate experiments in adult education—with an international dimension to it.

"I am convinced," he said in a letter to Robert O. Anderson when he formally accepted the presidency of the Institute, "that we can make Aspen the outstanding international center in the humanities. . . . We should aim for the highest possible quality in everything we do. We don't want large numbers; we want Aspen to be distinctive in its purposes, people, and its influence on the intellectual life of our time."

Soon afterward Anderson made a down payment of his own on this aspiration and hoped that it would also stand to the credit of the Aspen Institute. He created what was meant to be an annual Aspen Award of $30,000, which would go to an individual anywhere in the world judged to have made the greatest contribution to the advancement of the humanities. In defining the humanities as "these studies and activities concerned with the nature, interests, and ideals of man," Anderson made clear that the search for the recipient would not be confined to the academic community alone. "The Aspen Award," said he, "is designed to recognize those creative persons who are contributing most to the clarification of the individual's role and his relationship to society." World leaders in intellectual and cultural fields would be asked to nominate candidates for the award in the humanities, the final decision to be made by an authoritative international committee of judges. It was hoped that the recipients of the award would spend some time in Aspen, where they would be available for discussion and in other ways would help spur the growth of the Aspen Institute into an international institute in the humanities.

In a cover story devoted to the Aspen Award in the Humanities, the *Saturday Review* struck a note that was echoed in other press comments at the time:

To thoughtful people concerned over the humanities in a world increasingly dominated by science and its awesome achievements, the news from Aspen was a hopeful inspiration. The magnitude of the Award, and the prestige conferred on those who received it, indicated that perhaps the long eclipse of the humanities is coming to an end. The fact that the award is of American origin, may help dispel the notion that the United States values most the things that can be counted or measured or weighed or clocked.

The vision behind the awards, however, was eclipsed by the selection committee's errors of judgment. Five awards were made, and they went in succession to Benjamin Britten, Martha Graham, C. A. Doxiades, Gilberto Freyre, and Edmund Wilson. Several could be justified by a strict test of merit; the others more closely resembled the award of a door prize at a raffle. In any case, all five, taken together, showed no coherent pattern of choice, no recognizable criteria for scaling contributions "to the clarification of the individual's role in his relationship to society." The fate of the award and its displacement by something else will be related later.

II

Soon after Alvin C. Eurich assumed the presidency of the Aspen Institute in November, 1963, he and his wife established a home in Aspen. The wives of the principal figures in the history of the Institute have always made distinctive personal contributions of their own to the felicities of the place. So it was in the case of Nell Eurich. As a former dean in Vassar College, she took a look at the Aspen Public High School, took a second look, and things began to happen. They kept on happening until she reorganized the entire curriculum of the school.

Her husband, meanwhile, busied himself with the affairs of the Institute. At first, there were limits to what he could do immediately to enrich the programmatic content of the Institute, since the design of a full-scale program for any given year requires a lead time of many months. Topics worth considering, accessible people, printed material, available funds, and housing facilities must be combined in ways which conform to the priorities of the Institute as a whole, and which take into account the currents of human traffic which flow in and out of the place. In consequence, the program for 1964 reflected in the main the plans drawn prior to the hour when Eurich formally assumed the presidency of the Institute.

The first of his immediate concerns was to broaden the Institute's financial base of support for its existing programs and for programs being contemplated. Anderson, through his extensive business connections, had always tried to induce corporations to send promising managers to Aspen to participate in the Executive Seminars or in other programs. No records had ever been kept of the total number of persons who participated in activities of the Aspen Institute. In the case of the Executive Seminars, however, existing records showed that for the period 1951–64 more than 400 corporations—ranging in size from Lilliputians to Leviathans —had participated in them and secondly, that more than 2,000 "alumni" of the Executive Seminars held places of leadership in business, labor, government, the professions, the universities, and the arts and sciences. They did not form an "Aspen Mafia," but attempts had been made to preserve the link between these alumni and the Institute by holding special "refresher" seminars for them in Aspen, Washington, or other major metropolitan areas such as New York and Chicago.

The fees charged for participation in the Executive Seminars never covered operating costs, much less left a surplus that could be applied to other activities of the Institute. At the same time, though the radial effects of these activities was being increasingly welcomed by reflective people, the bare-bones extent of outside financial support for Institute is revealed in figures which show that prior to 1964 only a handful of corporations or foundations ever gave as much as $5,000 to the Institute. A few more made contributions in the range of $1,000, but the bulk of the grants from these two sources were in amounts of $100 or less. Much the same was true of financial contributions by individuals. Gifts in

Program on Communications and Society conference on "Problems of Reporting."

Introduction to Asian Civilizations, moderated each year by
Phillips Talbot (right center).

International workshop: "The Intellectuals and Power—Their Role and Responsibility," July 6–9, 1973, at Aspen. Left to right: Saul Bellow, author; François Bourricaud, University of Paris; Thornton Bradshaw, president, Atlantic Richfield Company.

Annual Aspen workshop on Arms Control.

Continuing workshop of National Alternatives and Their Impli-
cation. Lester Brown, Senior Fellow, Overseas Development
Council; Sylvain Bromberger, Graduate Studies, M.I.T.; and
Richard Gardner, Columbia University Law School.

Informal discussion on International Affairs.

Annual Aspen Institute International Board

stees meeting in Helen Laughlin Commons.

Peter Brook, Aspen Institute Artist-in-Residence.

Eisenhower Exchange Fellows in seminar discussion, May 2, 1972.

Robert O. Anderson and Thornton Bradshaw.

Dean Acheson, former Secretary of State, Special Participant,
1966. A few of the many leaders who have helped shape the Aspen
Institute are shown here and on the following pages.

Gaylord Freeman, chairman, First National Bank of Chicago.

Soedjatmoko, former Indonesian ambassador to the United States, Aspen Institute trustee, Scholar-in-Residence, 1973.

Thurgood Marshall, Associate Justice, United States Supreme Court, Special Participant, 1963.

Robert Kennedy, as United States Attorney General, participated in conference on "Hostile Foreign Students and the U.S. Image Abroad."

Lionel Trilling, Columbia University, participant, 1963, and
Scholar-in-Residence, 1974. 195

Representative Gerald Ford, participant, 1960 and 1961.

Walter Reuther, president, United Auto Workers' Union, former Institute trustee, member of the Institute advisory board, and Aspen Executive Program Special Participant.

Leonard Bernstein, composer, conductor, director, New York Philharmonic, Special Participant, 1965.

Herbert Bayer, artist, trustee, and Aspen Institute Founding
Fellow.

199

Marion Countess Doenhoff, publisher of *Die Zeit*, Aspen Institute
trustee.

Daniel Schorr, Washington correspondent of CBS News, frequent
Institute participant since 1969.

Lady Barbara Ward Jackson, president, International Institute for Environment and Development, London, Special Participant, 1974.

Robert S. McNamara, former secretary of defense, Aspen Institute trustee, and frequent participant in various Institute programs.

Paul Horgan, author, Aspen Institute Founding Fellow, Scholar-in-Residence, and honorary trustee.

Maurice S. Strong, executive director, United Nations Environment Programme, Aspen Institute trustee,and a leader of several Institute programs.

John G. Powers, Academy for Educational Development, former trustee, and currently special advisor to the Institute's president.

Shirley M. Hufstedler, judge, United States Court of Appeals, Los Angeles, Aspen Institute trustee.

Herbert Schlosser, president of NBC, and participant at the Institute's annual Broadcasters' Workshop.

excess of $500 were rare, and rarer still were they in excess of $1,000. Contributions from individuals, when they were forthcoming at all, generally were in amounts of $100 or less.

The Aspen Institute needed money, and with Eurich on the scene, searched for respectable sources and devices to meet the need. In this way, in 1964, the Institute created the Aspen Society of Fellows with a membership limited to "one hundred persons engaged in strengthening the humanities to give greater meaning to man and wiser direction to society." A public announcement added an explanatory word:

> Attention to the humanities must not be evoked entirely by an appeal to practical necessity. The humanities are based upon our finest self-expression. And these creations can inspire and move man to action only if he approaches them with an unquenchable curiosity to know more about himself. For this reason, the Aspen Institute believes that support for the humanities must come from voluntary private as well as public sources, and from individuals as well as corporations. This belief is the foundation for the Aspen Society of Fellows.

In the years ahead, the Aspen Society of Fellows—the name would be amended in 1973 to distinguish the members from a newly conceived identity for Aspen Fellows—would hold an important place in the operational structure of the Institute. But it would not be until Joseph E. Slater assumed the presidency of the Institute that its programs were positioned in ways that they attracted direct or indirect financial support from an impressive range of co-operating agencies.

III

In the history of the Aspen Institute, 1965 stands out as "The Year of Eurich," when things began to "snap, crackle, and pop" on all sides. With the support of Anderson and other trustees, he launched an Artists-in-Residence program, which was destined to grow into an Artists and Scholars and Special Guests-in-Residence program. The start in 1965 was modest—four contemporary painters of the New York School.

At the same time, the Institute mounted four concurrent art

exhibits which were widely publicized, captured the attention of art critics, and drew streams of visitors to Aspen. All available wall space in the buildings on the Institute's campus were commandeered to form an *ad hoc* art museum. One of the exhibits was a rare showing of the 1964–65 works of the American artist William de Kooning. Another exhibited the art owned by Institute trustees and reflected tastes ranging from paintings by Kandinsky, Klee, Miró, and Chagall, to sculpture by Remington, Lucchesi, Arp, and Calder, the most advanced "pop" art. There was also a special exhibit of Japanese works of art owned by trustee John C. Powers, former president of Prentice-Hall Publishing Company, collected by him during his long stay in Japan, where he had business interests. The fourth exhibit consisted of the works of Artists-in-Residence Friedl Dzubas and Allan D'Arcangelo.

Here was an exciting, movable feast of the plastic arts—a reminder that the human eye is the most valued of all the senses—since it can take in a world of things with minimum effort. The movable feast, however, was not another case in which the best things in life are free. Insurance on the works of art bit into the Institute's thin bank account, while the man-hours spent in organizing and maintaining the exhibits meant less time a short-handed Institute staff could give its basic program.

Meanwhile, in 1965, the curtain was raised on a friction-laden experiment which bore the name of the Executive Seminar on Asian Thought. The regular Executive Seminar, established in 1951, continued to draw its reading materials solely from Western sources, some modern, some dating from ancient Judea, Greece, and Rome. By 1965, however, because of the radical changes that had been under way in the Far East since V–J Day, the main-springs of thought and action in the cultural contexts of Japan, China, and India could not be ignored by Americans. Much less could they be ignored by American businessmen who were engaged in international trade and finance with an economically resurgent Japan.

An Aspenite who wished to introduce American businessmen to Far Eastern culture was John G. Powers, who has already been identified as a trustee of the Aspen Institute and a former president of Prentice-Hall who had lived in Japan for a long time. With the encouragement of Alvin C. Eurich, a fellow board member at Prentice-Hall, Powers in August, 1965, organized an Aspen seminar in which interested business executives were introduced to aspects of Oriental culture, expressed in philosophy, religion, fine arts, sculpture, architecture, music, theater, textile design, and calligraphy. In addition to academic experts, one of the people who joined Powers in conducting the experiment was Phillips Talbot, Assistant Secretary of State for Near Eastern and South Asian Affairs. (He would re-enter the Aspen story four years later.) At the end of the 1965 trial run, participant reactions—all positive —accounted for a public statement in which Eurich explained that the seminar on Far Eastern thought was a natural outgrowth of the Institute's organic humanistic concerns:

If man is to understand more fully the direction in which he is drifting, and conceive clearer goals for himself, he cannot remain confined by the blinders of Western thinking. No one nation, no one culture, no one language, no one civilization can claim any longer to possess universal truth. Quite the reverse: it is impossible to see reality steadily, and to see it whole, through the categories, concepts, and ideals of any one cultural tradition.

There must be a meeting and a marriage of the major cultures of the world, a fruitful interaction in which the best of each nation's insights and values can be available to all men.

The Executive Seminar on Far Eastern Thought was repeated for several years in a row on a personal experimental basis. On that same personal basis, John G. Powers, in the fall of 1966, began to lead parties of American businessmen and their wives to Hakone, Japan, for an annual seminar on Japanese thought. At the Aspen end of things, however, many problems had to be solved before the Executive Seminars on Far Eastern Thought gained a semblance of stability within the Aspen Institute. Many other problems— some springing either from forthright differences of opinion or from emotional unease—would haunt the attempts to introduce Japanese, Chinese, and Indian texts into the regular Executive Seminar.

The *quantity* of activities the Institute generated and sustained on a narrow financial base impressed onlookers. Robert O. Anderson, however, was troubled by their *quality*. The disconnected string of special conferences the Institute had been offering increasingly since the start of the 1960's seemed, in his words, "to be like buckshot spray fired at any flight of birds that came along." Was it possible, he asked Eurich, to classify groups of particular problems under a common identifying name? If the answer was yes, then each group could be the subject of continuing conferences, seminars, and workshops extending for a number of years. Interim research and exploration could go on between annual meetings, but every meeting would have a nucleus of continuing participants who could convey to others what had been learned or clarified in earlier sessions. The new round of inquiry could then start at a higher rung of perception. Beyond that fact, all the participants—whether they later framed legislative proposals, testified before Congressional committees, wrote books, made broadcasts, issued reports, served on advisory committees, or engaged in other activities—would be better armed to bridge the gap between thought and action.

Eurich not only fully agreed with Anderson's line of argument, but the follow-through he initiated with the approval of the Institute's trustees marked a major advance in the Institute's programmatic development up to that time. Specifically, he formulated an Institute program known as "Man in 1980," which was to co-ordinate sustained inquiries into salient problems facing man and society in the decades ahead. In 1965–66 this meant special conferences on Population Problems in the Americas, Planning for Higher Education, Educational Development Below the College Level, and Moral and Ethical Values.

In retrospect, each of these now appears as only a small-scale effort, and for the moment proved to be short-lived. This does not, however, discount their importance. They not only were instrumental in drawing a wider circle of people into the orbit of the Institute but provided helpful precedents for the larger and sustained projects which the Aspen Institute would pursue under the presidency of Joseph E. Slater.

There is no room here to detail the substantive nature of each of these special conferences. All one can do for illustrative purposes is to single out the conference on American Higher Education, for which fifteen college and university presidents, along with foundation representatives, met in Aspen in June, 1965, for an unprecedented two-week examination of their common concerns.

The conference was moderated by Lord James, vice-chancellor, University of York, England. Among the participants were George W. Beadle, University of Chicago; Louis T. Benezet, Claremont Graduate School and University Center; Mary I. Bunting, Radcliffe College; Paul J. Braisted, Hazen Foundation; Victor L. Butterfield, Wesleyan University; Merrimon Cunningham, the Danforth Foundation; Lee A. DuBridge, California Institute of Technology; Samuel B. Gould, State University of New York; Fred Harvey Harrington, University of Wisconsin; Father Theodore M. Hesburgh, University of Notre Dame; Samuel M. Nabrit, Texas Southern University; John W. Nason, Carleton College; Rosemary Park, Barnard College; John A. Perkins, University of Delaware; Seymour A. Smith, Stephens College; and Lloyd E. Warner, Colorado College.

How, they asked, would the currents of new social, political, and economic forces affect the colleges and universities? What effect would forces such as population growth, increased leisure time, and industrialization have on the university of 1980? These questions, in turn, pointed up the need to clarify the responsibility and purposes of universities and the point of balance between quality and quantity in education. They also pointed up the need to analyze the changing nature of the university community itself. How much emphasis could the university properly place on the vocational needs of society? In an age of scholarly specialization, could anything be done to encourage a greater synthesis of knowledge and an increase in the ability to understand what lay beyond one's own profession?

The questions were of critical importance, and would become increasingly so, partly for reasons of arithmetic alone. For
between 1955 and 1965, the number of high school graduates increased more than 85 per cent, and the number of those graduates
going to college increased 110 per cent. The number of institutions
of higher learning increased from 1,850 to nearly 2,500, and average enrollment doubled. Total higher education outlays, public
and private, showed signs of increasing at two and one-half times
the rate of increase in the gross national product. Increased access
to higher education, however, did not automatically lead to the
completion of a successful education. Fewer than half of the
young people who entered college each year completed two years
of study, and only about one-third ever completed a four-year
course of instruction.

These figures went hand-in-hand with a disturbing cultural
and political development. It was that, while many students found
traditional academic programs uncongenial, many others—drop-
outs and good students alike—found that the university or college
community represented a life-style of great appeal. They preferred
it by far to the outside world, which they viewed with deepening
suspicion and hostility, especially after the manpower needs of the
Vietnam War led to radical changes in the basis of student de-
ferment from Selective Service. So, whether students were drop-
outs or deliberately extended the length of their academic programs, they remained clustered in the shadow of the university, as
though it were an emotional haven rather than an educational
center.

It is hard to gauge the depth reached by the special conference
at Aspen in exploring the many challenges to higher education.
Existing records of the event amount to little more than a few
fragments. Yet the nature of the questions posed at the conference
are of historical interest because of the light they shed on claims
later made by the student leaders of the "Berkeley Free Speech"
movement and by those who led the Students For Democratic
Action in the last half of the 1960's, that *they* were the first to challenge the existing structure and purposes of the American uni-

versity. Actually they were anticipated in the summer of 1965 by reflective, self-critical university presidents who met in Aspen.

While all this was under way in 1965, the Aspen Institute for Humanistic Studies continued, as before, to absorb a substantial part of the housekeeping costs of the Aspen Center for Theoretical Physics. It could thus claim at least a modest share of the credit for the national and international recognition the physics center had won after only four years of existence. In the summer of 1965, for example, the sixty-five physicists who worked in the Aspen physics center completed and had accepted for publication more than twenty papers which added to human knowledge about high-energy physics, solid-state physics, nuclear physics, and the theory of low-temperature liquids.

Papers of this kind seldom shake the scientific world with the force of a Copernicus, Kepler, Newton, or Einstein. Some win assent for the small proofs they offer in support of claims for small discoveries. Others, floating a small hypothesis, are quickly sunk by a broadside from an informed critic. Yet, without the impetus they give to thought, the scientific world would stand still. With them, even though most scientific papers are doomed to oblivion, their *substance* is incorporated into the general stock of knowledge and forms a support structure for the flashing moment of a major scientific breakthrough. So it was when the Aspen physics center gained its first Nobel laureate in the fall of 1965, when Professor Richard P. Feyman won a Nobel prize for his work in quantum electro-dynamics.

In 1966, the Man in 1980 conferences attempted to deal more firmly with the issues raised in exploratory discussions of the preceding year. Support for the venture was now forthcoming from the Danforth Foundation, the Kettering Foundation, and the Pabst Foundation. The Conference on American Higher Education brought Sir Eric Ashby, vice-chancellor of Cambridge University, to Aspen to lead a two-week discussion by fifteen university presidents on the theme, "The Relationship of Colleges and Universities to Government." The event itself marked the introduction to the Aspen Institute of two men who later would become associated with it as program directors. One was Douglass Cater, then a special assistant to President Lyndon B. Johnson, with a special responsibility for matters involving education and communication. The other was Frank Keppel, then the United States Commissioner for Education and subsequently the Assistant Secretary for Education in the Department of Health, Education, and Welfare. Cater has since recalled that the conference "shed a world of light" on the nature of the problems that engrossed his own attention as a member of the White House staff.

As in the previous year, conferences were also held in 1966 on Educational Development Below the College, and on Moral and Ethical Values. But the fact that the conference on Population was not repeated vaguely suggested an encroaching new instability in the Institute's design for a long-range program. In offset on the positive side, however, the United States Steel Foundation had made a $150,000 grant to the Aspen Institute, payment of which, spread over a ten-year period starting in 1966, enabled the Institute to expand the infant Artists-in-Residence program by adding to it an infant Scholars-in-Residence program. Noted scholars in the humanities and social sciences, along with novelists, playwrights, poets, and composers of music, could now come to Aspen not only in connection with the Institute's seminars and special conferences, but to work for varying lengths of time on their own projects.

IV

By the fall of 1966, Eurich had done much to shore up the structural foundations of the Institute and had set in place part of the scaffolding for promising new ventures. Yet a point was reached where he apparently concluded that there was little more he could do for and with the Institute under the prevailing conditions—it had no endowment and put itself at hazard when it planned activities for more than one year at a time. Eurich was increasingly drawn back to New York City, partly in connection with the affairs of *Atlas* magazine, but mainly to promote the Academy for Educational Development which he had created while in Aspen.

After many earnest and amicable discussions between Eurich and Anderson, a meeting between the two men in November, 1966, brought matters to a head. Eurich would resign as president of the Institute, but would remain on its board of trustees. It was hoped that his successor in the presidency could be found by the start of the next year's summer season in Aspen.

Subsequently, at a special meeting of the board held in early December, Eurich informed the other trustees of his personal plans. Anderson was not present, but when the future of the Institute came under discussion, his views were conveyed to the trustees through Eurich. They were to the effect that as a means of insuring the permanence of the Institute, serious consideration should again be given to the old idea of forming a close association with an established college or university. Later, when Anderson learned that his views had stirred up a hornet's nest of angry objections, he wrote Eurich that he was not surprised by the reaction of the trustees. He recognized that it was "natural" for them to feel "a pride of authorship in the Institute" and "to fear that its special character would be lost" if it were made part of an established institution of higher learning. But, said he, since a different course had been decided on, he had some pointed advice to give:

We should start examining the task ahead of us and, particularly, *the extent to which our Trustees can be of assistance.* I think you should be prepared to suggest a skeleton staff for Aspen at our next meeting. . . . I have no reservations about the Institute's ability to move in the direction we selected for our future success, provided *we all recognize the fairly limited scope of the operations we are embracing.* In some respects, it has certain advantages, and a much closer and more personal identity for both participants and Trustees, as the latter will have to be called on to take an active role on many occasions.

When a regular meeting of the trustees was held in late December—with Anderson present—the central item for discussion was the "balanced budget" on which he and Eurich had previously agreed. In essence, it pointed to a skeletal Institute staff and the elimination of special conferences, so that, as Eurich expressed it, "the Institute would be placed on a sound financial basis without major support from one person for the first time in its history." The discussion, however, did not remain focused on the budget. Wounding remarks were apparently made about other matters, as is suggested in the tenor of a note Anderson wrote Eurich in late January, 1967:

> Since our December meeting, the Institute has been very much on my mind and *particularly what role, if any, I should play beyond this year.* I still feel that there are wide differences of opinion between the Trustees and myself that are going to be extremely difficult to reconcile.
>
> First and foremost, I must reject the concept expressed several times in Board meetings and as yet not really rejected by the Board that the Institute should serve essentially as a civic focal center for Aspen and become a guiding hand in the community. I did not comment on this at the meeting as I find it hard to believe that anyone can consider this a major purpose. I have always believed and repeatedly stated that every Trustee should take an active interest in the town either individually or through organizations and the media. In the past, we have been rebuffed whenever the Institute tried to inject itself into local situations, and it has created much ill will and suspicion regarding the Institute's motives. Aspen, as a town, has reached a point where it can and should guide its own destiny. Its childhood is over and it must now rise or fall on its own capabilities and efforts.
>
> Quite aside from this, it would appear that my recommendations for the operation and improved financial outlook were clearly rejected. Over the years I believe I have gained some experience and knowledge of the Institute and particularly some of its peculiarities. Its operating problems are as unique as the Institute itself and need continual appraisal and solution. Above all, I have learned the hard way that there are a large number of things one does *not* do.
>
> ... *I left our meeting more discouraged than I have ever been with the Institute, as I realized how little the Trustees appreciate the difficulties the Institute has been through....* The Institute has always been long on hope and confidence, neither of which were much in evidence ... In retrospect, I feel more strongly than ever that the plan we recommended offered a balanced fiscal situation and *the maximum degree of financial independence from either myself or any other source of funds.*

Eurich sent a copy of this letter to William F. Stevenson, who was then in Florida, as well as a copy of a letter he had lately received from Gaylord Freeman. In it, Freeman had vividly described the unsettling impact of the Executive Seminars on business executives—and their importance for that very reason. But he went on to observe that some of the trustees who had long been associated with the Institute—and especially with the seminars—had lost their original excitement. Under the circumstances, he added, perhaps the future of the Institute lay either in an association with a university, if not Chicago then the University of Colorado, or of "going amateur." Stevenson, on his part, demurred from the views expressed in the two letters. In a note of his own to Eurich he said:

> As to Gale's letter, I think he outlines very well the meaning of the Institute to business executives. That has always been the vital thing to many of us as you know. I'm sorry he feels he has "run out of gas." But I don't understand why that fact or even your leaving, unfortunate as that is, means that we have to join [the University of Chicago] or turn "amateur." As you keep telling us, we've never been in better shape. So why isn't it clear that we should move forward, not backward? There are still many of us who "haven't run out of gas" yet!
>
> As to Bob's letter, I'm sorry that he feels some trustees are unsympathetic to his concept of the Institute's function. I believe most of us fully agree with his ideas. We have a wonderful thing going and it must go on!

Stevenson thus reaffirmed his own long-standing attachment to the Institute. But by no word or gesture did he indicate a personal interest in filling the post which Eurich was vacating. His fellow trustees, however, in a seeming conspiracy among themselves, now began to work on him to accept the presidency, though with no initial success. Stevenson maintained that after a strenuous life he was ready to retire, spending part of his time in Aspen and part in his regular home in Florida. This, in turn, evoked another kind of appeal from the trustees. No man of Stevenson's quality, they said, with his history of public service, had a right to retreat into privacy. He was intimately familiar with the operations and purposes of the Institute, and could take on the presidency without making any major readjustments in his life-style.

Stevenson, though not taken by storm, was brought to a point where he laid his cards on the table face up. He would accept the offered post, said he, on condition that everyone understood the limits of what he could or could not do. He could not criss-cross the country on fund-raising expeditions. Other trustees would have to attend to such matters. What he would and could do would be to conduct a "holding operation" for perhaps a year, until a new and permanent president was found. No new programs would be launched. The Institute would be stripped down to the rock on which it was originally built—namely, the Executive Seminar, and this he would happily supervise.

His candidly stated terms were understood and accepted by the trustees, but they were reviewed again by Anderson and Stevenson when the two men met alone in Philadelphia on February 16, 1967. The encounter went smoothly, and the substance of the agreement reached was compressed into a brief note which Anderson sent Stevenson the next day. It was agreed that Stevenson would be elected president at the May meeting of the trustees and would assume his duties in Aspen by mid-June. He would remain in Aspen until late August and probably be abroad during September. He would be provided with a "summer assistant to help handle some of the social and general welfare aspects of the Executive Seminars." His hours would largely be determined by his own "assessment of what needed to be done." He would receive a modest basic salary. It was hoped that his eventual successor "would be found during the balance of the year and not later than the next year."

And so the deed was done.

12. FINGER IN THE DIKE

I

In May, 1967, as planned, Stevenson was elected president of the Institute. The budget required economies in many directions, but without peril to the Executive Seminars, to the "Tuesday night lectures," or to the use of the Institute's facilities for such activities as the medical conferences or the Conferences of Young Presidents which paid their own way. The Executive Seminars were in fact enriched by measures which increased the number of women, blacks, and students among the participants. The Tuesday night lectures were also enriched by raising the standards for choosing lecturers, while the program of refresher seminars for Aspen "alumni" was energetically pushed.

On the other hand, savings were made by reducing the Institute's staff to a skeleton force of not more than five people. One was Joan Fitzpatrick, who bore the title of secretary, but was, in reality, the assistant president. In Stevenson's absence, she sat at his desk and kept things moving. Another important staff member was King Woodward, who had been with the Institute since 1964. He served as its conference manager—a euphemism for his work as the quartermaster general, overseeing the logistics of the buildings and grounds and of everything else: housing and transportation, the availability of conference rooms, necessary texts, and so on. Then there was Muriel Vroom, who had charge of all the minute details which went into recruiting businessmen and special guests for a balanced composition of participants in the Executive Seminars. Patricia Clark looked after the "social and general welfare" needs of the participants, while Henry Lee had the responsibility for reproducing all the reading materials and getting them into the hands of seminar participants in advance of their arrival in Aspen.

Savings were also made in connection with the affairs of the Aspen Center for Theoretical Physics. Most of its main costs were covered by the National Science Foundation, but the Aspen Institute for Humanistic Studies had acted as a "service organization" to the physicists at the center, arranging their housing and meeting other needs of a clerical nature such as the duplication of papers. These services could no longer be provided by a short-handed staff operating with a very tight budget. But when Stevenson informed the physicists of this fact, the reaction at their end was a tempest in a teapot, leading to a temporary breach between the physicists and the Institute for Humanistic Studies.

It should be said here that though the original physicists drawn to the center had also entered into the life of the Institute for Humanistic Studies, the very success of the center for theoretical research found later groups of physicists doing what the musicians in the festival orchestra and music school had done. They steadily reduced their direct contacts with the Institute and turned their attention inward on themselves and their work. After 1969, however, when Robert O. Anderson and Joseph E. Slater both joined the board of directors of the Aspen Center for Theoretical Physics, concerted efforts were made to reknit the physicists into the fabric of the larger "Aspen family."

A saving proposed by Stevenson—but not acted upon until after 1969—involved the suspension of the Aspen Award in the Humanities which was created in 1963. Stevenson had long been critical of the judgment shown by the committee which selected the recipients. In his view, Robert M. Hutchins was, above all other candidates, supremely deserving of the award. Yet the committee, because of the personal animus of one member toward Hutchins, had repeatedly passed him over in favor of other figures. The incidental result was that, after the initial flurry of excitement when the award was first established in 1963, the press gave little attention to announcements concerning recipients.

Still, neither the controversy concerning the choice of persons thought deserving of the award nor the elimination of special con-ferences, such as those the Institute had previously sponsored, affected the Executive Seminar. It continued to be an exciting ex-perience for participating businessmen, who, in the absence of other Institute activities, held the center of the stage. This, in Stevenson's words, was "the old Institute which he loved." It was the Institute which he held together for two years—or three sum-mer sessions in Aspen—while the national environment, wherever one looked, seemed to be a boiling sea of rancors, partly because of the Vietnam conflict, partly because of racial strife, and partly because of a *Kultur Kampf* among generations and within families.

It was a time when few people caught in the eye of any one storm—whether they were white radical students or black mili-tants, parents or teachers, school administrators or reporters, busi-nessmen or political officials, policemen or National Guardsmen—were inclined to see their personal experiences objectively. Each of these, in his illusion of central position, tended to assume that the whole of the United States was just one vast hurricane with no stretches of calm between.

As the demonstrations and disorders crowded against each other on the televised evening news, it seemed that academic life in particular had lapsed into a Hobbesian state of nature where there was no common power able to make laws and enforce peace. At the same time, another image of American youth—on and off campus—was repeatedly featured by the televised evening news. It was the image of the American youth who, as the child of middle-class affluence, was committed to a sweeping cultural revo-lution against everything associated with his middle-class origins—its concern for appearances, its materialism, its sexual mores, its pious homilies and moral ambiguities, its drive for success, its science, technology, trade, industry, administrative and political structures. Whether the cultural rebel was called a dropout, cop-out, hippie, or flower child, he seemed bent on retreating into a subcultural community not only free of all controlling organs, but also based on ecstatic utterances and visions, psychedelic pleasures, and music whose beat, twang, and blare would induce ineffable feelings of freedom and union for "happenings" with no thought of consequences.

These two pictures of American youth—one a campus revolutionary primed for violence, the other a flower child destined to wilt from the consumption of drugs—merged in the minds of television viewers who witnessed the clash between the young and the police in Grant Park in Chicago at the time of the 1968 National Democratic Convention. More than that, the merged picture gave currency to the macabre conclusion that the United States as a whole was moving inexorably toward an apocalyptic abyss, either by the route of a violent overturn or by the route of cultural decadence.

II

Cutting across the picture just sketched was a growing controversy over private philanthropy and the foundations. Back in the nineteenth century when Henry David Thoreau wrote an essay on philanthropy, he set two views in opposition to each other: "Philanthropy," he said, "is the only virtue which is sufficiently appreciated by mankind." But he added that when the integrity of philanthropy is marred from any cause, "there is no odor as bad as that which rises from goodness tainted." By 1969, the second of the two views had gained the ascendancy in an influential segment of American opinion, and of Congressional opinion in particular.

Philanthropy in general and charitable foundations in particular—without regard to their individual nature—became the object of a blanket indictment by Congressional "populists," and in a meeting of extremes, by right-wingers. To the populists, the foundations were "tax dodges" which denied to the Treasury funds desperately needed to support massive governmental efforts to solve acute social problems. To the right-wingers, the foundations were "partisan political instruments" which used "tax-exempt dollars to promote extreme ideologies of the left." The polar opinions which joined in these indictments of the foundations lumped together those that were blameless with those whose conduct made them vulnerable to a finding of guilty as charged.

Private philanthropy and the foundations were not without defenders. They admitted the existence of many instances and forms of abuse. But they went on to contend that the best of private philanthropy and the foundations could more readily sponsor experiments in the realm of social change than the government. Government, by its nature, cannot readily operate on a small scale. It must generalize, whereas human life is infinitely varied in its nuances. Further, the consensus mechanisms of large established institutions of government are not always the best and are certainly not the only way to initiate measures that lead to orderly social change. Competing bureaucratic interests may keep the governmental instruments for change immobilized on dead center or may lead to the premature death of a program or may open the throttle to the broad application of a program based on untested theories.

Further, government programs rarely cover a field of social change in a uniform way. They tend to be centered on one corner of the field to the neglect of others which seem politically less important or less controversial to policy makers and legislators. At the same time, the pressure for even-handedness in government support leaves little room for the support of exceptional talent or of unusual approaches to the business of social change—approaches that can set new standards of excellence for public programs. Finally, government agencies, in their scramble for funds, are more concerned with trumpeting the virtues of their programs than they are with evaluating them. They thus deny to themselves and to the public the corrective measures that could follow if their programs were subject to critical and independent appraisals.

The best of private philanthropy, however, can be free of these disabilities. It can spot emerging problems, take the long view, diagnose the gestating revolutions of the future, understand earlier the roots of tomorrow's issues, and test new and different solutions to determine if they justify broad public support. They can also provide support for experiments with embryonic ideas in an environment where the unfamiliar often meets with general hostility.

The pros and cons in the controversy about philanthropy and the foundations came to a head when Congress passed and President Richard Nixon signed the Tax Reform Act of 1969, which contained a mixed bag of features. Some aborted the birth of new foundations. Some, on the other hand, provided for salutary and long-overdue reforms bearing on the need for public accountability in the operations of foundations. But the Act also contained an ambiguous provision banning so-called legislative activities by foundations. Insofar as the purpose was to bar foundations from engaging in electoral contests or in elective politics, the merits of the provision were clear-cut. Yet the confused legislative history of the provision against "legislative activities" left another critical matter in doubt. Did the legislation bar foundation-financed studies of public-policy issues?

The law permitted foundations to make "available the results of nonpartisan analysis, study, or research." It did not, however, clarify the highly ambiguous word "nonpartisan." Did it mean that no conclusions could be drawn from any studies that were undertaken or that a study must shun any significant public questions that could become partisan issues in the future? Did it bar any communications with legislators or government officials who might participate in the formulation of legislation? Did it bar any legislators or government officials from communicating their own expert knowledge to persons conducting a foundation study? The insecurity in the answers to these questions was compounded by the deliberations of the Conference Committee of the House and Senate.

The committee, in considering the provision of the law just mentioned, indicated that it was not meant to prevent the examination of broad problems such as those which the government might be expected to deal with ultimately. In the next breath, however, the committee added the qualifying statement that "lobbying on matters which have been proposed for legislative action" would not be permitted. But what, then, constituted "lobbying"? Where was the line to be drawn between "lobbying" and "education"? For that matter, where should the line be drawn between the fields of interest of foundations and those of governments? Practically every area of significant foundation activity was one in which federal, state, and local governments were also active, generally on a far larger scale. This was true both of the conventional fields of philanthropy—health, education, welfare, science, and technology—and of such newer areas as urban problems, civil rights, the arts, the environment, and population control.

It was unrealistic to expect that foundation programs should not have direct impact on government programs. Nor, for that matter, did it make sense to deplore the intertwining of the private and public sectors. The intertwining was a healthy feature of American society, for the larger and more complex government becomes, the greater is the need for private contributions to the whole of the decision-making process.

III

All that has just been said provided the backdrop against which William E. Stevenson held the Aspen Institute together as its president. At a time when urgent new issues were piled on top of old unresolved issues, the new tax law saddled private philanthropy with uncertainty about how to move between permissible and nonpermissible lines of action in connection with public-policy matters. One thing, however, was clear to Stevenson. By the terms of his original understanding with Anderson and the other trustees of the Aspen Institute, his successor as president was supposed to be found within a year. Yet as the months dropped away and as one year gave way to the second, he appeared to be locked into the post in perpetuity. Possible successors were approached or discussed now and again, but no one seemed to be in a hurry to change the existing leadership of the Institute. Stevenson must, therefore, take the initiative in finding a successor. And he did. His search led him back to Joseph E. Slater, who, on an earlier occasion, had declared himself unavailable for the Aspen Institute's presidency.

13. JOSEPH E. SLATER:
PAST AS PROLOGUE

I

When Joseph E. Slater's friends describe him in shorthand, the phrases they use sound like this:

—"a master of the art of combination"—
—"America's No. 1 generalist"—
—"a man born to have no rest himself, and to allow none to others"—
—"a stranger to cynicism"—
—"a genius at discovering approximate solutions to impossible financial problems"—
—"a three-stage rocket with all three stages firing simultaneously"—
—"the nation's most imaginative philosopher of philanthropy"—
—"an exceptional talent for friendship"—

When Slater's friends use longhand to describe him, they say that "though he talks with the rapid-fire discharge of an automatic weapon, the recurrent subjects of his speech have the high flight of imperial themes—the relationship between liberty and learning, the unities of human life, the fate and freedom of societies faced by the necessities of choice." They also say that the central purpose of Joe Slater's life has been "to create a network of institutions and people who can generate and transmit tremors that will ultimately 'change things' in an orderly way." To all this, one should add Ann Slater's candid judgment of her husband: "Joe is devoted to the life of the mind, but he is primarily a man of action who serves the life of the mind through his work as an *intellectual entrepreneur.*"

Taken together, the shorthand and the longhand descriptions convey some sense of what Slater is like as a person. But the key to his impact on the Aspen Institute lies elsewhere. It lies in his career prior to 1969—since each piece in that career was part of a mosaic, and he repeatedly used each piece once he and Robert O. Anderson began their collaboration in "refounding" the Institute. It lies, more specifically, in the way his interests and convictions brought him to the right place at the right time when conditions were ripe for new institutional inventions. The details of his pre-Aspen career, as sketched below, merit attention because all have a bearing on his work as president of the Aspen Institute.

II

Slater is a "mountain man" whose early years were spent in Salt Lake City, his birthplace. From there he went on to the University of California at Berkeley, won Phi Beta Kappa honors, and joined the faculty as an instructor in economics. After Pearl Harbor, he joined the navy, was commissioned an ensign, and was sent to the Boston Naval Yard to help supervise cargo loadings. He was not in his own eyes an overlooked John Paul Jones or Horatio Nelson. But his job was limited in drama to preventing cargoes from being dropped into the sea by inept crane operators. Since this was not enough to hold his interest, he cut through walls of living red tape and landed in a London office. Here he worked for a while on plans for post-war Europe and then moved on to join Robert Murphy's staff in Versailles.

No one in his ambience, not even those whose epaulettes twinkled with stars, brought expert knowledge to the work of framing a prospective military government for a defeated Germany. Everyone was an amateur. Yet precisely on this account, imaginative young men who might live with doubt, but had a strong will to decide, could imprint their thoughts on the shape of the plan. As one of these, Slater helped design the structure for the Disarmament and Armed Forces Secretariat of the Allied Control Authority. Later, in Germany itself, he was among the small group of officers who were sent to Flensburg on the border of Denmark, where the remnants of the German government had fled.

Here, following the surrender of Admiral Doenitz and General Keitel, Slater participated in the "sealing" of all the German ministries, and was also among the officers who supervised the dismantling of the German Navy. Although these were heady experiences for a young man in his early twenties, they were no more than an appetizer. Between 1945 and 1948, Slater helped plan and establish the Economic and Financial Directorates of the Four Power Allied Control Authority in Berlin, and the Bi-Zonal Economic Council for Germany. The quality of his staff work caught the eye of General William H. Draper, Jr., the economic director on the American side of that authority, and he made Slater an executive aide and United States secretary to the Economic Directorate. On his side, Slater found in Draper one of his mentors in the immediate postwar years and one of his collaborators in later ventures.

There was no let-up in the work to be done in Berlin, but Slater found ways to relax which did not entail burning the candle at both ends. Music was his main recreation. He would slip off to Leipzig merely to talk to Gunther Ramin, who was the last in the line of successors to Bach in the Thomas Kirche. He would stage parties for displaced children in his home and would entertain them with music. He would also open his home to German musicians so that they would have a place to give concerts of chamber music. In between, he studied German, and though he spoke it with a very heavy Utah accent, he mastered its nuances so that he could understand what was being said in German political cabarets.

One of the friends Slater made at this time—who re-entered his life at recurrent intervals in later years—was Rowan Wakefield. It was through him that he was introduced to a young woman, Annelore Kremser. She had come to the United States from her native Germany in 1934, but had returned to Berlin at the end of the war to work in the Economic Section of the Office of Military Government (OMGUS) and to search for her family. Shared interests were the matchmaker for the marriage in 1946 between Joe and Ann, and the dowry of mind and spirit she brought with her was not purchasable on any market. She would be, as a family friend said, "50 per cent of the Slater team."

Slater spent the year 1948–49 in Washington, where he shared in the creation of the United Nations Affairs Division of the U.S. Department of State's Political and Security Planning Staff. But in 1949 various people who knew of his work in Berlin were instrumental in bringing him to Bonn when John J. McCloy was appointed U.S. High Commissioner for Germany. On the latter's behalf, Slater wrote the United States position paper regarding the structure of Allied Control. He also organized the office of the Secretary General of the Allied High Commission, and served as *the* secretary general in it—meaning that he dealt with all aspects of German life, not merely those of an economic and financial nature. Of no small importance for the future was the personal bond forged during this period. "Ever since 1949," so Slater would later say, "Jack McCloy has been the dominant figure in my life."

In 1952, Slater moved from Bonn to Paris, where he spent a year in helping to organize and launch yet another institution of which he was also the secretary general. This was the Office of the Executive Secretary of the U.S. Representatives in Europe—consisting of the representatives of the U.S. Departments of State, Defense, and Treasury to NATO and to the Organization of European Economic Co-operation. With General William H. Draper, Jr., in over-all charge, it was not only the largest United States office overseas, but the only operation where the total United States mission was developed into a single, unified organization and not into a series of separate units reflecting the institutional positions of each constituent governmental department.

Slater's experiences during the "constituent era" when major institutions of the postwar world were taking shape, had important effects on the direction of his later career. For one thing, a number of the young people with whom he formed international friendships would eventually emerge as leaders of the first rank in their respective countries; some he would later bring under the roof of the scientific and cultural institutions he would help establish, and some he would draw into the Aspen Institute as members of the board of trustees.

For another thing, he saw in close detail how the foremost representatives of the American private economic sector who held commanding governmental positions in postwar Europe—William H. Draper, Jr., Paul Hoffman, and John J. McCloy—came to grips with infinitely complex problems in a chaotic world. All three, taken together, taught Slater that great men are not cynical, but are primarily teachers and builders, with a quiet passion to create something better in place of things which exist. They also taught him never to despair when institutions are under siege. To lift the siege, one should find "good people" who can be trusted around the clock and who can be given a task which "will make their adrenalin flow." Their joint efforts will eventually prove the means for converting seemingly hopeless situations—as in the case of Europe right after the end of the war—into one more promising.

In addition to what Slater learned from men such as Draper, Hoffman, and McCloy, he saw that other public-spirited American businessmen such as Clarence Randall, who were not in a position to accept "permanent" posts overseas, made important contributions to the conduct of America's foreign relations by short-term periods of concentrated service abroad. He would later adapt this pattern of fluid contacts to the affairs of the Institute.

One more important consequence of Slater's experience in postwar Europe is worth noting. Most Americans of the time still drew sharp distinctions between domestic and foreign affairs as if each comprised a self-sealing world of its own. They also believed that the cardinal issues of the hour were rooted solely in an East-West clash over forms of social organization and, in any case, could be dealt with one by one. Slater, however, began to see the matter differently. Through the work that fell to him, he was introduced to an emerging new truth—that in the world ahead any particular problem would tend to be indivisible with a cluster of other such problems, and these, in turn, most likely would be transnational, transregional, and trans-societal.

His early views on this point were further clarified during the years 1953–57 which he spent as the chief economist for the Creole Petroleum Company, whose headquarters were in Caracas, Venezuela. Creole at the time provided over $400 million in net annual income to its parent company, Standard Oil of New Jersey. Aside from Slater's regular work as an adviser on its economic and financial affairs, with the approval of the company he organized and launched the Creole Foundation—whose grants of over $3 million a year made it the largest major foundation of an American corporation operating overseas.

To give money away is easy [so Aristotle observed twenty-two centuries ago]. It is in the power of every man. But to decide to whom it should be given, and for what purpose, and how—this is not easy. It is not in the power of every man. Hence it is that such excellence is rare, praiseworthy, and noble.

This ancient view also informed Slater's first venture in philanthropy and those that followed. He realized from the start that the grants of the Creole Foundation would contribute little to the general welfare in Latin America if available funds flowed at random into outstretched tin cups. More would be achieved if the funds were concentrated on a selected number of programs, embracing well-defined sets of interacting trans-societal problems, where any point gained would provide a grappling hook to get at other points. To this end, he formulated a long-range plan of action for the Creole Foundation. His conceptual approach in the matter provided the governing precedent for his later work in the field of philanthropy.

Above all other vocations, public service was for Slater the most exhilarating use a man could make of his life, and he awaited the first opportunity to return to it. The opportunity arose in 1957 when John J. McCloy became the president of the Ford Foundation and sought Slater out to determine if he was interested in resuming their old association in a new context. He was. He resigned from the Creole Petroleum Company and joined the Ford Foundation in New York as the deputy director of its program in international affairs.

Three men of his own generation who were then at the foundation—Philip Coombs, Shepard Stone, and Waldemar ("Wally") Nielsen—would figure in Slater's career in the years ahead. Coombs, who was then active in the field of international education, would go on to become the Assistant Secretary of State for Education and Cultural Affairs in the opening years of the Kennedy administration; Slater would serve for a while as his deputy. Stone, who in 1957 was Slater's immediate superior as director of the Ford Foundation's program in international affairs, would subsequently become president of the Association for Cultural Freedom. Later, in 1973, when Aspen Institute Berlin was to be established as the European affiliate of its parent institution in the United States, Stone would help organize Aspen Institute Berlin and serve as its first director, besides joining the Aspen Institute's board of trustees.

Nielsen's future relations with Slater would be of a special kind—more subtle than the others and yet of unsurpassed importance. On a purely personal basis, he would undertake special tasks for Slater, would keep him abreast of developments in the world arena—including those rooted in the proliferation of multinational corporations—and would eventually help formulate the terms for an Aspen program in international affairs. In addition, he would provide Slater with fresh insights on the internal changes within the "nonprofit world" and how these were bound to affect the interplay between that world and the world of government. But above all, Nielsen was to Slater a prophet of warning and encouragement—a candid, plain-speaking friend, who either corrected his errors of perception or braced his nerve for high-risk ventures.

It was Slater's conviction that any man entering the field of philanthropy who immobilizes himself in it makes himself vulnerable to a deformation of perception. "If you really want to be any good in this field," so he explained, "you must move in and out of it—to replenish your stock of ideas." John J. McCloy was of the same mind, and it was with his approval that Slater in 1959 took a leave of absence from the Ford Foundation in order to serve as the secretary of President Eisenhower's Commission on Foreign Assistance.

The commission, which was to reappraise all aspects of the United States foreign-aid program, was better known as the Draper Committee, after its chairman, William H. Draper, Jr., for whom Slater had worked in Berlin and Paris. (McCloy also served on this committee.) It was in connection with the work that fell to him as secretary that Slater came to know a staff aide and Regular Army officer whom he would bring into the work of the Aspen Institute in 1972. This was Amos Jordan, a West Pointer, Rhodes Scholar, intercollegiate boxer, and Doctor of Philosophy. Jordan, in time, would become the chairman of the Political Science Department at West Point, a brigadier general, and would eventually serve as the executive officer of the Aspen Institute from the late fall of 1972 to the early spring of 1974.

After the Draper Committee submitted its report to President Eisenhower, the sequel called for negotiations with the White House over the nature of the recommendations in the report and their application to the actual work of the Development Loan Fund, which was then the major arm of the United States foreign assistance program. To help conduct these negotiations, Slater agreed to serve as the deputy manager of the fund, under the chairmanship of C. Douglas Dillon. As a closely related matter, he also undertook a special assignment with the President's Scientific Advisory Committee. What this entailed was the formulation of recommendations for research and development projects bearing on the process of foreign aid—ranging from agriculture and home construction to the use of the new media of communication, such as radio and television, in order to promote mass literacy and education in the developing nations.

With the completion of these tasks, Slater returned to the Ford Foundation, only to take another leave of absence after John F. Kennedy was elected President in 1960. One of the new President's many appointments was, as has been mentioned, Philip Coombs, of the Ford Foundation, as Assistant Secretary of State for Education and Cultural Affairs. Coombs had long contended that education and cultural exchanges should be put in the mainstream of foreign affairs, as against the tendency to view them as sideshows. He assumed that the new President actually meant what he said when he associated himself with those same views. So, to help give programmatic expression to them, he persuaded Slater to come into the State Department as his deputy, and the latter soon swept through the place with the energy of a Kansas twister.

Among other things, he created eleven Standing Working Groups in the State Department covering all conceivable aspects of education and cultural exchanges—plus a few that were inconceivable to anyone else. But when he reached the limits of what one man could do in a drive *against* the citadels of inertia, he returned to the Ford Foundation and to a taxing assignment entrusted to him by McCloy. He was to direct a study for the trustees concerning the policies and programs the foundation was to pursue in the decade 1962–72.

In his approach to the task—and with the Foundation's $3 billion endowment at stake—Slater drew on what he had already formulated for the Creole Foundation, for the Draper Committee, for the Development Loan Fund, and for the Educational and Cultural Division of the State Department. "The realists of the world," he would say, "are the most earth-bound and short-sighted of men. In the name of realism, they almost invariably make costly mistakes. I believe in scanning the whole landscape so as to avoid a foreshortening of the horizon, followed by a focus on projects that are 'doable' because good people are ready to work at them. I don't believe in second-guessing what you can't pay for. But I also believe in retaining sufficient flexibility in any set of plans so as to take advantage of any targets of opportunity that come along."

Slater's ten-year plan of action was approved by the trustees of the Ford Foundation, following which he was made the director of the foundation's International Affairs Program. Taking his new assignment together with his previous work in 1957–59 as deputy director under Shephard Stone, he played a major role in establishing such institutions as the following: Institute for Strategic Studies (London); the Overseas Development Institute (London); the International Program of the CED; the Latin American Affairs Program of the Royal Institute of International Affairs (universities in Europe and Japan); the International Comparative Music Institute (Berlin); the United Nations Institute for Training and Research; the China and Atlantic Programs of the Council on Foreign Relations; the Italian Council on Foreign Relations; the Southeast Asian Training and Research Center at Kyoto University; the China Institutes of the Universities of Leeds, Hamburg, Munich, and Berlin; the Korea Center for Asian and International Studies; and the School of Oriental and African Studies at the Royal Institute of International Affairs.

III

Slater had visited Aspen as a boy in the 1920's and again in the 1930's, but his first encounter with the place as an adult was in the summer of 1967, when he arrived at the Aspen Institute as a scholar-in-residence. Previously, at the Ford Foundation, he had been thinking about a new institution he wanted to bring to birth as an extension of his three-way interests in international communications, foreign affairs, and educational exchanges. But he still needed a time and place, free from the pressure-cooker atmosphere of his New York office, where he could produce a document which would clearly state the nature, structure, and purpose of the new institution he had in mind. He discussed his need with Alvin C. Eurich whom he had known since the years when the latter was with the Ford Foundation, and at Eurich's invitation he came to Aspen as a scholar-in-residence to work on his project.

Slater's arrival in Aspen with his wife, Ann, took place several months after William F. Stevenson had succeeded Eurich as president of the Aspen Institute on the understanding that he would conduct a holding action until someone else was found to assume the presidency. As a scholar-in-residence, Slater sat in on several sessions of an Executive Seminar then under way, delivered a Tuesday Night Lecture, and was introduced to Robert O. Anderson and several Institute trustees not previously known to him. His main attention, however, was centered on the business of conceptualizing an institution that eventually materialized as the International Broadcast Institute, based jointly in Rome and London.

Stevenson, meanwhile, continued to scan the horizon for prospective successors to the presidency of the Institute. At one point during the summer of 1967 he asked Slater if the post would be of interest to him. No formal offer was implied. The question was only part of a probing action that extended to other men as well. Slater's reply was in the negative. He explained that until he brought the gestating International Broadcast Institute to birth, he was not in a position to think of anything else. That seemed to be that. But not quite.

The Tuesday Night Lecture which Slater gave at the Aspen Institute was titled "Biology and Humanism," and two points were central to all the others he made. First, the world was caught up in a biological revolution as great as any in physics, and the revolution involved "men, not things." It was imperative, therefore, to force the nature of that revolution into the light and to weigh its profound implications for man and society. The second point was projected against the background screen of the Vietnam War. The best way to open lines of communication between the United States and Communist China, said Slater, was by joint bio-medical efforts, since shared human needs transcended differences in political, economic, social, and cultural ideologies.

Jerome Hardy, publisher of *Life* magazine, was in the audience on the night of the lecture, and subsequently invited Slater to join him at dinner. The purpose, it turned out, was to talk about the affairs of the Salk Institute for Biological Studies, of which Hardy was a trustee. He revealed that the Salk Institute, which then consisted of a number of laboratories and research fellows, was in financial difficulties, was at odds with itself, and lacked leadership. Hardy himself was a member of a search committee for a new president and, in this role, put a question to Slater. Would he consider filling the post so as to pull the Salk Institute together?

The answer was the same as in the case involving the Aspen Institute. He could not consider anything new until he launched the International Broadcast Institute.

Later that fall when the Broadcast Institute was a going concern, Slater was formally offered the dual post of chairman and president of the Salk Institute. He now accepted the offer, effective in January, 1968, while continuing his working relationship with the Ford Foundation. Soon afterward, to strengthen the leadership of the Salk Institute, he separated these dual roles. While personally retaining the presidency, he persuaded John J. McCloy to assume the chairmanship, a post the latter would hold for five years. He also recruited other friends from the past for service as policy-minded members on the new kind of board of trustees the Salk Institute needed. One of the new members, Slater's friend since Berlin days, was Sir Alan Bullock, then the vice-chancellor of Oxford University.

Slater was not a biologist. Yet he became a galvanizing needle not only on the administrative side of the Salk Institute but in its substantive affairs as well. Thus he presently formulated an eight-year program of action, two under the ten-year plan he had previously formulated for the Ford Foundation. Moreover, to help keep the needle steady, in February, 1968, he brought John Hunt into the Salk Institute as its executive vice-president for operations. This was no small source of support considering the latter's unique background and talents.

An Oklahoman by birth, Hunt had graduated from the Lawrenceville School in 1943 at the age of seventeen, promptly enlisted in the wartime U.S. Marine Corps from which he was honorably discharged in 1946 as a second lieutenant of infantry, went on to Harvard where he concentrated in English literature and the classics, graduated from Harvard in 1948 and continued his post-graduate studies at both the University of Iowa and the Sorbonne. Between 1951 and 1956 he taught Greek, French, and English at an experimental preparatory school in Kirkwood, Missouri, and on the side served as the director of admissions, and the coach of the track and basketball teams. Also on the side, he wrote a novel, *Generations of Men,* which was awarded the prize of the Western Writers Association of America as the best western historical novel of 1956, besides being included in that year for the final listing of twelve novels to be considered for the National Book Award. A later novel he published in 1968, *The Grey Horse Legacy,* would be chosen as an alternate selection of the Literary Guild.

In 1956, Hunt began a new career when he entered the complex world of international organizations, with their cadres of temperamental soloists. His initial entry point was as the assistant to the executive director of the Paris-based Congress for Cultural Freedom. Now the International Association for Cultural Freedom, it includes writers, scholars, scientists, and public figures from various parts of the world; it has an international secretariat representing many national and linguistic backgrounds; it publishes more than twenty magazines—monthly, bimonthly, and quarterly—in ten languages; and its many-sided programs are carried out by affiliated groups throughout the world. In 1958, Hunt became the executive director of this organization, a post he held for the next nine years. The Ford Foundation had been an American funding source for the organization. Shepard Stone had become its president, and it was through this institutional and personal connection that Hunt and Slater first came to know each other.

At the Salk Institute, Hunt's talents as a novelist—his insights into human character and motivation—enabled him to decode what Slater, in rapid-fire speech, said he wanted done. This was all the more important for another reason. Although Slater had been thoroughly trained in staff work by Draper and McCloy, two masters of the craft, he was far from being an "administrative functionary." Administrative mechanisms were important to him only insofar as they advanced his interests in public policies and in the substantive programs which expressed those policies. Hunt, the novelist-executive, understood the style of the man with whom he was now associated, and knew when and where to resist it or to allow it free reign.

The first of many things to be done in and with the Salk Institute reflected Slater's concern over the social and human implications of the scientific advances being made in the general field of molecular biology. To provide the Salk Institute with an instrument for a systematic inquiry into those implications, Slater, with Hunt's executive support, created the Council on Biology in Human Affairs. To enlarge the frame of inquiry, Slater later helped create the Stockholm-based International Federation of Institutes for Advanced Studies—a web of organizations whose multidisciplinary interests provided the infra-structure for a "free floating university." At the same time, an aspect of the neurological studies under way at the Institute gained new importance when Slater linked the studies to his long-standing interest in the "early learning process" in children. He was convinced that if pre-school learning for children was soundly conceived from a biological and psychological standpoint, the effect would be to reduce the scale of later needs to subject the children to "remedial learning," thus saving educational institutions a heavy drain on their resources.

Of the many things done in other directions, there is space here to mention only one of particular importance. Slater had called a meeting attended by a number of Nobel laureates in biology to discuss the question of whether the Salk Institute should get into the field of reproductive biology. The general reaction was negative, because, it was explained, scientific research in the field lacked "elegance." Slater, not satisfied with the explanation, subsequently discussed the matter with William H. Draper, Jr., and the latter had a suggestion to make. Professor Roger Guilleman of Baylor University, who was working on the trigger mechanism in the brain which is responsible for the menstruation cycle in women, should be invited to speak to the Nobel laureates. The necessary arrangements were presently made, and Guilleman, within the first half hour of his presentation, convinced the skeptics in his audience of both the worth and the elegance of the research that could be done in reproductive biology. The Nobel laureates now agreed that the Salk Institute should get into this field, whereupon Draper helped Slater get grants from the Ford and Rockefeller foundations and AID that enabled Guilleman to continue his research work under the aegis of the Salk Institute.

IV

Following the 1968 Presidential election which gave Richard M. Nixon the keys to the White House, a sequence of impulses which began with William E. Stevenson crept up on Slater. Stevenson by now was well into his second year as president of the Aspen Institute and was increasingly troubled by the fact that no concerted effort was being made to find his successor. He was due to attend a Denver meeting of a learned society where he knew Slater would be present, and in advance of the event discussed with Alvin C. Eurich the possibility of interesting Slater in the Aspen Institute presidency. "Joe would be great," said Eurich, "but I doubt if you can get him." Stevenson, not discouraged, made an approach to Slater when the latter and his wife appeared in Denver. He recalled their brief conversation in the midsummer of 1967 concerning the presidency of the Aspen Institute, reviewed what had happened since then in the affairs of the Institute, and then asked if Slater would reconsider his earlier expression of disinterest in the presidency. This time around, the reaction, in which Ann Slater shared, was strongly positive.

This was enough for Stevenson. On December 18 he wrote Robert O. Anderson a long letter itemizing various matters to be discussed when the Aspen Institute's executive committee met at the end of the month. One item posed the question of whether to pass up the making of an Aspen Award in the Humanities in 1969. In this connection, Stevenson plainly indicated his displeasure with every aspect of the award—the composition of the selection committee, the way the committee had narrowed the scope of persons eligible to receive the award, the kind of choices they had made, the lack of an endowment which would guarantee the continuity of the award by putting it on a basis comparable to the Nobel Prize, and so on.

"As you know," Stevenson wrote, "I feel that Robert

Hutchins is an example of the type of person who is highly qualified for the award from all possible aspects." He added the hope
that the award could be made to Hutchins over the weekend of
July 4, 1969. The time would coincide with a modest celebration
he was planning with the Music Associates in order to commemorate the twentieth anniversary of the founding of the Aspen Institute. Stevenson concluded his letter by underlining "another
important item" which the executive committee should discuss—
namely, *"the continuing executive leadership of the Institute."* He
added by way of emphasis:

I do not need to review our various conversations about my presidency,
it being well understood, I think, and recorded in the minutes, that I
took the job only temporarily, pending the selection of someone else.
As I see it, John Hunt would be an excellent possibility to carry on the
work. I think he would come as Vice President or Executive Director
and work under some more senior leader such as Joe Slater.

At the executive committee meeting held in December, Anderson indicated that he was still weighing the question of whether
or not to resume the Aspen Award in the Humanities, though
his decision in the matter would soon be forthcoming. When the
discussion turned to the other major item of business—the continuing executive leadership of the Aspen Institute—Stevenson
reported on his Denver conversation with Slater and strongly
urged that he be made a formal offer of the Institute's presidency
without delay. The members agreed, and it was left to Anderson
to pursue the matter in ways which he deemed best.

Anderson had created the Anderson Foundation as a conduit
for his existing philanthropies, including the Aspen Institute, and
for those he might make in the future. He had not as yet, however,
fleshed out the operating structure of the new foundation nor
given it a clearly defined programmatic focus. This fact accounted
for the open-end question he put to Slater when the two men met
in New York several days after the inauguration of President
Richard Nixon on January 20, 1969. "Joe," said he, "assume you
were free to design the mechanism and the action programs for

the Anderson Foundation, what kind of humanistic problems would you tackle?"

Slater had no need to ask for time "to think it over." Drawing on his experiences in government, the Creole Foundation, the Ford Foundation, and the Salk Institute, he ticked off some fourteen specific humanistic issues which clamored for attention. He then went on to orchestrate his long-standing contention that the individual now feels entrapped by the very bigness of society, by the sense of being denied a voice in the choice of policies that affect his life, by the sense that even the implications of the choices to be made are beyond his grasp. "What the individual deplores," said Slater, "he deplores narrowly from a parochial perspective, and the world cannot afford that kind of narrowness any more. All the great issues of the day are not unique to this or that local community, or to the United States itself. They penetrate the frame of all societies." Thus, said Slater, he would have an operating foundation such as Anderson's concentrate on a critical number of areas, embracing interrelated and trans-societal issues, and would seek to illuminate from within the nature of the alternative choices they pose.

"Well," said Anderson at the end of the recital, "you would have a chance to work in the fields you indicated if you accepted what I am now offering you—the presidency of the Anderson Foundation. The offer carries with it as well the presidency of the Aspen Institute."

Slater frankly admitted his interest in the prospect. But would his acceptance of the offer entail severing his connection with the Salk Institute? He hoped not, since by continuing in its presidency, he might be able to bring the Salk Institute and the Anderson Foundation together in support of humanistic programs where they had a joint interest. Anderson, the free-style swimmer, answered that Slater should consider himself free to work out with the Salk Institute any arrangements that would best serve the purposes he had in mind. The same held for the amount of time Slater spent in Aspen proper. He could continue to be based in New York and could come to Aspen for such periods and on such occasions as he judged were necessary.

Several days later, though Slater was fighting the flu and the weather was wretched, he flew to Los Angeles to meet with Anderson in the latter's office. He was prepared to accept the presidency of the Anderson Foundation and the Aspen Institute, and added that the trustees of the Salk Foundation agreed to his continuing as *its* president. One more thing remained to be done at this meeting. Slater wrote down on a sheet of paper between eight and ten points which reflected the essence of their previous conversation in New York. Anderson looked at the sheet for several minutes, reached for his pen and wrote: "OK. ROA." The estimated date when Slater could assume the presidency of the Anderson Foundation and the Aspen Institute would be around July 1, 1969. Anderson promptly phoned William E. Stevenson in Aspen to share the news with him. Stevenson was both pleased and relieved.

Though it anticipates future developments, several things should be said here. First, Slater's hopes of bringing the Salk Institute and the Aspen Institute together in support of joint projects did not materialize. He eventually resigned the presidency of the Salk Institute but retained a link with it as a trustee and Special Fellow. Second, John Hunt also resigned from the Salk Institute in order to return to his writing. But he later accepted a position with the Royaumont Institute, the oldest foundation in France. The primary mission of Royaumont was to encourage progressive movements in the human sciences, but the directors had come to be dissatisfied with the way the mission was being executed. They asked Hunt to assume responsibility for managing the international program of the institute. And so he did. In co-operation with friends from the Salk Institute, he organized and then became the executive vice-president of the Royaumont Center for the Science of Man. The center, in Hunt's phrase, was dedicated to the "recovery of man," by bringing the life sciences such as the new biology into a working relationship with human sciences such as anthropology and psychology. Hunt would eventually be brought into the family of the Aspen Institute starting with a probe in 1973 and then full time, starting in the spring of 1974.

A final point must be made here. At the center of everything that was to follow in the history of the Aspen Institute was the relationship between Anderson and Slater. The close collaboration which marked that relationship owed much of its binding force to the symmetries in their prior interests and experiences. Slater, for example, knew the oil business and had created the Creole Foundation on the basis of income from it. Anderson, on his part, had given much thought to the uses of private philanthropy and had supported his own philanthropies largely from oil income. Again, as a matching piece to Slater's role in promoting the arts with the support of governmental resources and private philanthropy, Anderson was chairman of the Businessman's Committee on the Arts, was of immense help to Roger Stevens in the creation of the Kennedy Center, was on the board of the Museum of Modern Art, and so on.

Further, both men shared a keen interest in communication and education. Slater, for example, had tried to bring the communications community and the educational community together in order to promote "early learning." He had initiated the creation of many overseas educational institutions and had brought into being the International Broadcast Institute. He was concerned with the whole field of public broadcasting, and had worked on a Ford Foundation project in 1962 which contemplated the creation of a "fourth network" to demonstrate over a period of time what sustained quality broadcasting could achieve. Anderson was equally interested in all such matters, being, among other things, a director of the Columbia Broadcasting Company. Finally, Slater had been daily at grips with issues of science, technology, humanism—and economics—in all the posts he had held since the end of World War II. Many of the same issues had been of vital concern to Anderson in his capacity as president of the Lovelace Clinic and as a trustee of the California Institute.

When these and other points of symmetry are viewed as a whole, one can understand why it was seldom necessary for these two men to start a discussion with the ABC's of an issue to be decided. They could more often start with the XYZ's. So often, in fact, that it was not unusual for Anderson and Slater to dispose of fifty separate items of business in the course of a two-hour conversation—or at the average rate of a little over two minutes per item. To give but one example, a decision to establish Aspen Institute Berlin would be reached in the summer of 1973 through a quick exchange of notes between the two men while they sat around a conference table as participants in an Aspen Conference on The Role of the Intellectual.

14. THE FIVE-YEAR PLAN

I

Joe and Ann Slater were warmly introduced to the Aspen community during the Fourth of July week-end events which William E. Stevenson had arranged to celebrate the twentieth anniversary of the founding of the Aspen Institute. Robert M. Hutchins, the featured guest on the occasion, was not, as Stevenson had hoped, the recipient of an Aspen Award in the Humanities. But it had been settled in February of 1969 that, through a bequest from Robert O. Anderson, Hutchins would receive a specially created Aspen Founders Award of $10,000—in return for which he was expected to make a speech during the twentieth-anniversary celebration. When he was first informed of this decision, Hutchins wrote Stevenson:

> I am overwhelmed by your letter. . . . Or perhaps that honorarium is a misprint? I can remember when my father told a man who was about to offer me a $1,000 fee for a speech that no speech by a member of his family could be worth more than $500. My father was right. . . .

The speech Hutchins gave on the anniversary week end when he received the award began on the same self-deprecating note:

> I do not deserve this honor. It belongs to others. The patent insincerity of these words, when used by recipients of Oscars, Emmies, Grammies, and gold phonograph records, should not render them unavailable on occasions when they were demonstrably true.
>
> This is such an occasion. The persons who conceived and carried through the great celebration here twenty years ago were Arnold Bergstraesser, Antonio Borgese, and Walter Paepcke. My role may be expressed in terms of a neo-Kantian categorical imperative, one I fear Kant would not have recognized: so act as to gain a maximum of credit with a minimum of work.

The remainder of the speech was an ardent and eloquent analysis of the ways in which the purposes of the American university had been corrupted by the subordination of the university to the service of the industrial state—and this at a time when the very nature of the industrial state was being set on its head by the accelerating march of science and technology. The post-industrial society he envisioned could be "one in which men set seriously to work to straighten out their relations with one another and in which they sought, not material goods, but moral, intellectual, or what might be called cultural goods." Such a society could be a learning society. "Its object could be to raise every community and every man to the highest cultural level attainable." In such a society the role of educational institutions would be "to provide what is notably missing from them today, and that is the interaction of minds."

Civilization and culture [Hutchins continued] cannot be preserved and expanded without another institution that is missing. Today we have no centers of independent thought and criticism. The multiversity is not independent; it is the result of the parallelogram of forces at work in the community. It is not engaged as an institution in thought or criticism, though isolated members of it often are. It is dedicated to training and what is called service. It is not a center; it is compartmentalized both vertically and horizontally into departments and divisions that are in competition for money and students. A multipurpose institution can by definition have no unifying principle.

For a democratic country in an era of overwhelming change to have no way of applying some of its best minds to a concerted attempt to comprehend what is going on in the world seems to verge on suicidal insanity, the more so when we realize that the centers required could be small and relatively inexpensive. At the pinnacle of our educational system we need as many groups of this kind as we can muster. I hope that eventually, along with the college of which Walter Paepcke dreamed, one may be established at Aspen.

It seems fairly clear that the transition from an industrial to a post-industrial age will involve severe dislocation. . . . The way to fortify ourselves is, therefore, to establish wherever we can colleges of liberal arts and those centers of independent thought and criticism for which I would prefer to reserve the name of university. If [these] can become incandescent, if they can be points of light, then culture and civilization can be preserved and expanded as they have been by small groups during dark days in the past.

The lines of this "$10,000 speech" ran parallel with the views of Anderson and Slater when they set the purposes of the Anderson Foundation and the Aspen Institute. The procedures they had originally agreed upon, however, were modified not long after Slater had set in place the structure for the Anderson Foundation. President Nixon had just signed the Tax Reform Act of 1969. Among other terms, the Act provided that if a person gave anything of appreciable value to his own foundation, he would be entitled to only a 50 per cent tax deduction on the bequest. He would be entitled, however, to a 100 per cent tax deduction if he gave it to some other charitable institution.

When Anderson and Slater studied the new law, they agreed that it amounted to a "birth control pill" for new foundations, and that the Anderson Foundation should be phased out of existence —a process that permitted a number of significant grants to be made until 1971. They also agreed that the Aspen Institute should henceforth carry forward the "thought leading to action" programs that were to receive financial support from Anderson personally. In this connection, Anderson also encouraged Slater to draw on his experience in planning long-range programs for both the Ford Foundation and the Salk Institute, and to prepare for submission to the trustees of the Aspen Institute a Five-Year Action Program (1969–74) framed in the light of four questions: Which functions of the Institute should be continued? Which were in need of greater organizational strength? What adjustments in policies and programs were necessary if the Institute was to have any utility in the face of the profound changes that had overtaken the world since 1949? What kind of financial and operational structure did the Institute need to sustain its work in the years ahead? The Five-Year Action Program was to be formulated in time for a meeting of the Institute's board of trustees set for the end of 1969.

Meanwhile, with Anderson's backing, Slater initiated a venture that was to have a world-circling career, though it was initially the subject of congratulatory regrets. Previously at the Ford Foundation and the Salk Institute, Slater's concern with environmental issues brought home to him both a negative fact and a positive idea. The negative fact was that the old-line conservation organizations tended to focus only on single aspects of the environment and even then from a perspective that seldom went beyond a particular region in the United States.

The positive idea was inspired by an analogy to the Institute for Strategic Studies which Slater had been instrumental in creating in London with Ford Foundation support. That institute, under the direction of Alistair Buchan, a journalist who had distinguished himself as a Washington correspondent for the *London Observer*, was a service organization which periodically provided interested parties with a world-wide overview of security issues and their underlying facts. A counterpart service institute, said Slater, was needed to conduct an international overview of environmental issues, to identify problems and their linkages, to mobilize and present in lucid form sets of facts on which an informed national and international debate on policy issues could go forward.

Anderson saw the merits of the proposal and agreed to underwrite the costs of the first step toward the new international institute Slater had in mind. The first step was to conduct a world-wide survey to determine who was doing what, well or poorly or nothing at all, in the environmental field. A conservationist who was thought to be highly qualified was engaged to make the survey, but he either misunderstood the assignment or could not discharge it in other than conventional ways. His final report was of no use as a building block for a new international institute of strategic studies dealing with the environment. It could only provide the basis for a "consciousness-heightening" event known as Earth Day, financed by Anderson.

Slater would not settle for so ephemeral a result. He flicked over the extensive index of names and talents he carried around in his memory, picked out the name of Thomas W. Wilson, Jr., and in late 1969 put in a telephone call to him. Wilson in public and private life had dealt with many aspects of policy analysis and formulation. He had been a staff member of the planning committee of the War Production Board, director of the Combined Economic Warfare Agency (Middle East), member of the Allied Commission on Reparations, and special adviser to W. Averell Harriman during the Marshall Plan. In the United States diplomatic service he held the rank of minister and was a member or adviser to numerous United States delegations to the United Nations and other international organizations such as NATO. Late 1969 found him back in the State Department serving as senior planning adviser to the Office of Counsellor. Here he had tried for some months to get the Secretary of State to move on the international front in environmental matters, but without success. The telephone call from Slater reached Wilson at a time when he had served notice that he meant to leave the State Department shortly.

"Tom," said Slater at the other end of the phone, "we've been trying at the Aspen Institute to get a handle on the environment issue and to do something positive about it. But no one seems to know where to begin. I'm going to see Bob Anderson tomorrow morning for breakfast, and I think he'd be willing to finance a survey to find out who is or isn't doing one thing or another. We need the right man to conduct the survey. Are you interested? After I see Bob, I am due to leave for Frankfurt. But I'll call you from Kennedy Airport at three o'clock in the afternoon."

The call from the airport came through on schedule.

"Tom," said Slater, "Anderson says okay; he will finance the survey. What do you say?"

Wilson said okay, too, adding that he could start work in early February, 1970.

II

Between one thing and another, including the quick trip to Frankfurt, Slater worked with Anderson on drafts of his Five-Year Action Program. The text, as submitted to the Institute's board of trustees at the end of December, 1969, was unanimously approved. Although a statement concerning the "public posture" of the Institute appeared at the end of the document, it is worth noticing first because it conformed to a policy Anderson had laid down years before the 1969 tax law was enacted, and also because the new law made that policy mandatory. The relevant passages read:

> The Aspen Institute must not allow the potential reaction of the general public or of any vocal segment of broad or local interest to be of cardinal influence in the carrying out of its programs. At the same time, it cannot discharge its proper role upon the basis of criteria that informed members of the public do not readily understand.
>
> The Institute should pursue such a course that its broad objectives and operations will be generally comprehended and supported so that elements of its program will be largely accepted even when they are not universally approved. The Institute must retain its non-partisan character nationally and internationally. It should rely on the quality of its activities and its expanding, convinced alumni for the support and understanding which it requires.

The public posture, as defined, was the more necessary since two vital sections of the Action Program clearly indicated that the Institute meant to focus on explosive issues of social change. As if in a rapid-fire echo of Slater's recurrent speech, one of the two sections consisted of a long list of needs and developments that had come to affect the human condition in the two decades since the founding of the Institute. Nor did the list stand alone. Coupled with it was an inventory of the possible subjects for seminars that might be sponsored by the Aspen Institute—subjects which were trans-national and trans-societal in nature, and which also had profound humanistic implications.

The changes and needs in combination—Slater wrote— pointed to the road ahead for the Institute. It must reaffirm its commitment to humanistic studies, to the body of knowledge which included history, literature, the arts, religion, and philosophy; to the social and cultural applications of science; to the individual in relationship to himself, to his fellow man, and to his environment; to the endless pursuit of freedom from outmoded dogma, freedom to go beyond convention, freedom of the imagination and the will, freedom from the certain tyrannizing aspects of technology and materialism, "freedom also to be in conflict with oneself." Further, as part of the same commitment, the Institute must try to light up the means by which individuals and groups of individuals could discharge their personal responsibilities in the common task of improving the quality of human life and the safeguarding of human freedom. This was all the more important since, as Slater observed:

There now exist strong tendencies for both humanistic thought and man as an individual to be engulfed by overwhelming scientific and technological developments and by an inhumane bureaucracy, as well as by massive and impersonal urban complexes. The humanities must seek a more vigorous role in preserving, forming, and giving a new vitality to the social, moral, and aesthetic values of our culture. This will require closer mutual understanding and cooperation between those concerned with the humanities, our social and political leaders, and increasingly, men of science to examine how these forces can work together to help resolve human dilemmas and the increasingly complex and urgent problems facing mankind.

On these counts the Action Program stressed that the continuing involvement of "men of affairs" in the Executive Seminars would "remain the central activity of the Institute" and would have the first claim on its attention. In fact, the Institute's Executive Seminars "were bound to be more important in the future" because all governmental, political, and business systems "were being profoundly questioned." Perceptive industrial and business leaders recognized "that they were no longer the symbols which many young people wish to emulate." Though they were now less certain than ever before about their position and the worth of their contributions to American society, they nonetheless wanted to play a large and direct role in the search for solutions to the great social problems of the day. What the Aspen Executive Seminars could do in support of businessmen who were so disposed was to help them understand the fundamental issues involved in the work of social change.

Furthermore, an effort should be made to secure the participation in the Executive Seminars of young people and of representatives of deprived minority groups who "could challenge the dogmas of others—and have their own dogmas challenged in return." To the same end, special fellowships and other funding arrangements should be created in order to bring into the seminars the brightest young leaders in American society and in societies abroad. They should be drawn not only from the realms of business, education, research, communications, and government, but should also include lawyers, doctors, engineers, architects, theologians, writers, and articulate performing artists.

In an added reference to the Executive Seminars, Slater argued that in view of the changes which had overtaken the world since 1949, readings should not be confined to Judaic, Greek, and Roman sources. Asian writings should also be taken into account, and in two suggested ways. For one thing, the Far Eastern Seminar (Asian Thought) which had been suspended for two years should be reinstated, and its future activities should be planned and assisted by a panel of the nation's most knowledgeable experts on Asian thoughts. Secondly, the Japan Seminar should not only be continued but should be made a regular part of the Institute's program. In addition, significant works by Chinese, Indian, and Japanese authors should be included in the readings of the regular or core Executive Seminar.

In another direction, it was noted that the activities of the Aspen Center for Physics showed that summer study groups for periods of three weeks to three months could be both effective and comparatively inexpensive. The same arrangement should be adapted to the work of the Aspen Institute for Humanistic Studies. It should form summer study groups—whether *ad hoc* or for a series type of conference—that would examine critical problems of humanistic concern whose solutions required collaboration between representatives of business, government, civil, and academic life. In matters bearing on the relationship between science and society, such study groups could be co-ordinated with or cosponsored by a number of other agencies: the National Academy of Sciences, the American Academy of Science, the National Academy of Engineering, the Aspen Center for Physics, or the Salk Institute's Council on Biology in Human Affairs. The Institute should also be prepared to host an annual meeting of the leading communicators in the country—particularly from radio and television—in order to evaluate the media and develop both general and specific recommendations for the improvement of program quality in broadcasting.

A number of important details which do not appear in the body of the Action Program were brought out by Slater in the discussion at the trustees' meeting. He took the dual list of social changes and proposed conferences and regrouped them into the six action-oriented programs similar to those he had outlined almost a year previously in his conversation with Anderson. They were programs bearing on:

Communications and Society
Environment and the Quality of Life
Education for a Changing Society
Science, Technology, and Humanism
Justice, Society, and the Individual
International Affairs.

Some of these, in their nomenclature, recalled the tentative, intermittent earlier ventures of the Institute, most of which lasted no more than a week in a year, with no follow-up. Now, however, all the programs amounted to a new "constitution" that was to inform the life of the Institute in the years ahead. It was understood that at recurrent intervals, the Institute would hold exploratory conferences to assess the substance for an action program that could be presented to the foundations for funding. No program, however, would become fully operational unless it was adequately funded in advance for a projected number of years, and unless a program director could be found who was equal to the responsibilities that would fall to him. In any case, until these criteria for new ventures were met, the Institute should confine itself to only a few activities and do them well, rather than compile a paper record of business on many fronts solely for "public relations" purposes.

As a closely related matter, Slater urged that the Aspen Humanistic Award be ended. It could not be justified on the ground that it embodied high, exacting, and recognizable standards of excellence. If an award was to be identified with the Aspen Institute, let it be one which honored a humanistic statesman, and was granted not annually but only when an individual performance merited it. The $30,000 that had been set aside annually for the Aspen Humanistic Award could be better spent in bringing more promising young scholars and artists to Aspen. Matters would be so arranged. Jean Monnet was to be the first recipient of the Aspen Humanistic Statesman Award; Willie Brandt, the second.

It was understood that Slater, with his intimate knowledge of the foundation world, would try to arouse the interest of foundations in particular aspects of the Institute's work and to make them collaborators in formulating and executing particular projects. He would also promote various forms of collaboration with other institutions in the United States and overseas. The nature of the joint ventures might vary from case to case. Some might entail a consortium of institutions. Some might be limited to one-shot or short-range projects; others to projects to be carried on over a period of three or four years. In any event, a system of collaboration with outside institutions pointed to a pattern of mutual benefits. On the one side, the system would enable the Aspen Institute to function with a small staff and small budget and yet generate activities it could not carry forward on its own. On the other side, co-operating institutions could maximize the efficient use of their own resources by avoiding duplications of efforts and by bringing their own ideas to bear on the design of a common task—although they might subsequently concentrate on a particular aspect of that design.

III

The best-laid plans of mice and men do not always go astray. Some of the efforts envisioned in the Five-Year Action Program materialized ahead of schedule, some on schedule, and some are now moving from a state of "becoming" to a state of "being." Yet none of the gains made in the affairs of the Institute in line with the Action Program, came about easily. At intervals Anderson and Slater met to consider a recurrent question. Should the Institute "continue"? Could it "continue"? In fact, it was not until November, 1973, that Anderson thought that the Institute could survive his own lifetime. Meanwhile, there were false starts, disappointments, many zigs and zags to get around obstacles. There were also particular efforts where the results so far attained raised the difficult question whether "a glass should be described as being half *full* or half *empty*." A case in point, to be noted presently, concerns the divided reactions to the attempt to introduce Asian readings into the core Executive Seminar. Yet for all the caveats and provisos that qualify any claim of success, the story the following pages tell is the story of how the Aspen Institute developed since 1969 in ways which conformed to the main thrust of Slater's plan.

PART IV: **Being and Becoming**

15. THREE-WAY STRETCH

I

In preparing the Action Program, Slater had concluded—among other things—that if the suspended Seminar on Asian Thought was to be revived, its structure should be institutionalized. But how? The question led him to Phillips Talbot, a friend of many years. As noted earlier, in 1965, when Talbot was Assistant Secretary of State for Near East and Southeast Asian Affairs, he had been a "resource person" at the first Seminar on Asian Thought held in Aspen, and thus gained some sense of both the inherent capabilities and limitations of the enterprise. He had subsequently served as the United States Ambassador to Greece and was now the new president of the Asia Society.

When Slater and Talbot met to discuss the question just indicated, they agreed that the answer might lie in an arrangement by which the Asia Society would assume the responsibility for organizing an annual Aspen Seminar on Asian Thought—meaning that it would recruit the moderators and resource guests and would design the reading list. It would also identify texts from Chinese, Indian, and Japanese sources that could be woven into Western-oriented lists of the core Executive Seminar. The Aspen Institute, for its part, would recruit all other participants for the Seminar on Asian Thought and would meet the financial costs of the enterprise. The proposal was subsequently approved by the trustees of the two institutions, with Slater joining the board of the Asia Society and Talbot the board of the Aspen Institute—as if in an exchange of "hostages." To support the Asian Seminar, Slater approached the Luce Foundation, and some of the necessary funds were forthcoming from that source.

The restructured Seminar on Asian Thought was first offered

in Aspen in 1971, and has been repeated every year since then, though the venture remains "experimental." Artists and scholars-in-residence, such as novelist Herman Wouk and Robert Mann of the Juilliard String Quartette, have said that they found participation in the Asian Thought seminars an "enlightening experience." But there have been difficulties in getting business executives to sign up or to stay the length of the seminar when they do. Joseph Slater, however, remains hopeful and determined. "It may," said he, "take ten years to bring the Asian Seminar to a point where it fulfills its inherent potentialities, and I mean for it to have that time."

The introduction of Asian texts into the readings of the core Executive Seminars also presents a mixed picture. Moderators such as Mortimer Adler, Jacques Barzun, and William E. Stevenson, who are masters of the Great Books of the Western World, are not comfortable with the Asian texts. Neither their structure nor their substance conforms to Western concepts of "philosophy"—itself a Greek word—representing organized systems of thought where parts are related to wholes, or where proofs offered go to show *this* and not *that* view of reality is either true or false. The Asian material is more like precepts or aphorisms for conduct, sometimes clear, sometimes deliberately ambiguous, and, in most cases, disconnected from each other. It is thus a frustrating experience to try to deal with the material in a dialectical manner as one can deal with a text say, by Plato, Aristotle, Hobbes, or Locke. The seminar participants themselves often complain that they find it hard to locate points of accord or discord between the expressed views of Asian and Western writers.

Still, if the Asian texts are not philosophy in a Western sense, they *are* thoughts and as such do reflect the *thoughts* of half the world. On this ground, the Aspen Institute is likely to experiment a good while longer with a mixed reading list of Western and Asian texts. The search is always on for seminar moderators who are equally at home in the worlds of Western and Asian thought and who can relate the two to each other in ways which force hidden things into light. It will be for the future to show whether the core Executive Seminar can prove Kipling wrong in saying that "East is East and West is West and ne'er the twain shall meet."

II

The Action Program pointed to a possibility that the Institute could be the host for an annual meeting of the leading communicators in the country—particularly from radio and television—in the hope that the event would help them develop both general and specific recommendations for improving the quality of broadcast programs. The idea here was akin to, but separate from, the larger concept of an ongoing Institute program on Communications and Society. More specifically, the idea was an extension of Slater's involvement while at the Ford Foundation with all aspects of public broadcasting and of his protracted efforts to bring together the separate worlds inhabited by communicators and educators.

For several years prior to 1970, on the initiative of Jack Schneider, president of CBS, elements of the broadcasting industry met annually at a conference center in Asilomar, California, to discuss problems of common interests. Robert Anderson, as a director of CBS, attended these annual meetings and came away from them in a troubled frame of mind. The discussions at best amounted to in-house "shop talk"; at worst, they degenerated into a shouting match over wages and hours. In his view, all elements of the broadcasting industry—the heads of commercial networks, producers, directors, writers, advertisers, as well as people involved in public broadcasting—were in need of something better that was not provided. Was there, he asked Slater, any way in which the Aspen Institute could serve the needs of the broadcasters' conference? The answer was in the affirmative. All elements of the broadcasting industry could be periodically brought into intense face-to-face encounters with leaders of thought and action *outside* the broadcasting industry—scientists, educators, sociologists, philosophers, economists, top-level government officials, international civil servants—such as the Aspen Institute regularly mobilized for its own programs.

Slater's suggestion was conveyed by Anderson to Jack Schneider, who, in turn, arranged to shift the broadcasters' conference from Asilomar to Aspen. In this way, under a change of name as well as of venue, an annual *Aspen* Broadcaster's Conference came into being, starting in May, 1970. The industry has a mechanism for choosing participants from within its own ranks, but the Aspen Institute suggests the theme and provides the participants from outside the industry. The events are not exercises in locker-room exhortations, nor evangelical inspirational affairs, nor devices for "selling" a point of view to the industry. No one tells the industry what to do or how to do it—whether the central theme of a conference is "The Future of Commercial Entertainment Television" (1970), "Credibility of News and Public Affairs Programs" (1971), "Years of Decision" (1972), "Mankind and Freedom—Planning for 1984" (1973), "Values and Scarcity" (1974), and "American Self-Renewal in an Interdependent World" (1975). Speakers and other participants provided by the Aspen Institute present or dispute the facts germane to a theme, define the questions posed by the facts, and present or challenge alternative lines of public policy bearing on the social realities under consideration. But it is for the industry to decide how it will deal with the questions of choice that come to the front at a broadcasters' conference. The Aspen Institute, on its part, takes seriously its self-assumed responsibility for regularly exposing the leaders of the industry to the best available *diverse* sources of informed opinion about public-policy issues that do in fact call for acts of choice.

III

The foregoing matters were first being set into place when a new line of impulses flowed from Slater's arrangements with Thomas W. Wilson at the end of 1969 to survey the activities or non-activities in the environmental field.

Wilson began work in early February, 1970, soon after the

National Environmental Policy Act had just been signed into law. He spent three months assembling raw material for his survey and an added two months in whipping it into shape. He found a great swirl of activity under way, all in an early stage. Everywhere in government, in corporations, and in the academies, people were being tapped on the shoulder and told, "Hey, from now on, you are in charge of environment." He was also impressed by two other aspects of the early picture. They were the general tendency to conceive of environmental issues in terms limited to the technical and legal aspects of air and water pollution control and, as a related matter, to see the implications of these issues only within the narrow boundaries of a single community, state, or region. The first tendency raised the danger that the social and humanistic dimensions would be neglected; the second pointed to an equally serious neglect of the internationally unifying force implicit in the concept of Spaceship Earth.

Wilson's completed study—with a forty-page annotated bibliography—would presently be published under the title, *International Environment Action: A Global Survey*. But he had a strategic suggestion to make when he turned the manuscript over to Slater. The Aspen Institute, he said, should leave the specifically technical aspects of environmental problems to the scientists and engineers who already were beginning to deal with them. If the Institute wished to work an untouched part of the environment field, it should concentrate on its social fall-out—on the long-term implications environmental issues had for the individual, society, value systems, and the institutions of decision-making. It should do this, moreover, not in any parochial context, but in a global context, taking into account the unitary nature of the biosphere and its interactions with a man-made environment.

The perspective here was set forth by Wilson in the first chapter of his global survey, which the Aspen Institute published in the summer of 1970 as a pamphlet, *The Environment: Too Small a View*. He argued straight-off that the structure and quality of our institutions would turn out to be a critical variable in the success or failure of society to cope with emergent issues of the human environment, issues which are inseparable from fundamental decisions on how society is to be managed for what purposes:

The "crisis" [Wilson wrote] has more to do with economic-political-social change than with more and better sewage treatment and smoke abatement, essential though these may be. It is a crisis not just for the environment but for traditions and institutions as well.

The first chapter, in pamphlet form, was widely distributed among government officials and opinion leaders and was excerpted for publication in newspapers, magazines, and books. Closer to home, its treatment of the social and ethical aspects of the environmental issues was discussed at an international conference from August 29 to September 3, held in Aspen and co-sponsored by the Aspen Institute and the International Association for Cultural Freedom. The title of the conference was Technology: Social Goals and Cultural Options, with the participants numbering seventy-five notables—scientists, economists, historians, philosophers, journalists—American and non-American alike.

James Reston, who was present, reported in his column for *The New York Times* that his fellow conferees were agreed on the goals of human society and on the fact that "the human family was approaching an historic crisis which will require fundamental revisions in the organization of society." "But," said he, "on the means of achieving even the minimum goals of a livable diet for all men, clean air and water, and reasonable security from death by curable disease or war," the conference was "a babble of disagreement."

Some participants argued, for example, that "since the problems of technology, war, and human suffering were connected, a whole new system of world controls must be devised." Historian Henry Steele Commager, who shared this view, doubted that civil actions in the United States against industries that pollute the air and water would suffice, adding that "only criminal penalties—sending the heads of offending industries to jail—will meet the scope of the problem." Others argued that "nothing will be done if an attempt was made to do everything." Then there were the views expressed by Dr. Salvador E. Luria, the biologist and 1969 Nobel Prize winner in medicine:

The problem of how the fruits of science are going to be used, is an ethical rather than a scientific problem; a problem of values, of wisdom, or responsibility. For the first time in his history, man has learned enough about his environment, with which he is engaged in an unending game, that he may deal his own hand. But he has not learned enough about himself. Man is like a card player engaged in a game for high stakes without being sure of his own nerves and, even worse, without reliable knowledge of the rules of the game. . . . We may gamble on the wrong card and face nuclear or biological disaster. Or we may stumble on the right play, and then, the only reward will be to go on playing.

Slater, not being a cynical or despairing man, saw no reason to retire from the environmental field because the seventy-five leaders he assembled for a two-day special Aspen conference produced only what James Reston rightly called "a babble of disagreement." The event, as he saw it, confirmed what he had told Wilson months before, that "no one had a handle on environmental issues." It reinforced the case for the creation of an international institute on environmental issues, as well as for a protracted Aspen program on the environment and the quality of life. It added point to Wilson's advocacy of a world-wide response to the crisis of the environment. Finally, despite the sketchy results, the event in Aspen put the Institute into an advanced position where it could help prepare the conceptual basis for the United Nations Conference on the Human Environment set for Stockholm in June, 1972.

The United Nations, in common with most national governments since the end of World War II, had been preoccupied with economic development and had given little thought to environmental problems. Its specialized agencies, admittedly, dealt with selected aspects of the human environment such as conservation, resource management, and public health. Yet there was no overall direction for these separate efforts, no real sense of urgency, and no institutional instrument for concerted action. President Kennedy had tried to change the picture for the better when he addressed the General Assembly in September, 1963, and called for a global effort "to defend the human environment—to protect the forest and wild game preserves now in danger of extinction—to improve the marine harvest of food from our oceans—and prevent the contamination of air and water by industrial as well as nuclear pollution." Nobody at the United Nations responded to his call; Kennedy was dead nine weeks later, and his call seemed to die with him.

The picture within the General Assembly remained a model of congealed inertia until 1968, when Sverker Ostrom, the Swedish ambassador to the United Nations—with whom Slater had quietly worked—introduced a proposal for a UN conference on the human environment to be held in Stockholm. In the long debate that ensued, spokesmen for "third world nations" charged that any UN-backed measures for the defense of the environment would be at the expense of their own economic development. Although this note of fear would hang in the air, at balloting time a majority of the General Assembly approved the Swedish proposal, and a UN conference on the human environment was set for Stockholm in June, 1972. Maurice Strong was later recruited from his position as head of Canada's International Development Research Center to become secretary-general of the conference.

Strong, another of the friends Slater had made in years past, stood on untrodden procedural ground in organizing the Stockholm conference. One of his first moves was to recruit Wilson as a personal consultant. Strong knew that the institutional problems of environmental control were far more complex at the international level than at the level of national governments, and the leading reasons for this were as plain as an axe handle. International controls would entail intergovernmental agreements. Different nations differed in their environmental priorities. The need to provide broad national representation in the agencies of the world community would introduce eccentric or obstructionist elements into their administrative structures. Above all, international environmental management would tend to impinge upon traditional concepts of national sovereignty.

In Strong's view, the complexities of the case precluded any prospect that all things out of joint in the world environment would be set right once the Stockholm conference was held in June, 1972. It was possible, however, that the conference could lead to the adoption of a work program to be pursued in post-Stockholm years. If so, then the formulation of such a program by the Secretariat for discussion and disposition by the delegations at Stockholm implied two preparatory lines of action. One was to identify a few priority areas for international agreement as quickly as possible. The other was to define an action program for post-Stockholm follow-through work, the responsibilities for which should be vested either in existing institutions or in new ones to be formed.

To adapt, alter, or design international or intergovernmental agencies for the purposes indicated would require sustained probing and imaginative mental efforts. This was clearly understood by Strong, a rare bird among international civil servants. Being also a man not addicted to illusions, he also knew the answer to the question he put to himself. Was the UN Secretariat, unaided, equal to the tasks it faced in preparation for the Stockholm Conference? The answer was no. It was chronically understaffed and underfinanced, and, besides, most of its international civil servants found it convenient to restrict the flow of their thoughts to safe and conventional channels.

To get at the sources of unconventional thinking which were indispensable if the Stockholm Conference was to have any kind of success, Strong ruffled the dovecotes in the structure of the UN by doing something unorthodox. He reached above the heads of official national or international bodies and into private organizations, including the Aspen Institute for Humanistic Studies. In accounting for the gesture, Strong had this to say:

The world community, like national governments, is now faced with increasingly complex issues cutting across the traditional lines of academic disciplines, specialized areas of knowledge and sectoral organization. I have been convinced for years that governments and international agencies must break down the old frontiers between

271

"public" and "private" agencies and reach out to engage the leading talents of the nongovernmental world if such problems are to be resolved or even managed in a tolerable fashion.

As things stand now, large reservoirs of existing knowledge and experience lying in the private domain are not being brought to bear in a systematic way on problems of the human environment. The gap between these resources and the political process of policy formulation and decision-making must be bridged with a system of co-operative working arrangements.

What is needed is much more than an enriched flow of scientific and technical information. Public administrators, often harassed by the pressure of day-to-day details, need the stimulation of steady exposure to innovative concepts, ideas and perceptions that are generated on the leading edges of intellectual endeavor. Above all, perhaps, the leaders of public institutions need to be reminded, over and over again, that their ultimate purpose is to help bring about a more humane international society that reflects the enduring ethical values of humankind.

The actual sequence which brought the Aspen Institute into the picture started with a request Strong made of Thomas Wilson. Could he help mobilize non-governmental groups and individuals who could contribute to the exploratory work to be done before the Stockholm Conference? Wilson, in turn, shot the request on to Joseph Slater. Slater, by now, had subscribed to Wilson's concepts regarding the kind of work the Aspen Institute could perform in the environmental field. But on a plane apart from the foregoing, there was his own long-standing idea which awaited expression in an institutional form—the idea for an institute of strategic studies about environmental issues. The chain reaction of impulses which ran from Strong to Wilson and then to himself convinced Slater that the time had come to move his idea from the realm of possibilities into the realm of realities. If so, however, he would need the support of Robert Anderson, and he got it.

Anderson agreed to provide the "seed money" for use in organizing and launching what would be known as the International Institute for Environmental Affairs (IIEA). The model would be the London-based Institute for Strategic Studies which Slater had helped bring into being when he was with the Ford Foundation. It was understood that the IIEA, from a corporate standpoint, would be independent of the Aspen Institute, though it would share with it a number of trustees to provide a link at the policy level. Further, it was understood that the Aspen program in the environmental field would be carried out through the IIEA, but would not lose its own distinctive identity. It was also understood that, initially, the most useful function the IIEA and the Aspen Institute program could perform was to lend support to the UN Secretariat for the Stockholm Conference.

Someone now had to be found who could fill the difficult post of president of the new organization, especially difficult because old-line environmentalists who had long been crying in the wilderness might very well resent the entry of the IIEA into their own domain. Thomas Wilson made it clear at the time that he was personally not interested in the administrative responsibilities that would fall to the president of the new organization. His interests lay in research, the formulation of policies and program, and writings designed to illuminate the problems of choice inherent in environmental matters for decision-makers and the general public. But he was not out of the IIEA picture.

In searching for a president of the IIEA, Slater had before him the example of Alistair Buchan, the former Washington correspondent of the *London Observer*, who was chosen to head the London-based Institute for Strategic Studies. Why not a journalist to head the IIEA? The question led him to pluck yet another strand in his web of friendships, and the strand led to Jack Raymond.

The two men had come to know each other after World War II when Slater was with the Allied Control Council in Berlin and Raymond was a foreign correspondent for *The New York Times*. Subsequently, Raymond was the bureau chief for the *Times* in Yugoslavia, the Soviet Union, and Roumania, and was then posted to the Washington bureau of the *Times*, with the Pentagon as his beat. He renewed contact with Slater during the period the latter worked with the Draper Committee and then in the State Department. Again, the two men saw each other periodically after Raymond left journalism in the mid-1960's to become the president of the New York–based Thomas Deegan Company, a large public relations firm.

It was Slater's practice to keep in touch with "good men" and to draw them, even tangentially, into the orbit of his own work. This was done out of motives of friendship, but for another reason as well. Considering the many projects he pushed simultaneously —some struggling to be born, some newborn, some on the road to maturity—there was no telling when he might suddenly need a "good man" to tap for this or that purpose. So it was when he invited his friend Jack Raymond to come to Aspen in the summer of 1970, and the invitation was accepted. There was no hint in the air that Slater had Raymond in mind for a specific place in the structure of the Aspen Institute. But several months later, in the first days of December, Slater met with Raymond in New York, brought him abreast of recent developments in the affairs of the Institute, and asked if he would be interested in assuming the presidency of the IIEA. The answer was yes, provided the terms were satisfactory.

Some time in mid-December, after a meeting in New York with Slater, Anderson, and Wilson, Raymond said he would accept the presidency of the new organization. It was also settled that Wilson would serve as the IIEA vice-president for program, to head its Washington office and to direct the international workshops to be held in Aspen on all aspects of the environment which affect the quality of life.

Wilson not only knew who and what made the wheels go round in Washington and in international organizations, but was also the kind of writer who could take a seemingly dry subject and convert it into an explosion of dry gunpowder. Soon there issued from him a succession of articles, speeches, and testamentary material for appearances before Congressional committees which lighted up previously hidden aspects of cardinal environmental issues.

There is no space here to review in chapter and verse everything he said and wrote. Yet his *leitmotif* at least should be noted because, as the months went by, it not only became the signature of the Aspen Institute's program on the environment, but was picked up and re-echoed among an ever widening circle of people. Wilson acknowledged the possibility that because of remorseless trends in population, industrialization, energy use, resource depletion, and environmental degradation, man could be doomed at some point to "overshoot" the carrying capacity of the biosphere, and the result could be a global catastrophe. Yet he observed that the ominous trend of things on the move in the environment were the result of the policies, decisions, and aims of human beings, the same human beings who could also revoke or alter the pace or direction of their actions. Hence, said Wilson, a world-wide catastrophe could be averted by timely actions framed in the light of three considerations: first, that all the prevailing trends in the environment raise fundamental questions of choice; second, that the crisis contained within each particular aspect of the environment merges into a *single crisis of choice*; and third, that the overriding aim of public policy must be to protect and, if possible, extend the freedom of choice about the way societies are going to evolve and the alternatives that are to remain open for individual life-styles.

The international risks inherent in the present situation [Wilson wrote] can be sensed if we imagine the disastrous consequences for a spaceship if it were manned by a crew comprised of a dozen astronauts, each with a different idea about where he wants to go and about the goal of his mission. Yet the imaginary picture is the real picture of how things now are with Spaceship Earth. It is manned by more than a hundred governments with different and often conflicting missions and with nobody in charge of the crew. International conflict is now no longer a matter merely of territorial claims, border disputes, or ideological struggle. Conflict is everywhere inherent in the interactions of biosphere and technosphere, especially in the interplay of environment, population and resources.

Wilson then went on to list the kinds of conflict which needed to be mediated through the political-social process. Included among these were conflicts over access to resources in global short supply or—from the other side of the coin—responsibility for supplying resources that were in excess in one area and required in others; conflicts over national activities that cause environmental damage in other countries or which contaminate the global atmospheric and oceanic commons; conflicts over alternative uses of land; conflicts over water allocation among competing purposes; conflicts over priorities in the use of energy; conflicts over environmental protection measures which appear to threaten jobs; conflicts over resource consumption among countries of different levels of development and among different levels of income within national societies; conflicts among political jurisdictions over such matters as waste disposal and storage; conflicts over real or imagined hazards to health and safety such as food additives and nuclear power reactors; conflicts over access to the living and other resources of the oceans and seabeds.

Wilson recognized that many of the particular activities underlying such conflicts had been decried by ecologists, environmentalists, conservationists, and others for many years. But, he said, they had not singled out either of two central social implications in the realities around them. First, at present and projected levels, each major area of activity impinges on the others and compounds environmental stress. All together, they contain the seeds of polarization, division, and disintegration of social structures, including the international order. Second, however, these conflicts —with their insistent demand for the exercise of human choice— do not confront us with either-or, black-or-white alternatives. There is no acceptable reason, for example, why even an overwhelming concern for environmental protection justifies a flat commitment to "no-growth." There are almost endless patterns of tolerable compromises, trade-offs, accommodations, and redirections that would not only avoid collision but might even help enhance the general quality of life.

The sum of what Wilson contended and refined entered into the ongoing purpose of the Aspen program on Environment and the Quality of Life. The purpose was to help bring to the surface the social implications of environment-related conflict, to help search for points of convergence and harmony among goals, values, and priorities, and to pose in unmistakably clear terms the choices to be made among alternative lines of action. All this, however, was for the future to show.

To round out how matters stood at the end of 1970, two things remain to be said. First, Maurice Strong was kept informed of every turn in the shaping of the IIEA. Moreover, as did Slater, Anderson, and Wilson, he passed on many helpful suggestions to Jack Raymond in connection with the latter's priority task—to organize an *international* board of directors.

When formed, the board had two co-chairmen, Robert O. Anderson and Roy Jenkins, a leader of the British Labor party. Serving under them were five vice-chairmen, one for each of five regions in the world. There was also a general board of directors of more than twenty persons, plus an Advisory Council in which the dominant figures were Robert S. McNamara, president of the World Bank, and Maurice Strong.

If Maurice Strong, to repeat, rendered important help in finding and recruiting qualified individuals for the governance of the IIEA, he was, in turn, helped by a timely piece of advice he got from Wilson. Strong had previously stressed the need to provide the Stockholm conference participants with a "conceptual framework" for their deliberations. Moreover, said he, the design of that framework would draw upon the world's leading intellectuals. To Wilson, a battle-wise survivor of limitless kinds of committees and meetings, the announced project had an ominous ring, and he paid Strong the compliment of friendship by telling him so directly.

"Maurice," he said, "I don't know who the world's leading intellectuals are, but if you find them and bring them together under one roof, the result would be a shambles. Each one would have his own professional and personal approach to the human environment and the proceedings would turn into a shouting match. And the last place they would look for guidance would be from an international civil servant."

"But the conference *needs* a conceptual framework."

"Agreed," Wilson replied, "so it does. But it won't come into focus as a result of a mass meeting. The conceptual framework should be laid out first in a draft manuscript written by no more than two collaborating authors. At the same time, we can set up the most distinguished group that can be found to serve as consultants who will review and criticize the draft by correspondence. In that way, *we can have the contributions of the world's greatest experts without ever bringing them together in one place.*"

Strong agreed to this approach, and Wilson's plan of action was soon put into effect by a concert of hands. The World Bank and the Ford Foundation provided the financial support; Barbara Ward (Lady Jackson) of Great Britain and Professor René Dubos, each a commanding figure among the world's intellectuals, were persuaded to write the draft text; and the IIEA, with the advice of international professional societies and others, formed a world-wide committee of "corresponding consultants"—152 world notables, representing natural and social scientists, historians, educators, philosophers, and philosopher-statesmen.

There are some tribes in which a newborn son and heir apparent to the chief is passed around among lactating women so that each who suckles him can later claim part of him as their own. In some such similar way the notables to whom the Ward-Dubos draft text was sent, and who responded with comments on it, could claim a measure of co-authorship of the book that was eventually published under the title, *Only One Earth.* Here was the conceptual framework for the Stockholm conference. Maurice Strong was delighted. In a preface he wrote for *Only One Earth*—the book was published in nineteen countries in fifteen languages with many printings—he underlined the UN's debt to the IIEA for its "highly effective management of a complex process with no precedents to provide guidance." But the IIEA and the Aspen Institute would have other tasks in helping to prepare the grounds for the Stockholm Conference.

16. MORE OUTWARD-BOUND GESTURES

I

Amid the many things that were in motion in 1970, Slater cast about for ways to mount an Aspen program on Communications and Society. What he wanted in this respect went beyond his long-standing interest in the educational uses of broadcasting media. It also went beyond the Aspen Broadcasters' Conference in May, where the participants met not to argue over hours and wages but to be exposed to the substantive issues of national life that affected their own industry. Yet what he wanted beyond all this escaped precise definition.

As in the case of all other Institute programs, the one point that stood out clearly in Slater's thoughts was that the program on communications and society should address matters seldom touched by other people who worked in the communications field. Some of these other people, for example, conducted audience research—who was using the media and how. Some focused on content analysis—what was in the media and how the media reflected popular culture or ideological biases. Some people, found mainly in the journalism schools, studied the professional life of newsmen. And then there were the psychologists who focused on attitudes and attitude changes influenced by the media. Each of these efforts, standing alone, carried worth on its face. But taking them all together, what did they add up to? Did they exhaust all that was worth doing? Did they get to the heart within the heart of the problems concerning communications and society?

All this had long been in Slater's mind, but the questions took on new meaning in the fall of 1970 when the communications world was agog over two separate events. One, which unfolded against the background of the Congressional elections then under way, was Vice-President Spiro Agnew's resumption in a more virulent form of his attacks on the networks generally and the "Eastern press" specifically. The other was a major advance in the technology of cable television which held out the promise of "television abundance." Both matters figured in Slater's conversations with two knowledgeable men who were part of his network of friends—Edward Barrett, former dean of the School of Journalism at Columbia University, and Sig Mickelson, former president of CBS News, who had become vice-president of the Encyclopaedia Britannica Company. Barrett and Mickelson suggested, and Slater agreed, that the two developments just mentioned warranted holding a week-end conference in Aspen on Communications and the Media. The conference, small in size and wholly informal in nature, was quickly arranged through telephone calls to possible participants.

In this way, Douglass Cater showed up in Aspen. He had been there before in connection with the 1966 conference on education, as a participant in the Executive Seminars, and more recently as a scholar-in-residence; he was also one of the persons who in the late 1960's had been offered and turned down the presidency of the Aspen Institute. Since his figure will loom large later in the Aspen story, it is best to pause here for a moment to identify him more fully.

Cater, born in Montgomery, Alabama, and educated at Phillips Exeter Academy and at Harvard, had been the Washington editor of *The Reporter* magazine and one of the most respected members of the Washington press corps. One of his books, *The Fourth Branch of Government*, published in 1958, was regarded by competent judges to be the most penetrating study to that time on the role of the press in the nation's capital. He had observed how the image of government, projected by the media, was being accepted as reality, not only by the lay public but by those involved in government itself. He further observed that the vast power communications media have to shape government—policies and leaders—was not what was usually denominated as "editorial power." It was the power to select which of the words

spoken and which of the events that occurred in Washington during a day were to be projected for mankind to see. It was also the
power to ignore—and words and events which failed to get projected might as well not have occurred.

What Cater saw of these matters when he was outside the
White House looking in, he saw from another perspective when
he was in the White House looking out, starting in 1964 when he
was recruited by President Lyndon B. Johnson for a staff position.
As a special assistant, Cater concentrated on the President's programs in the fields of education and health; not the least of the
things he did was to shepherd through the Congress the act which
created the Public Broadcasting Corporation.

Despite or because of the day-to-day tensions of life in the
pressure cooker of Lyndon B. Johnson's White House, Cater often
reflected anew on the theme of a free press in a democratic society.
He concluded that what he had written on the subject in his 1958
book was confirmed by what he saw from within the government.
The only difference was that his direct White House experiences
at the crossroads where the *political* problems of communications
and education intersected with a rapidly growing communications
technology worked to expand the conceptual frame in which he
appraised the structure and the role of the press in American life.
Where his chief concerns had once been centered on the relationship between the press and the government, he now took in the
wide world of communications and their impact on the wide
world of society.

At the small conference in Aspen held on a week end in the
fall of 1970, Cater listened attentively to what was being said as the
talk swayed between denunciations of Vice-President Agnew and
prophecies about the implications of cable television. But then, in
the slow, seemingly hesitant way which tends to conceal the precision of his thoughts, he began to speak his own views. The time
had come, he said, to shed the conventional *ad hoc* approaches to
particular aspects of communications whose importance seemed
to vary from one moment to the next. The fundamental and long-
range need was to create an institution that would inquire into,

clarify, and formulate the terms of the policy choices posed by the interplay between American society and the communications media.

Slater, all alert, knew that what he had just heard gave form to the same idea he had carried around in an inchoate state for some time. "Doug," said he with reflex quickness, "if you will provide a design for the institute you propose, the Aspen Institute will try to get the money for you to launch it." The offer was accepted.

In the months that followed, Cater consulted more than one hundred representatives of government, the media, and interested outside parties. In the act of doing so and without conscious design, he formed a kind of subcommunications network linked to his own person. But he did more than just consult. He studied the history of past efforts to provide a review mechanism for the press, including the 1947 Luce Commission on the Freedom of the Press. He examined the experimental press councils in Oregon and California, as well as the ombudsmen appointed by the *Washington Post* and *Louisville Courier-Journal* to respond to public grievances. He surveyed the content of community journalism reviews. By the spring of 1971, all this and more became the basis for his report to Slater, entitled "Design for a Communications Media Council."

The council would be a non-governmental institution, perhaps fraternally associated with the Brookings Institution in Washington. Though it would act on its own when no one else was in motion, it would always seek to encourage and support the activities of others. Its governing powers would be vested in a small body whose members would meet regularly and involve themselves substantively in policy matters—an "elitist" accent justified on the ground that communications problems require sophisticated judgments as well as a capacity to devise careful strategies. However, said Cater, "the public interest in the media is too laden with controversy to be represented by a single spokesman. Not even a council will automatically be accorded the right to speak for the public interest. It will have to earn that right by the wisdom of its actions."

What kind of actions?

Philosophers from Aristotle to Adler would have found no fault with Cater's six logical categories. Thus, as the source of an *overview*, the council would survey and assign priorities to problems of communication media policy affecting the public interest. As a *clearinghouse*, it would be a point of confluence for significant research and information and would offer guidance to activities in this area. As a stimulant to *research and innovation*, it would initiate expert studies of critical problems and policies, would encourage projects making use of new technology, and would award fellowships to spur creative thinking about the challenges of communication. As a *forum*, it would organize task forces, seminars, and conferences on media problems, and would bring into the academy those who raise high standards for the media. As a *critic*, it would assess the performance of the media, schools of communications, and government agencies involved in communications. As an *advocate*, it would issue policy statements and reports on major communications issues, would testify before media gatherings as well as agencies at all levels of government, and would participate in judicial proceedings on issues of general public interest.

Cater recognized that the council must set its own priorities and that its effectiveness would largely hinge on its choice and timing of issues. But his report revealed an extraordinary range of pressing topics in all corners of the communications field. Expressed in shorthand form, the topics included technology and the media, public broadcasting, lifelong schooling via the media, public affairs programs, fairness and access to broadcasting, economics and the media, government and the media, media and society.

To launch the Media Council with an annual budget of $1 million—and to prevent it from becoming a one-man show—Cater proposed that the foundations which were prepared to finance the council should establish a founding committee composed of one representative from each foundation and one outsider designated by each. The founding committee would then appoint the chairman and members of the council, which would include practicing journalists, executives, and professionals from the media, but no one with any proprietary interests. The executive director of the professional staff would come from this list. The founding committee would also initiate a thorough review and assessment of the council at the end of its fourth year of existence.

Cater regularly informed Slater where he stood in his work, and from one stage to the next gained much from Slater's questions and suggestions. In his final "Report on the Design for a Communications Media Council," the structure, governance, and scope of the council were stated so that each part interlocked with all the rest. Yet when the proposal was submitted for review to the heads of major foundations, the only one who was prepared from the outset to join the founding committee was Lloyd Morrisett, the president of the Markle Foundation. Successive approaches to other potential sources of funds got nowhere, and a point was reached where Cater reluctantly concluded that his Communications Media Council was an idea whose time would never come. Why then should he immobilize himself in watchful waiting in Washington? He had been offered a Regents' Professorship at the University of California in San Francisco as part of an arrangement where he would work with Dr. Philip Lee of the medical school in developing a Health Policy Center. He accepted the offer and moved with his family to San Francisco. But that was not quite that.

To Slater, the quality of hope was not just a prejudice of the mind. It was a positive duty, and, out of obedience to it, he reconsidered his strategy. It occurred to him that if the general foundations, other than Markle, balked at helping to support a Communications Media Council budgeted at $1 million annually, perhaps something else could be done that was worthwhile on its own terms. Perhaps it might be possible to identify in Cater's comprehensive report certain high-priority areas of activity around which an Aspen program on Communications and Society could be built and sustained at a relatively modest cost.

The new approach was discussed with William Benton, who had a lifelong interest in communications through the Benton Foundation. [The Benton Foundation would come in time to acquire his own stock in the Encyclopaedia Britannica Company and its related enterprises.] Benton agreed that his foundation would grant $100,000 to the Aspen Institute, spread in installments over three years, to support its work in the communications field. With this pledge as a spur to action, other things now unfolded at a fast clip.

In July, 1971, Slater chaired a meeting in Aspen attended by Cater, Barrett, Mickelson, Elie Abel, dean of the Columbia Journalism School, and several other men who had conferred the previous fall. In three days of concentrated work, with Cater's report as the reference point from which decisions were made, they agreed on four interrelated, high-priority topics that would provide the focus for an Aspen program on Communications and Society. The four topics were *government and the media, television and social behavior, public broadcasting,* and *the cable and the new technology.* Taken together, they would comprise a much smaller institutional structure than the one contemplated for the Communications Media Council. Yet within the frame of these four priority topics, it would be possible to come to grips with most of the fundamental policy issues in communications posed by Cater. It would also be possible to initiate conferences, seminars, and workshops centered on any *one* of the topics as funds became available expressly for *it*—without waiting until funds became available for concurrent work on all four.

The plan of action was presented to Lloyd Morrisett, who was in Aspen at the time. In a follow-through on his earlier expression of interest, Morrisett arranged a $133,000 grant from the Markle Foundation to the Aspen Institute, payable over four years in support of the newly designed program on Communications and Society. Douglass Cater was then asked to assume the directorship of that program, and the condition he set—namely, that he would be able to work out of a university base—was agreed to by all parties. He then negotiated the terms for an appointment as a visiting professor at Stanford University, a leading national center for communications research. Then he moved to Palo Alto, where he established the headquarters for this Aspen program.

Although he was denied his Communications Media Council, the months Cater had spent preparing his report paid off in the speed with which he drew other people into the infant program and defined a first round of activities for it. His report was to govern the future of what he did in the field of communications and society, just as Slater's Action Program governed the evolution of the Aspen Institute as a whole. More than that, Cater would be a major source of influence and have a major impact on all aspects of the Aspen Institute. Slater would regularly say of him: "Doug Cater is my ideal working partner."

II

On the basis of Cater's prior work, by the fall of 1971 he was well on his way toward the formation of an advisory council whose members could be counted on to bring many perspectives to bear on policy issues in communications. The members, in addition to Slater, Barrett, and Mickelson, would soon include Elie Abel, dean of the School of Journalism at Columbia University; Harry Ashmore, president of the Center for the Study of Democratic Institutions; Charles Benton, president of Films, Inc.; Louis G. Cowan, professor, Columbia Graduate School of Journalism, president of the Broadcast Institute of North America, and former president of the CBS Television Network; Peter Goldmark, president of Goldmark Communications, former president of CBS Laboratories, inventor of communications systems, including long-playing records; Kermit Gordon, president of the Brookings Institution; James Killian, a director of the Corporation for Public Broadcasting, former chairman of the Carnegie Commission on Educational Television, and the former president of the Massachusetts Institute of Technology; De Vier Pierson, a Washington attorney who had served in the White House under President Johnson; and Ithiel de Sola Pool, professor and former chairman

286

of the Political Science Department in the Massachusetts Institute of Technology and a specialist in communications and public opinion. Also by the fall of 1971, Cater had under development a number of projects he had touched on in his report on the Media Council, but which were now to be pursued under the rubric of four categories comprising the Aspen Institute Program on Communications and Society. More about this presently.

17. STOCKHOLM AND SEQUEL

I

In the months leading to the summer of 1971, Jack Raymond worked on the organization of the IIEA, while Thomas Wilson, based in a small Washington office, more sharply defined the purposes of the Aspen program on the Environment and the Quality of Life and prepared for the first international environmental workshop set for Aspen between June 10 and August 1, 1971. The theme of the workshop, "The International Management of Environmental Problems," reflected the Anderson-Slater decision reached in December that the most immediately useful thing the Aspen program on the environment could do would be to help set the stage for the UN conference in Stockholm. To the same end, Wilson served as a link between the Aspen Institute and the UN conference secretariat in his role as a personal consultant to Maurice Strong.

The 1971 workshop was co-sponsored by the IIEA and the Aspen Institute for Humanistic Studies. Supplementary help was provided by the Aspen Center of Physics, of which Anderson and Slater were now trustees, and by the Council on Biology and Human Affairs of the Salk Institute—an earlier Slater-Hunt creation. If the workshop was to succeed, it had to be organized so as to embrace a great diversity of participants, without becoming a great cackle. The procedural solutions that were devised have since been adhered to in all international environmental workshops so far held in Aspen. First, a small core group, after preliminary meetings and the assembly of documents, would work throughout a seven-week study period in Aspen. Members of a rotating consulting group would join the workshop, several at a time, usually for three or four days each over a period of about five weeks. A special

288

review group would then meet for a week to consider a discussion paper distilled from the proceedings of the consulting period, and ensuing criticisms or suggestions would be taken into account in preparing the final version of the workshop report.

The first workshop held in Aspen in the summer of 1971 made a direct substantive contribution to the preparation for the Stockholm conference, and especially to the *institutional* needs implied in Agenda Item VI: "Organizational Implications of the Action Plan." Over a period of seven weeks, representatives from a dozen nations came to Aspen to work with Thomas Wilson, and at one point with Maurice Strong, in producing a report for the guidance of the conference in Stockholm. The report, "Science and International Decision Making: A Basic Paper," was republished in its entirety by the subcommittee on International Organizations and Movements, Committee on Foreign Affairs, U.S. House of Representatives. The central recommendations found their way into the Plan of Action adopted by the Stockholm conference, subsequently approved by the General Assembly of the United Nations. As part of the ripple effect of the workshop, Wilson also served as the study director for a report by the National Academy of Sciences prepared for the Department of State on "Institutional Arrangements for International Environmental Co-operation." Other workshop participants played major roles in seminars organized by the American Society for International Law, by the Center for the Study of International Organizations at the University of Sussex, and by the UN conference secretariat.

Jack Raymond's contributions were of a different kind, and they occurred later on—on the eve of the conference and during the meeting itself. For example, he got the International Chamber of Commerce to convene and pay the costs of a day-long meeting in Paris, where representatives of the international business community could hear from Maurice Strong and others the reasons why they should support the UN program on the environment. Around 150 leaders of international business enterprises came to Paris for the meeting, with the ITT sending eight vice-presidents.

For extra measure, Raymond got the French magazine, *Realité*, to pick up the tab at the George V Hotel where the magnates were entertained at lunch. The success of the Paris event was later repeated in New York, where Raymond persuaded the National Conference Board to arrange a similar meeting for other international business leaders. This time around, he accorded *Newsweek* magazine the honor of paying for the luncheon.

In this way, at the cost of two international briefings, he started a process by which the International Chamber of Commerce eventually found itself doing something it had not originally contemplated. It formally pledged support for the UN program on the environment and organized an Environmental Problems Project of its own to work in ongoing co-operation with the United Nations Environment Program (UNEP) established by the General Assembly after the Stockholm conference.

Raymond had another idea. He had been casting about for ways to finance a "Distinguished Lecture Series" on the environment to be held in Stockholm coincident with the conference. Nothing, however, seemed to jell until he was visited in his New York office by a delegation from the International Population Institute. The Institute, a delegation spokesman explained, had been trying to get the population issue on the agenda of the UN environment conference, but without success. It was feared that the environment conference could be wrecked if it were asked to deal with the explosive implications in population trends. The final word to this effect had just been conveyed to the delegation from the Population Institute by Whitman Bassow, the senior public affairs officer in Strong's secretariat. Bassow had also added a suggestion: "Why don't you call on Jack Raymond? He might have some ideas concerning ways and means to bring the population issue to the attention of the Stockholm conference."

When all this was explained, Raymond reached for a document on his desk containing his design for a Distinguished Lecture Series. "All right," he said, as he showed the document to the delegation, "I'll tell you what to do. If you can fund the distinguished lecture series, I will see to it that one of them will be focused on the population issue." The deal was made on the spot. Raymond's plan called for eight lecturers of international standing, supplemented by sixteen "introducers" of similar distinction. Invitations to speak on particular aspects of the environment were accepted by Gunnar Myrdal, Thor H. Heyerdahl, Lord Zuckerman, René Dubos, Barbara Ward, and Aurelio Peccei. Of the invitations sent to scientists or humanists in the Eastern bloc countries, there were no responses from the Poles or Russians, but there was one acceptance from Roumania. The program set, Raymond wrote to the Swedish Royal Academy to ask if its auditorium —where Nobel prizes are awarded—could be used for the lectures which the IIEA and the Population Institute meant to sponsor at the time of the UN conference in Stockholm. The initial answer in the affirmative was later countermanded by an official of the academy on the ground that the list of lecturers and "introducers" did not give due representation to Eastern European countries.

It now became imperative for Raymond to send his assistant, William Dean, to Stockholm, to find a suitable place for the lectures. Days later, Dean called Raymond in New York from Stockholm to say that all likely halls had been pre-empted for use by the UN conference. "Listen," said Raymond, "you haven't looked everywhere. Go straight to the Grand Hotel in Stockholm. Walk in off the street, and ask for the use of the Grand Ballroom. My guess is that no one from the UN Secretariat has thought to commandeer it."

How did he know? He didn't. But as an experienced former foreign correspondent, he assumed that Stockholm, like every other major city in Europe, *must* have a Grand Hotel, and the hotel *must* have a Grand Ballroom. Also as an experienced foreign correspondent who had covered many international conferences, he assumed the UN Secretariat would think only in terms of august official structures as places where events could be staged and would overlook the unofficial halls deliberately designed to provide meeting places for large groups of ordinary human beings. His assumptions proved correct. Dean found the Grand Hotel, walked in, found the Grand Ballroom, saw that it would do, asked if it was engaged, was told that it was not, and engaged it right there.

Raymond was not through yet. When he arrived in Stockholm, he struck a bargain with Maurice Strong concerning the start of the Distinguished Lecture Series. All plenary sessions of the UN conference were held in the Swedish parliament building, and at the end of the opening one, Strong rapped his gavel to say: "Our first plenary session stands adjourned, and we will now convene right here to hear the first of the distinguished lecturers in the series sponsored by the International Institute of Environmental Affairs and the International Population Institute." The éclat with which the lecture series was launched in the Swedish parliament—despite the initial rebuff from the Swedish Royal Academy—paid off in the audiences which defied an eccentric summer heat wave in Stockholm to pack the Grand Ballroom for all the remaining events in the series. To reach a world-wide audience, the remarks of all the lecturers and introducers were subsequently brought together in the book, *Who Speaks for Earth,* which was published in early 1973.

II

The work performed in support of the Stockholm Conference by the IIEA, by the Aspen workshop, and by its participants in other roles, offered a striking case history of how nongovernmental organizations can contribute to the public policy-making process. The analysis and recommendations that emerged from Aspen were significantly reflected in the background papers prepared by the conference secretariat, in the course of debates of the preparatory committee, in the recommendations that emerged from the Stockholm conference, and in the subsequent actions of the UN General Assembly when it created the United Nations Environment Program (UNEP), with Maurice Strong as its director.

III

But even as the Stockholm Conference itself was moving toward a successful conclusion—despite threatening intervening moments —things were in readiness in Aspen itself for a follow-through once the conference was over in June, 1972. Without taking time out, the IIEA and the Aspen Institute immediately and jointly rolled into the second Aspen international environmental workshop, this one being focused on "The Environment, Energy, and Institutional Structures." The initial interest in energy was based on the assumption that when the subject emerged as a public policy issue—as it has since done with a vengeance—it would become apparent that the environmental problem was vastly more complex than air and water pollution and solid waste disposal.

Accordingly, the Aspen workshop—supported by a grant from the Rockefeller Brothers Fund, supplemented by help in the form of contributed personnel from the Danforth Foundation and the Conservation Foundation—undertook the difficult task of developing a world overview of the tangled global energy problem. The object was not to expose new technical aspects of the matter at issue, but to try to place the energy issue in the relevant contexts of environmental and international affairs, to probe the implications for institutional adaptations, and to recommend the first steps for political action that would be valid regardless of disputes about supply-demand data and technological prospects in the energy field. It was hoped that as in the case of the lead-up to the UN conference in Stockholm, the formulation of a non-technical overview might make a useful complement to the more detailed, more technical, and usually more circumscribed studies undertaken within governments and private research facilities. It was thought that if the UN ever got around to holding a conference on the energy problem, then the work done at Aspen in preparing an overreaching conceptual view of the problem might be useful.

The energy workshop in 1972 was conducted within the same general format that had been devised for the 1971 workshop in the environment, with an extraordinary range of people participating in the core group, the consulting group, and the review group. A paper prepared by Thomas Wilson based on the materials and ideas considered during the seven-week workshop was published under the title, *World Energy: The Environment and Political Action*. Its full text deserves to be read as a prophecy because it anticipated a year in advance the garish shape of the international crisis that followed the Arab oil boycott at the time of the 1973 Arab-Israeli war, followed by the precipitate increases in the price of oil. There is space here, however, only for references to several key points in Wilson's text, starting with this one:

In the framework of traditional concepts of sovereignty, national security, trade rivalry, and commercial competition, the world energy outlook presents a picture of present contradictions and potential dangers. One does not have to be a prophet of doom to foresee the emergence in the not-too-distant future of politically divisive competition among high energy-consuming nations for access to dwindling fuel supplies—confrontations between major consumers and major suppliers—conflicts between resource-rich and resource-poor developing countries—opportunities for economic and political blackmail—even temptations to resort to the use of force to assure reliable supplies of energy materials, unless steps are taken to insure that the energy problem does not drift into a crisis in world order.

To Wilson, the world energy problem was in large part *"political* in character and *global* in reach"—a matter for "Foreign Ministries as well as resource agencies, an issue for the world's political leaders as well as for scientists, engineers, and economists." Hence, though Wilson detailed a number of short-, medium-, and long-range measures to cope with energy shortages, his main accent was on the need to adapt and reform existing institutional structures so that they could deal with energy matters on national and international levels. But what if the need for adaption was ignored? What if national governments and the international community depended on a policy of muddling through? The consequences sounded in Wilson's warning note:

In the event of a physical crisis governments will react with crash decisions and arbitrary solutions which foreclose other options and which are all too likely to require policing and enforcement. Thus the ultimate price may be measured not so much in physical terms as in the loss of freedom of action—and perhaps other freedoms as well. . . .

It can be said with assurance that the more acute the energy problem becomes, the fewer choices will remain, and the more likely it is to induce crash reactions, coercive solutions, and painful adaptions. And without adequate time for study and discussion, crash reactions are all too likely to be technically wrong as well as politically repugnant.

The warning note, sounding out of Aspen, met with no immediate response in any quarter, not in the United States, not in any other national government, not in the United Nations. A policy of "muddling through" continued to be the general order of the day, until events suddenly transformed the note Wilson struck into a world-wide shriek.

IV

The international workshop on energy ran concurrently with a discussion in Aspen about the future status and role of the IIEA. Earlier, at the Stockholm conference, an irrepressible question had cut across all the points at issue. Was it possible to reconcile the conflicting interests in environmental protection and the industrialization of the underdeveloped countries? Jack Raymond, while still at Stockholm, contended that the IIEA must come to grips with that question, and his conviction accounted for his proposal to Anderson and Slater. The headquarters of the IIEA should be moved from the United States to Europe; at the same time, he should relinquish its presidency in favor of someone who was not an American. Anderson favored the proposed move but wanted Raymond to continue as president of the IIEA.

Subsequently, in Aspen, Roy Jenkins, the co-chairman of the board of the IIEA, joined in re-examining the whole of the case. Raymond, who had spent many years in Europe as a foreign correspondent, was reluctant to return there with his family, but agreed to do so for the time required to establish the headquarters of the IIEA in a place such as Geneva. When it appeared that Nairobi instead would be the new home, he resigned the presidency of the IIEA to clear the decks for the next phase of its work.

Later on, toward the end of 1972, Maurice Strong approached Barbara Ward, who indicated her willingness to head the organization on condition, first, that the IIEA should seek to meld the issues of development with those of the environment, especially with respect to the less developed countries; and second, that its headquarters be established in London. Her terms were accepted. In 1973, the IIEA, renamed the International Institute for Environment and Development, with Barbara Ward at its head, began to work out of London. It would continue to collaborate with the Aspen Institute—whose own program on the Environment and the Quality of Life, under the direction of Thomas Wilson, would henceforth be centered on its annual international workshops.

V

The dynamics of these workshops offer a striking illustration of a point made earlier in these pages: that any cardinal problem of contemporary human existence now shares a common frontier or merges with other cardinal problems. Thus an initial focus on environmental pollution was expanded to take in the implications of a growing energy crisis, and these two concerns led by a logic of their own to a concern over the exponential growth in the world's population, and from there to a concern over the capacity of the world to feed its people.

Limitations of space allow only a few bare-bones references to the latter matters. First, the 1973 summer workshop in Aspen was preceded by a spring-time tune-up international seminar on population problems held in Rensselaerville, New York, under the co-sponsorship of the Aspen Institute and the Institute on Man and Science. With Professor Richard N. Gardner as chairman, the forty participants included senior officials of various UN agencies concerned with population matters, representatives from all the major geographical regions of the world, and specialists from nongovernmental agencies. Some of these later came to the summertime workshop in Aspen, the purpose of which was to contribute to the preparation for the United Nations World Population Conference set for Bucharest in August, 1974—much as the Institute's earlier efforts had contributed to the preparations for the Stockholm Conference on the Environment.

Further, since the UN's World Population Conference in Bucharest was due to be followed in November of the same year by a special UN World Food Conference in Rome, a major part of the 1973 summer workshop in Aspen centered on the crucial relationship of population growth to food supplies. Work on the linkage between the two was led by Lester Brown of the Overseas Development Council, and a member of the core group of the population workshop. With the collaborative support of the Aspen Institute and the Development Council, he presently brought together materials on population, food, and related issues and developed them into a full-length book, *In the Human Interest*, published in the spring of 1974.

At the same time, the action-oriented ideas bearing directly on population problems that were clarified at the 1973 workshop were published by Thomas W. Wilson in his report, *World Population and a Global Emergency*. The report itself soon became a focus for the discussions at a series of national and international meetings leading up to the Bucharest conference. It was made available to every delegate to the conference, to all the nongovernmental organizations participating in the parallel Population Tribune, to delegates to the Youth Conference on World Population, and two hundred members of the press from the developing world who were brought to Bucharest for the UN event.

Wilson recognized that the Action Plan contained in his report was focused on only one-half of the population problem, on ways and means that could help curtail future population growth. It did not deal with the other half of the problem. How was one to avert social and political disasters in the decades ahead because of the pressures generated by the built-in momentum of the existing population? How was one to provide schools, shelter, health services, water, sewerage, jobs, and, above all, food, for the masses of people who are destined willy-nilly to arrive on Planet Earth as children of the people already on it? What, in fact, were the "outer limits" to the carrying capacity of Planet Earth, not only with respect to a population load, but also with respect to matters such as contemporary stress, climatic changes, toxic substances, energy, soil and water, and the management of environmental and social problems?

The questions were of pressing concern to Maurice Strong, executive director of the United Nations Environment Program (UNEP). In conversations with Anderson, Slater, and Wilson, he said that he and his deputy, Mostapha Tolba, would welcome a chance to meet with leading representatives of the world's scientific community in a setting where each, within his own field of competence—and all collectively—could give him face-to-face advice on the outer limits of the biosphere to bear man-imposed burdens, where the thresholds of those limits might lie, and what triggering mechanism might set in motion irreversible damage to the life-supporting natural system. The response was an experiment in "consultative education" which the Aspen Institute and the UN Environment Program then arranged.

On the days of August 19–25, the Institute brought Maurice Strong and Mostapha Tolba together with nineteen leading scientists from the United States and fourteen countries of Africa, Asia, and Europe. Among others, the participants included Nobel laureate Sir Peter Medawar; Kenneth Hare of the Canadian Department of Environment; René Dubos; Carroll Wilson of M.I.T.; B. R. Seschachar of India; G. E. Blackman of Oxford University; H. Flohn of the Meteorological Institute of the University of Bonn; Adriano Buzzati-Traverso of Italy; F. Hoveyada, Iranian ambassador to the UN; and Walter Orr Roberts.

The process of "consultative education," compressed into six days at Aspen, had few if any precedents elsewhere. Here, all of a sudden, was a school with a faculty comprised of some of the world's leading scientists, all learning from one another, and all brought together to "teach" the two "students" facing them: Strong and Tolba. The larger result was a set of recommendations for priorities for further UNEP–endorsed studies and activities, together with estimates of research needs and proposals to meet them. Of special interest—because of its bearing on the further development of Aspen Institute programs—was the contribution of a group of participants under the leadership of Walter Orr Roberts. In stirring and disturbing ways, they illuminated the crucial relationship between climate and man, with particular attention on the way actual or potential climatic changes—of natural and man-made origins alike—bore directly on problems of food and famine.

18. COMMUNICATIONS
AND SOCIETY

I

To keep the narrative line clear, the immediately preceding pages dealt only with developments in the program on the Environment and the Quality of Life. The Aspen Institute, however, was never engaged in just one thing, one at a time. It was engaged in many things simultaneously all the time—as was true with what will be dealt with here.

After the fall of 1971, the Aspen Institute Program on Communications and Society, under the direction of Douglass Cater, branched and flared in many directions. The varied activities, however, drew their unity from a common objective that was stated by Lloyd Morrisett when a grant from the Markle Foundation, coupled with one from the Benton Foundation, made the program operational. The objective, said Morrisett, was "to bring together men, ideas, and institutions to pioneer in the communications field, to identify the main communications issues confronting society, and to develop effective programs to implement sound policies."

The progress made so far by the program can be gauged in several ways. First, through its workshops and conferences to date, the program has drawn into its orbit over five hundred leaders in the communications field and has thus expanded the community of those vitally concerned with humanistic and social claims on communications. Second, through the creation of Aspen Communications Fellows, the program has been notably enriched by regular participants such as Professor Ithiel de Sola Pool of M.I.T.; Bill Moyers of public broadcasting; James Hoge, editor of the *Chicago Sun-Times*; Professor William Rivers of Stanford; Daniel Schorr, Washington correspondent with CBS news; Lou Cannon, correspondent, *Washington Post;* Henry Geller, former Special Assistant for Planning and former General Counsel, FCC; and Anne Branscomb, an attorney specializing in communications problems. At the same time, as an effective alternative to staff expansion, short-term fellows—Paul Weaver of both *Fortune* magazine and *The Public Interest,* William Harris of M.I.T., Charles Clift of Ohio University, Andrew Margeson of the Woodrow Wilson School at Princeton, and Paul Fitzpatrick of the University of Colorado—have actively contributed to the work of the program while carrying on their own interests.

Third, program publications—seven major books, five occasional papers, and six special reports—have not only been widely distributed among key policy-makers in both governmental and private sectors, but comprise a new curriculum on communications policy for classroom use. For example, the publications series has already been adopted in its entirety for a course being given by Professor Percy Tannenbaum at the University of California, Berkeley; and a curriculum guide to the Aspen series for use by schools of communication is currently being prepared. Two hundred professors throughout the United States and Canada were recently invited to become active participants in the Aspen Institute Communications Policy Clearinghouse. The informal communications network that Cater had initiated in 1970 was ready to pay dividends. His activities in the four priority areas continued to acquire current information about important research and conference efforts by the policymakers in the communications field. He was now prepared to share that information with a large group of interested parties and also to act as an open and direct line between other people or organizations. Members of the clearinghouse receive complimentary copies of all program publications and reports. They, in turn, are expected to respond to questionnaires and periodically report about trends in research or developing issues in their areas of specialty.

But above all, the Aspen program, through its workshops and critique conferences, has directly contributed to the formulation of public policies in ways which take into account the humanistic and social components of communications questions. At the same time it has contributed to a growing public awareness that communications—heretofore a neglected area of citizen interest and concern—represents an enterprise even more fundamental than formal education to a free and open society. Some sense of the case —supported by the Benton, Markle, Ford, and Rockefeller foundations and the Rockefeller Brothers Fund—can perhaps be gained from what follows.

II

Television and Social Behavior. The impact of television violence on the social behavior of children had long been a source of concern to parents, psychologists, educators, and some political leaders. No major move, however, had been made to get at the realities of the matter until 1969 when Senator John Pastore of Rhode Island proposed that the Department of Health, Education and Welfare undertake a study of the content of television programs to determine "whether there is a causal connection between televised crime and violence and anti-social behavior by individuals, especially children." President Nixon endorsed Pastore's proposal and HEW Secretary Robert Finch complied by directing the Surgeon General to assemble a committee of "experts" in behavioral sciences, mental health disciplines, and communications to come up with the soundest answer to the question that scientific evidence would allow.

Months before the report was issued, however, it was apparent that it would receive critical review from at least three constituencies. Among the social scientist community, skepticism was stirred when the then Surgeon General, William Stewart, appointed several employees and consultants of the networks to his television committee and allowed the industry to veto seven distinguished social scientists who had been doing research in this area. The broadcasting industry, for its part, was known to be highly suspicious that television was being made the scapegoat for society's ills. At the same time, senators and representatives were likely to be contemptuous of an inconclusive report for which so much time and money had been expended.

It was with all this in mind that Cater, in the fall of 1971, laid plans for a critique conference in which the Surgeon General's report, when eventually published, could be coolly appraised and the need for further research on television's impact on social behavior could be defined. The need was all the more urgent in view of the events that intervened before the conference was held in Palo Alto in mid-February, 1972. For example, in early January, one week before the Surgeon General's committee finally signed the transmittal letter for the report, *The New York Times* scooped the rest of the press with a misleading page one story:

The office of the United States Surgeon General has found that violence in television programming does not have an adverse effect on the majority of the nation's youth but may influence small groups of youngsters predisposed by many factors to aggressive behavior.

The article's headline was dead wrong: "TV Violence Held Unharmful to Youth." That no such conclusion had been reached was quickly made clear in a statement issued by the Surgeon General. But this did not check the rising commotion. *The Times'* interpretation was reprinted and widely distributed by the Television Information Service of the National Association of Broadcasters. Meanwhile, the new Surgeon General, Jesse Steinfeld, had reviewed volumes of research and concluded that "for the first time causality between violence-viewing on television and subsequent aggression has been identified." Senator Pastore agreed. He let it be known that he considered the report a "major breakthrough," and scheduled Senate hearings in late March, 1972, when the Surgeon General and his advisory committee members, network heads, critics, and other interested parties would be asked: "What steps can and should each take in the light of the report's findings and conclusions?"

In anticipation of Senator Pastore's hearing, the conference organized by the Program with Dr. Meredith Willson as moderator, met in Palo Alto at the Center for Advanced Studies in Behavioral Research. The participants included the Surgeon General of the United States; the vice-chairman and two other members of the Surgeon General's advisory committee; two social scientists who had been on the television networks' veto list; other psychologists and sociologists; the staff director of Senator Pastore's committee; and the presidents of three foundations—the Markle Foundation, the Russell Sage Foundation, and the Social Science Research Council—concerned with social science research. At the outset of the Palo Alto conference, the conferees pressed their differences in many directions. Yet by the end of the conference, they had reached a meeting of the minds on a number of key points, of which the following alone need be cited:

Since television outdistances school as the occupation of a child during his waking hours, it would be disaster for society to disregard the environment of television in which children grow up. While there had been a slight decline in television episodes of fatal violence, cartoon and comedy violence had increased, especially on the Saturday morning children's programs. Moreover, violence was typically portrayed in a painless way which did not convey the real suffering of the victim and his family.

The revelations contained in the Surgeon General's report made it clear that television not only offered but *imposed* on children vicarious experiences in no way comparable to those of earlier generations. The Congress, therefore, would be more than justified in periodically reviewing what the television industry was doing in children's programming and in the larger area of violent content viewed by children. None of this implied that a law should be passed to control the content of programming. The real question was whether the television industry itself could be more sensitive and self-conscious about its great responsibility.

Nicholas Zapple, the staff director of Senator Pastore's committee, having participated in the Palo Alto conference, learned much that helped him structure the committee's March hearings on the Surgeon General's report. In a matching piece, the substantive terms of the hearings followed the lines of a report on the Palo Alto conference which Douglass Cater submitted to Senator Pastore and amplified as an influential witness before his commit-

Mrs. Robert O. Anderson.

Mr. and Mrs. William E. Stevenson.

Mr. and Mrs. J. E. Slater.

Seminar participants walking through Anderson P

tween Aspen Meadows and Paepcke Memorial Building.

Robert O. Anderson (left) and Walter Orr Roberts.

Henry Steele Commager, frequent Scholar-in-Residence, in the
Institute's auditorium on August 7, 1974.

Elizabeth Paepcke addressing the twenty-fi

iversary celebration of the Aspen Institute.

Aspen Institute Berlin Education Works⟩

otograph by Bullmann

Annual meeting of the Aspen Institute Internatio

...ırd of Trustees, July 2–4, 1975.

Chief Justice Warren E. Burger with fellow judges at annual Aspen Institute International Board of Trustees meeting, July, 1975.

The Empress of Iran, honorary trustee, participating in the annual
Aspen Institute International Board of Trustees meeting, July,
1975.

Staff of the Aspen Institute for Humanistic Studies, summer, 1975.

tee. In particular, with the consent of Lloyd Morrisett and Orville G. Brim, he presented a letter they had written to the Surgeon General in which a statement they had made at Palo Alto was converted into a formal offer. Their respective foundations, Markle and Russell Sage, working in collaboration with the Surgeon General, were prepared to invest research funds in a project aimed at developing social indicators of violence on television and other social effects of programming. These indicators would be instructive to industry leaders, to program producers and sponsors, to citizens' groups, and to Congress. Measuring agencies, to be formed afterward, would be kept at arm's length, both from government and from the broadcasting industry. Senator Pastore promptly associated himself with the offer. More, he called on the Secretary of Health, Education and Welfare—and through him, on the Surgeon General—to join in the development of a set of violence indicators.

For the longer term, the Aspen Program itself undertook a critical review of the Surgeon General's inquiry and its aftermath. A draft manuscript, "TV Violence and the Child: The Evolution and Fate of the Surgeon General's Report," was written by Douglass Cater and became the subject of a critique conference held in Aspen in July, 1973. When the book was published by the Russell Sage Foundation in February, 1975, it contributed to the public debate that continued to rage within the media and government forums. Dr. Eli A. Rubinstein reviewed the book in the *Journal of Communications*. He said, "The book is a balanced, sophisticated, and comprehensive analysis of the many variables that interacted to influence the process and the product of the work of the Surgeon General's Scientific Advisory Committee on Television & Social Behavior. . . . Not until the publication of this book by Cater & Strickland have all the pieces been put together in a way that tells the story as fully and as correctly as one could realistically hope. . . . I recommend it highly to anyone who wants to learn more about the manifestly imperfect relationship between social science research and social policy. I commend it even more highly to the officials of the television industry to remind them that the work of the Surgeon General's Program is neither gone nor forgotten."

The next year, the Aspen program published *Getting to Sesame Street: Origins of the Children's Television Workshop*, by Richard Polsky. It traced in detail the birth struggle of this major innovation in educational TV programming, and thus shed light on a question not touched on in the Surgeon General's report: How can one encourage pro-social programming on television?

Many other questions involving television and society remained to be examined which fell outside the scope of the Surgeon General's report. What role could television play as a humanistic force? How could society cope with the detrimental effects of telecommunications? In the years of decision lying ahead, could television help light up the nature of the human choices to be made? What was the likely shape of the problems which would pose the need for strategic choices? The questions would thread their way through the future workshops of the Aspen program on Communications and Society.

III

Public Broadcasting. In the fall of 1971, the newborn Aspen program on Communications and Society initiated a study by Professors Wilbur Schramm and Lyle Nelson on the costs and structural problems of public broadcasting in the decade ahead. They were, of course, not alone in their interest in the matter. But the Schramm-Nelson report, when completed—and made the subject of a critique conference in Aspen in July, 1972—differed from its predecessors from the standpoint of focus and from the standpoint of the historical realities that had intervened since the earlier studies were made.

To begin with, the growth of noncommercial television during the sixties—from a few over fifty to more than two hundred stations—far outran even the most optimistic predictions. Financially, the decade of growth saw a capital investment of more than $150 million, a near tripling of employees, and a multiplication of annual operating budgets by a factor of more than five. Yet in spite of this spectacular expansion—and in a sense, because of it—educational television was in grave financial trouble. The average station found that the net increase in its revenue—8 per cent in the typical case—was insufficient to provide for technical improvements, much less to expand local program services or embark on color conversion projects.

There were other complications. Public television, from the standpoint of ownership and targeted audiences, was a mixed bag of "community stations," stations licensed to local school systems, state- and municipally-owned stations, and university-owned stations. All, however, had one problem in common. It was the financial pinch, caused on the one side by rising costs and on the other by increasing difficulties in securing funds from private or from state and local public sources. Stations therefore came to depend more and more upon the programs provided by the Public Broadcasting Service interconnections, by regional and state networks, and by other distribution services—at a time when these same national and regional resources were also being threatened by spokesmen for the Nixon Administration. The latter seemed bent on undercutting the whole basis for an interconnected system of public broadcasting, one that could develop national programming.

It was not the purpose of Cater and his associates in the Aspen program on Communications and Society to become preoccupied with the daily tactical maneuvers in the Washington arena where public broadcasting seeks to survive the ambushes set for its destruction. Their own aim was to try to chart a brighter, less conflict-ridden future for the still-evolving institution of public broadcasting. The starting point was the critique conference held in Aspen in the latter part of July, 1972, on the completed Schramm-Nelson study.

Preceding studies on the potential long-range financial commitments involved in public television generally used an approach based on the number of PTV stations required to serve the majority of American households, the costs of interconnection of these stations, and the amount required to provide a national program service for this "network." The approach was criticized for being "station"-oriented, and for not taking into account the potential of other perhaps more cost-effective alternatives such as cable-TV, videocassettes, or the long-range potential of direct reception from satellites. The Schramm-Nelson study, on its part, began with a consideration of the *service* itself. It asked: What kind of non-commercial television service could best meet the public interest, in what quantity and quality, and in what kind of mix between national, regional, and local programming? From there, the study moved to the question of how best to organize and deliver such service, and what it would cost.

To Schramm and Nelson, as to Douglass Cater, the debate about local versus national programming posed a false question of choice. Both kinds of services, as well as the overlooked regional services, were necessary. "On the one hand," so Schramm and Nelson asserted, "the evidence of stations' needs is too overwhelming to ignore the important local aspects of the nationwide problem. On the other hand, funds spent on national program production—programs which are then shared by all the stations—go much further toward the provision of high-quality service than if the same amount were spread over all participating stations. And thus, striking a reasonable balance between local, regional and national support becomes necessary."

The three-day critique conference held in Aspen to study the Schramm-Nelson report and to consider its implications was well attended by persons from the media, foundations, universities, and government agencies. The published report, which incorporated helpful suggestions made at the critique conference, was widely disseminated within the communications industry and in governmental circles, and was drawn on heavily by the subsequent Public Task Force Report on Long-Range Financing. "The report," said John K. Kiermaier, vice-chancellor of Long Island University and past president of WNET, New York and Eastern Educational Network, "is the most comprehensive summary I have seen of the past history of public television financing including trends by category funding and individual station types. . . .

Further, in outlining the scale of financing required to mount a flexible, diverse, and effective broadcast system, it allows still another necessary touchstone for intelligent debate."

To keep an "intelligent debate" alive, Cater, on his own, wrote articles for *The New York Times* and the *Washington Post* which provided timely analyses of critical points in dispute about public television. Further, along with other associates in his program, he developed an "issues" paper which served as a focus for the emerging organization of station chairmen as well as a subsequent issues paper prepared for the Committee for Economic Development. Also issuing from his program was a proposal for a station co-operative organization (PBS) to establish a marketplace system of funding for national programming, the Station Program Cooperative (SPC), and this organization is now in its second year of operation.

In all the foregoing ways, the Aspen program's studies, deliberations, and testimony have been a very considerable force in shaping public broadcasting's economic and political course.

IV

Government and the media. "By participating in Douglass Cater's seminars and workshops, I've telescoped by at least ten years the time it might have taken me to learn what I now know about the print and electronic media," said James Hoge, editor of the *Chicago Sun-Times* and a commentator on public affairs for WGN–TV in Chicago. The first of the workshops he had in mind was on Government and the Media, held in Aspen in August, 1972.

In view of the raw political climate in Washington at the time and the remembered climate of the waning years of the Johnson presidency, it would have been reasonable to make any one of three dreary predictions about what would happen when that August workshop brought together government officials, journalists, and media executives, communications educators, and attorneys. The workshop would degenerate into a slugging match between people who spoke for the government and those who spoke for the media; it would not go beyond a mouthing of hallowed attitudes, platitudes, and beatitudes about the First Amendment; it would become a monologue in which speakers intoned the orthodoxies of their respective institutional associations, without once stopping to listen and respond to what was said by a fellow monologist.

Evidence showing that none of these bleak prospects materialized can readily be found by a reader of the *Aspen Notebook on Government and the Media*, edited by William Rivers of Stanford University and Michael J. Nyhan, assistant director of the Aspen program (New York, Praeger, 1973); it contains, among other things, verbatim statements made at the workshop and the spirited colloquies they evoked. In Aspen—away from the adversary atmosphere of Washington—workshop participants were not held captive, at least not for very long, by the maxims of certified governmental wisdom, by the intramural pieties of the media, or by other distortions of perception inherent in institutional self-centered advocacy. The participants recognized that the issues of government and the media which were in urgent need of clarification lay beyond the classical definitions of the "shalts" and "shalt nots" of the First Amendment.

The integrity of the workshop owed much to the preparatory planning of a group of media experts Douglass Cater had earlier gathered around himself—Professors Ithiel de Sola Pool, Roger Fisher, and Sig Mickelson and communications attorneys Anne W. Branscomb and Lee M. Mitchell. Each helped prepare salient questions for submission to the workshop, and all endorsed Roger Fisher's proposal for a procedural rule that could help keep in clear view the public interest aspects of points discussed. The rule was that as successive problems were posed, participants should try to respond to each with at least one "yes-able proposition" pointing up the kind of action, if any, to be taken with respect to it, and by whom. In Fisher's definition, a "yes-able proposition" had these traits:

It is sufficiently specific so that it can be answered with a single word, "Yes" or "No." It is sufficiently palatable so that we might reasonably expect an affirmative answer. It is sufficiently operational so that, if any affirmative answer is obtained, we can expect that something we want to have happen will actually happen.

The workshop itself was divided into sub-seminars, one on government-media relations and one on regulatory issues. A third sub-seminar winnowed the wheat from the chaff of the things that were said and converted that wheat into propositions which were then put to the workshop as a whole. *Question*: How can the media provide the public with information it needs for the conduct of responsible citizenship? *Question*: How could one bring about a better governmental performance vis-a-vis the media? *Question*: How can regulation or deregulation be used to promote direct or indirect access to the media for a diversity of voices, ideas, opinions, and information—and for a similar diversity to be heard?

It was agreed that too great a proportion of media coverage was centered on a small sector of news-generating sources. All the media, for example, worked the White House. To keep the whole of the governmental picture in clear and realistic focus, it was proposed that more reporters should cover the Congress and the Supreme Court, and more should be regularly assigned to the great departments of government such as HEW and the regulatory agencies whose daily decisions profoundly affect the life of every American.

A natural question was implicit in the observation that many citizen groups keenly feel their lack of access to the existing media. In what ways could the media enhance the possibilities for the citizenry to express their own views in their own voices? Suggested answers included an expansion of op-ed pages (newspaper pages facing editorial pages, which usually carry letters to the editor) and similar access periods on TV; an expansion of letters to the editor columns, especially for letters criticizing the media itself; the easing or removal of restrictions on the acceptance for publication of advocacy ads, and the sale of TV time or spots for advocacy. Yet the prickly problems concealed in the latter proposal were also brought out in enlightening exchanges among participants in the workshop.

The seminar participants were divided in their views about the extent to which the media met the government's need for channels of communication with the public. This was particularly true of their responses to questions involving the communication resources at the command of a President and those at the command of his opposition. For example, is the President's power to command prime time simultaneously on all three networks desirable or excessive? Should the networks rotate among themselves the coverage of a President? Under what circumstances, if ever, do the media have an obligation to help the government get its message across? How can the opposition be given access to television in a degree that approaches an incumbent administration's access, with its enormous power to manipulate the news? But is there *an* opposition in the American system of government? If not, who identifies the opposition spokesman on any issue?

Throughout the entire workshop there was constant preoccupation with "access": access to the media for a diversity of ideas and individuals; access to government; access to opposition to government; access to diversity of program content; access to ownership by blacks, Chicanos, Indians, ethnic groups; access to dedicated channels for all sorts of minorities—racial, ethnic, political, educational, religious—plus the opposition to the government; access to channels for public broadcasting for advice and for creative outlets.

Meanwhile, the workshop groped for a nongovernmental force to weigh communications policy, assess present performance, set new standards, recommend rewards and incentives for superior performance, promote professionalization, analyze weaknesses, and suggest cures—but which would have no power of enforcement, except the power of recommendation. What seemed to be envisioned was a non-governmental counterpart of the Office of Telecommunications Policy, relying on knowledgeable and dedicated citizens, supported by private funds drawing on intellectual resources wherever they could be found.

Despite many disagreements among the participants in the workshop, they formulated twenty-eight specific "yes-able" propositions, along with variants and in some cases dissents. Some of the propositions required government action, some action by the media, and some citizen action. Taken together, they comprise the scaffolding for the possible construction of a new philosophy of government-media relations.

There were other outgrowths of the 1972 workshop. At one point, for example, the participants responded to a request to review the Twentieth Century Fund's proposal for a national press council. The unusual request pointed to the probability that the Aspen Institute, in the future, could be a source of independent appraisals of the work of other major foundations. More immediately, certain changes suggested in the course of the Aspen critique were adopted by the Twentieth Century Fund and were incorporated in the foundation of the National News Council, whose operations were later subject to continuing review by the Program.

V

Cable television and the new technologies. While most of the activities of the Communications Program concerned current policy issues, one project—the Workshop on Uses of the Cable— was intended to explore the implications of future developments in communications. As the first and only forum of its kind in the United States, its development has been shaped by Walter Baer, a former assistant to the President's science adviser, and by Richard Adler, a former instructor at Oberlin.

Several considerations prompted development of the enterprise. First, in contrast to broadcast television—which grew with little concern about its potentialities for the public good—many research and public interest groups have focused on the potentialities of the cable. Studies carried forward, for example, by the Sloan Commission, M.I.T., Stanford University and the RAND Corporation have contributed to a growing body of data on the subject. Also, a Cable Television Information Center, established in Washington, has been a source of counsel to local authorities concerned with aspects of the cable. Still, none of these efforts provided a forum where humanistic concerns could be identified, where expert knowledge could be exchanged, where national and international experiences—on the side of failure as well as of success—could be drawn on in formulating policy recommendations with respect to the new technologies for communications. It was to serve these unmet needs that the Aspen Workshop on the Uses of the Cable was formed.

The Sloan Commission, for its part, had observed that the cable, with accompanying new technology, pointed to the bright possibility of movement from an age of telecommunication scarcity to an age of "television abundance." But would the bright theoretical possibilities actually materialize in the world of real things? In *that* world, said the editor of *Radical Software*, an organ of video makers, "we have gone through the freakout, self-indulgent magic trip with the portopak which for all its stimulation and excitement, has left us somewhat cynical about its effectiveness." Why cynical?

The answer lay in the repetitive discovery that simply recording events is not by itself a communicative act. It could become a communicative act only if *human* claims were imposed on the new technologies for communication, only if it was possible to interest and involve the humanist in the potentialities of the new revolution in the technologies of communication. The Aspen Workshop on Uses of the Cable served as a vehicle through which the knowledge and skills of groups of people not previously involved in television—educators, scholars in all disciplines, and artists in all milieus—could contribute to the development of governing policies and the humanistic uses of the new technologies.

The scope of the work being undertaken can be sensed from the kind of questions that were the center of attention of the workshops thus far held. In the case of the one on Continuing Education, the participants—educators, cable operators, foundation and government representatives—dealt with matters of the following order. How could the cable make formal learning beyond the classroom more readily available to people who had not been well served by existing educational institutions? Could the medium of the cable work directly or indirectly to spur a redefinition and extension of continuing education? What areas existed in which unmet needs for continuing education could be filled by the cable? What were the prospects for sharing the instructional materials? In what ways do the characteristics of cable, such as multiple channels, selective audiences, and two-way capacity, offer advantages over broadcast television? How can televised programming be co-ordinated with direct student-teacher contact, written materials, and other media to create the most effective educational resource? What roles will existing institutions play in providing continuing education on the cable? What new institutions need be created? On what scale should we be considering proposals for cable-based alternative education systems? How can cable-based continuing education be paid for?

The views which surfaced at the conference about these and other questions—along with sets of proposals for specific lines of action—were subsequently published in *The Aspen Notebook on Cable and Continuing Education*. The worth of the enterprise was underlined in a post-publication comment by Professor Frank Newman, Director of University Relations at Stanford University and now president of the University of Rhode Island. Professor Newman, who was the chairman of the HEW Task Force on Higher Education, observed:

> *The Aspen Notebook on Cable and Continuing Education* is composed of realistic and probing analysis by people who have actually experienced the problems of using cable television. . . . It should be read by educators *before* they launch into non-traditional programs or institutions. It should be read by those in television interested in the potential of cable and broadcast TV for public affairs and education. It should be read by executives of "information companies" interested in providing the new materials useful in post-secondary education.

A second workshop, titled Humanities and Arts on the Cable, brought together humanists with representatives of all aspects of the performing arts—artists, impresarios, managers of cultural institutions, directors, and producers—to consider issues such as these: Is television a valid medium for programming of high intellectual and artistic caliber? Can it be used successfully as something more than an agent of popular mass culture? What specific content would best represent humanistic uses of the cable? What range of costs is involved? What existing institutions—universities, performing arts companies, libraries, museums, public broadcasting stations, commercial producers, cable-system operations—will or should be involved in producing new content for cable? Must new institutions be created?

Further: Is there or can a significant audience be created for the arts and humanities on cable? How can this audience be extended beyond the elite elements of the society? Is pay cable likely to be an important source of revenue for performing groups such as orchestras, opera companies, theatrical companies? What other sources of support—individual gifts, funds from cable operators, grants from foundations or arts councils, government subsidies—will be necessary or desirable? Given funding limitations, what is the proper balance between national and local productions? What impact would the wide availability of national, professional productions on cable have on the audiences for local, live performances?

All these questions were shot through with slippery imponderables. The workshop deliberations, in addition to inspiring the publication of a book, *The Electronic Box Office*, found the participants agreed on the following proposition. A national task force comprised of representatives of performing art centers, the humanities, public television, the National Endowments for the Humanities and Arts, the foundations, and the private sector —its mission to study the feasibility of a non-profit entity to promote high-quality cultural programming on cable television.

The task force was seen merely as a means to an end. The major finding of the project is that cable's abundance of channels, alone, will not ensure a greater diversity of programming. What is needed is a new market mechanism—specifically pay cable—to provide an alternative to the tyranny of lowest-common-denominator programming. Pay cable is the key because it will allow viewers to choose directly programming of special interest to special audiences.

In his introduction to *The Electronic Box Office*, Cater stated the conditions that must be met if the cable is to serve as a pipeline for new types of programming:

First, the regulatory framework must set technical standards to insure that video and, possibly more important, sound transmission is of the highest quality. Symphony and opera will hardly have a chance if the low fidelity of broadcast television is maintained.

Second, a new revenue base must be created through pay programming, and high culture must have equal access to its marketing mechanisms.

Third, humanities and arts programming will require sizable subsidy to ensure that the potential is fully tested. It is unlikely that this subsidy can be generated by the cable system itself. Public and private philanthropy will be needed.

Fourth, the development period will require special arrangements to ease copyright and union restrictions which might prevent experimental efforts from getting underway.

Finally, new entrepreneurs will be needed who are capable of linking cultural institutions with the new technology to create a critical mass of humanities and arts programming.

VI

Other developments saw the program pay increasing attention to the communications policy process itself—involving the FCC, Office of Telecommunications Policy (OTP), Congress, and the other government and non-government agencies. Marcus Cohn, president of the Federal Communications Bar Association and a participant in Cater's program, had used a telling figure of speech to describe the American communications policy process: "The captain doesn't have a compass. All he knows is that he is at sea with a lot of passengers pulling him one way or another. What he really needs is someone to give him guidance and direction."

Quick agreement with the idea behind the metaphor was voiced by Professor Ithiel de Sola Pool of M.I.T., and an intimate collaborator of Cater's. In Pool's view, despite the revolutionary implications of technological advances in communications, the critical policy questions posed by the revolution were lost in a dark continent. The questions received nothing remotely approaching the intellectual effort spent on the study of the transportation crisis, the energy crisis, the environmental crisis, or the population crisis.

We have, said Pool, a trifurcated system—broadcasting, telephony, and the postal service. Each grew separately in a way most appropriate for it. Now, however, new technologies were filling the gaps between them, providing new ways to do old chores, making the distinctions between modes less obvious, bringing the various modes into collision and competition, and highlighting the frustrating incompatabilities between systems. In Pool's view of the case, the issues involved in the relationship among the three parts of our communications system are both technical and matters of public policy. If so, said he, why not bring the Aspen program and the new M.I.T. Communications Policy Research Program together for a common exploration of these issues? Through joint seminars held in Cambridge, in Aspen, or elsewhere, the two institutions could explore *how to think* about the problem of moving from where we are to where we might want to be at some future point, to examine a more integrative approach to communications policy research, to critique the efforts to build a body of communications policy research, and to define salient questions that various research centers might wish to pursue on their own. Cater, who had been thinking along the same lines, readily embraced the proposal.

The first joint planning seminar between the Aspen Institute and the M.I.T. program was held in Cambridge in April, 1973, and brought together representatives from industry, government, and academic life. Except for the members from the Cambridge academic community, few of the participants knew each other beforehand. No such seminar had ever been held before. Yet soon after Pool posed a series of questions—about the social need for new communication facilities, their technological possibilities, their economic and regulatory aspects.

Subsequent to the exploratory meeting at Cambridge, the transcript of what was said was studied by a small committee, and the main points raised became the focus for an August, 1973, workshop in Aspen. At that workshop, engineers, economists, political scientists, British and American commentators, government officials, and executives for commercial communications systems and for public television jointly viewed communications policy issues from four angles—their technological prospects, economic tradeoffs, regulatory aspects, and social demands.

Subsequently, the Aspen program's expanding concern with the communications policy process itself accounted for two conferences it sponsored in 1974. One was in Washington, D.C., at the time of the cabinet committee report on the cable. The other was in Daytona, Florida, on the eve of the launching of the ATS–6 communications satellite. These were not self-contained experiences. They led to a plan, now an actuality, for the creation of a continuing seminar in Washington to examine critical communications issues. Participants would vary according to topic, but would associate policymaker and researcher, representatives of contending interests, spokesmen for citizens' groups, and others. Meetings arranged by a small Washington office would be focused on pending policy deliberations by the FCC and Congress or on new proposals stimulated by the Aspen workshop and other policy centers. In this way, it was believed that the Aspen program would be able to strike a better balance between current policy issues and longer-term activities. Forrest P. Chisman was named to direct the activities of the new office.

VII

Television as a social and cultural force. While the social or humanistic demands on communications technology were never far removed from the thoughts of Douglass Cater and his associates in the Aspen program, in 1974 they mounted a concerted effort to learn more about the substance of what was actually being communicated over the wondrous new technological media.

Their first step in a projected series of steps was focused on what was called Approaches to Television Criticism; the reasoning behind this order of priorities appears in an extract taken from what Richard Adler wrote:

If great poetry requires great audiences, something of the same might be said of television, and one major step toward the formation of such audiences which in turn can begin to influence the content of television programming is the development of an informed body of television criticism, applying to the contents of television the serious humanistic and aesthetic standards which are presently used in the continuing critical response to film, literature, music, painting, and the arts. It is largely by the sustained application of an informed and critical mind to the products of television, and the development of a critical tradition with respect to its programmatic content, that we can hope to develop audiences whose own standards can evoke an adequate response from producers whose defense of the cultural and educational inadequacies of contemporary American television consists chiefly of protesting that they are simply providing what the public wants.

A 1974 summer workshop was designed as a first down payment on the aims stated by Adler. General questions, formulated beforehand, included those in the following vein: What formal traits of television differentiate it from other media such as the film and print? What is the nature of reality as presented by television? Is television capable of conveying a coherent view of American history and culture? Can it present and interpret complex ideas—political, aesthetic, or philosophical—about our society rather than settle for a swift and superficial presentation of "facts"? Has television helped mold a national identity and culture? What are the positive and negative implications of increased cultural nationalization? What has been the influence of television on older cultural media such as print, theater, and film? What are the future implications? For example, can television contribute to the development of the American theatrical tradition, or is it inimical to it? Are there ways for television to contribute to the continuity and evolution of our society which it is not now utilizing?

Once the general questions were formulated, a number of

authors were commissioned to prepare papers for presentation and critique at the workshop. Among others, the contributing authors included Benjamin DeMott, professor of English, Amherst College; David Littlejohn, professor of journalism, University of California at Berkeley; Paul Weaver, associate editor of *The Public Interest*; Michael Novak of the Rockefeller Foundation; Michael Robinson, professor of political science, Catholic University; and Kas Kalba, lecturer in the Graduate School of Design at Harvard University.

The discussion they generated was highlighted at one point by a three-cornered rivalry between a fear, a disbelief, and a belief. The fear was that any official or unofficial attempt to make the media the instrument of "do-goodism" would result in the "do-badism" of curbed freedom of expression. The disbelief, expressed, for example, by conference participant Samuel Lubell, was that television had little autonomous effect on the behavior of voters, but rather confirmed pre-existing responses to candidates. The belief was that any writer, producer, or broadcaster of material for the media has some kind of message to convey, whether he admits it or not, and that it would therefore be well for him to be aware of the positive and negative consequences of his efforts.

At the conclusion of the workshop conference, program director Douglass Cater delivered a public lecture in Aspen on the subject of "Television and Thinking People." He examined the reasons why so little was known on television's impact on society, and argued that the impact had become too important to be ignored any longer. New approaches and new methodologies will be needed, said Cater, to produce a better understanding of television's influence on us and on our institutions.

Although only limited financial resources are presently available to support the purposes just indicated, particular individuals of high talent, grouped around Douglass Cater, have addressed themselves to ways and means for disseminating the results of the Institute's efforts. Richard Kuhn, for example, who oversees the publication of Aspen Institute books and monographs, brings to his task extensive experience with leading commercial book-

337

publishing companies. Bill Moyers, now of public broadcasting, after having served successively as press secretary to President Lyndon Johnson and then as publisher of *Newsday*, is currently preparing a series of telecasts based on "Aspen Conversations." And James Hoge, the editor of the *Chicago Sun Times*, has taken the lead in designing the form and substance of what it is hoped will emerge as a quarterly journal that will extend into print the inner life of the Aspen Institute as a whole.

In November, 1974, the Aspen Institute Program on Communications and Society began its fourth year. With renewed multiple-year support from the Ford and Markle foundations and the Rockefeller Brothers Fund, the Program is charting new areas of activity. Since its inception, the Aspen Program has sought to influence the communication policy process to become more than the adversary clash of special interests. With the establishment of a small Washington office, the Program is now able to strike a better balance between current policy issues and longer-term activities. Among the priorities of this office will be defining a strategy for political broadcasting in 1976. As a result of a planning meeting held at Brookings in March, 1975, the Program petitioned the Federal Communications Commission to reconsider its narrow interpretation of Section 315 of the Communications Act, concerning what constitutes bona fide news coverage of political candidates. A larger conference, in collaboration with the Washington Post, is planned for fall, 1975.

In retrospect, the history of the Program, viewed as a single whole, warrants the estimate made by Douglass Cater when he observed:

In a modest way, the Program, like the larger Aspen Institute, is a social invention that is relevant to our times. As I review the Program's activities so far, they have been heavily directed to social invention rather than to specific goals or performance standards for the media: the building of public broadcasting institutions which will be politically insulated and economically viable; the exploration of pay programming as a means of transforming television economics and consequently program diversity; the components required for TV production centers such as CTW or the Lincoln Center; the capacity of a Public Service Satellite Consortium to provide a delivery system capable of serving non-commercial uses; the role of a non-government institution, the National News Council, in providing grievance procedures which will reinforce rather than do damage to First Amendment freedom. Our Television Workshop has concentrated on ways by which informed criticism of that medium can become part of the education curriculum in the wider learning process.

The objective has been to improve the process by which communication serves society. This has led to criticism by some who believe that a foremost task should be to criticize specific media performance. This last is a worthy endeavor, but it is by no means as crucial in the longer run as the one the Program has undertaken.

19. NEW DIRECTIONS

I

Though Anderson and Slater were always in close touch with each other in matters bearing on the affairs of the Institute, they did not get bogged down in daily discussions of minutiae. Anderson, as chairman of the board of many enterprises knew that a subordinate executive who must justify each decision he makes during a day tends either to get defensive or to evade making hard decisions. Slater, on the other hand, knew that Anderson's position on any matter did not have to be confirmed in writing so that a document "could be brought in evidence" months later. A view when voiced would be remembered, and a promise made would be kept.

It was, however, the practice of the two men to meet after an interval of several months for a full-scale overview of the intervening events and to assess where the Aspen Institute stood, where it was trending, where it should go, and how it could best get there. In all of this, they accepted the risks of a possible failure as the natural "trade-off price" for a possible success. When they took the lead in initiating an experimental venture in the hope that it might succeed, there were no recriminations when the hope miscarried. The facts of the experience were noted and analyzed as a basis either for salvage operations or for new directions.

This was true, for example, of a venture known as APEX that was pursued between the spring of 1972 and the summer of 1973. The name itself stood for a troika arrangement where three institutions—the Aspen Institute, the Educational Testing Service, and its affiliate, the Institute for Educational Development—would each bring its special aptitudes to bear on a joint search for solutions to the problems of education and learning systems being posed by the scope and pace of change in all aspects of contemporary life. Yet the hopes which rode on the troika scheme did not materialize. Progress toward the end in view was stalled by differences in the work habits of the partners in APEX and in the cross-claims of their respective institutional constituencies.

A divisive point at issue, for example, was the question of how much time APEX should spend in formulating an "operational philosophy" before moving ahead with specific projects. Sam Gould, on behalf of the Educational Testing Service and the Institute for Educational Development, wanted to proceed cautiously—to grasp everything in its totality and only then to get out in the field for work on particular projects. Joseph Slater, on behalf of the Aspen Institute, contended that the year spent in conceptualizing the work of APEX had produced at least three clearly defined projects that could be mounted without further delay, just as the Aspen program on communications had been launched by focusing on four high-priority areas. In the case of APEX, one of the three projects lay in the field of early child learning; the second involved the relationship among education, work and the quality of life; and the third was the future of state higher education. With further experience, said Slater, new concepts could be formulated leading to new lines of activity in response to newly perceived needs. But a start could be made on those issues about whose importance there was no doubt.

Existing differences were forcefully but amicably stated on both sides, culminating in an agreement formally to dissolve APEX, effective on September 30, 1973; informal contacts and mutual consultation would continue. At the same time, of the three concepts which Slater had said were ready for field work, the Educational Testing Service picked up the one in the field of early child learning, claiming that it had the professional competence in this area which the Aspen Institute lacked. The Aspen Institute, for its part, pressed ahead with the programs on education, work and the quality of life, and with the one on the future of state higher education. Though something was thus salvaged from the APEX experiment, it still fell short of a full and mature conception of what an Aspen Institute Program in Education for a

Changing Society should be like. The need here would mark time until the hour when Frank Keppel agreed to serve as the director—and hence designer—of such an Aspen program.

Here is another example of a hope that did not materialize in its original form, but became the basis for something else. In 1972, the Aspen Institute, aided financially by the Rockefeller Brothers Fund, brought together a group of American leaders in science, technology, scholarship, government, business, and the foundations for an intensive series of discussions on the possibility of creating a "free-standing" Institute for the Analysis of Public Choices.

The participants agreed that public issues could no longer be studied as they used to be—one at a time, and at leisure. Not only were most major issues entwined with each other, but they changed at a speed greater than ever before, and thus foreshortened the reaction time. They further agreed that government officials found it hard to focus their thoughts on what might happen in the public realm, say, in the years 1985–2000. At best, they were preoccupied with immediate problems posed by the facts in the daily newspaper. At worst, they "ran things" by looking through the rear window, without trying to develop some capacity for sensing problems lying ahead.

Discussions about such matters led to a consensus on the proposition that the world-wide scientific and technological revolution under way called for new conceptual approaches and social mechanisms to help formulate the terms of public policy choices to be made in areas such as environment, energy, arms limitations, judicial practices, and educational innovations for an expanding world population. A consensus was also reached on the norms that were to govern actual operations of the proposed "free-standing" institute. For example, it should give priority to the issues of "growth and change" and should come to grips with them before partisan lines had jelled, selecting issues for which a comprehensive analysis could be most useful. At the same time, it could try to anticipate future problems, crises, and opportunities—this in order to permit an adequate lead time for analysis and effective communication with the public and other decision makers. Above all, it should try to light up from within, and bring a unified vision to bear on the interactions among policy problems that were elsewhere studied separately.

Because of financial difficulties, the envisioned "free-standing" institute did not immediately materialize within the orbit of Aspen-related enterprises. This did not, however, imply a harvest of dead leaves. Some of the written proposals that emerged from the exploratory discussions held in Aspen and elsewhere were picked up by Governor Nelson Rockefeller and were incorporated in what came to be known as the Rockefeller Commission on Critical Choices Facing America. There was another fruitful sequel as well. The discussions about the "free standing" institute influenced the nature of the tasks involving an examination of the implications of alternatives in all of the Aspen programs, particularly Science, Technology, and Humanism when that program was organized under the direction of Walter Orr Roberts.

II

But it was not all a case of salvage operations following disappointments. At recurrent intervals throughout its history, the Aspen Institute seemed to grope toward a destination suggested in Goethe's saying that "all things weave themselves into a whole." In early 1973, however, a statement issued by Slater marked the onset of a sustained, self-aware search for ways to inject the full force of the term "humanistic" in everything the Institute was currently doing or hoped to do. Slater's statement read in part:

> Few institutions in our society today deal formally with the humanities as disciplines. Even fewer seek actively to bring humanistic values and knowledge to bear on the complex, frustrating domestic and international problems which face American society and, indeed, all modern technological societies. Among available resources for dealing humanistically with social crises resulting from technological development and rapid social change, the Aspen Institute has a special role—not only in its concern for engaging leaders in humanistically oriented dialogue but also in the special relevance of many of its programs to the crisis of change.

343

Precisely because of its special role and opportunities, the Aspen Institute must carefully and deliberately nurture the human element in all aspects of its work. We must renew our emphasis on humanism in everything we do. To reinforce the Institute's programs through strengthening their humanistic content is a current goal of highest priority.

Many things followed from the sustained new attempt to weave all the affairs of the Aspen Institute into a single humanistic whole. There was, for example, the new form in which Slater pursued his long-standing concern over the social, political, and cultural implications of the advances being made in molecular biology. Previously, at the Salk Institute, it had been brought home to him that the more man understood about the molecular mechanism of life, the closer he moved to the role of a trustee of his own evolution. Secondly, the more man added to the body of knowledge about the functioning of the human mind, the greater would be the implications for his liberation or servitude. It followed, therefore, that the work of the molecular biologists was bound to confront scientists, humanists and policymakers alike with fundamental questions of value and social responsibility—questions that could not be evaded but that called for fateful acts of choice.

These convictions, carried over by Slater from his work at the Salk Institute into his work at the Aspen Institute, led to an event not unlike the unusual series of "tutorials" in the nation's capitol over V-J Day when nuclear physicists instructed members of the Congress about the immense implications of the new-born Atomic Age. Now, in early 1973, Slater organized a briefing for members of the United States Senate and the House of Representatives, in order to bring them abreast of the revolution in the biomedical sciences, and its implications for man and for future legislation. At the Washington end of things, the event was sponsored by the Senate Labor and Public Welfare Committee, with Senator Jacob Javits in the chair. The value the participating legislators placed on what they learned from the molecular biologists who appeared before them was expressed in a proposal they subsequently made, and which was agreed to by Slater. It was that the Aspen Institute would organize further briefings on Capitol Hill—perhaps several a year—so that lawmakers could be kept abreast of developments in biomedical research and of their "profound ethical and legislative implications."

Another move to weave things into a single humanistic whole had behind it years of talk within the Institute, along with direct approaches to it by other organizations, regarding the possibility of establishing Aspen-related programs—and especially the core Executive Seminar—in local communities and regions around the country. Against this background, in early 1973, Slater asked his friend John Hunt—who had taken leave of the Royaumont Center for the Science of Man—to work with the National Endowment for the Humanities on a feasibility study about the regionalization of the Aspen Executive Seminars. As part of his submission, Hunt had something to say about the need to work for "the recovery of man" in the face of a contemporary crisis in the human condition —a crisis which he defined like this:

The ubiquity of change, its relentless rhythms and the severe strains which it has imposed on man and society alike are now bringing about periodic institutional breakdown with increasing frequency— most strikingly in those highly industrial societies which are peculiarly vulnerable to sudden crises because of the extraordinary interdependence between man and the technological environment which he is fashioning around himself. . . .

In the midst of ignorant aggression against the very conditions of his continued existence, modern man has all but disappeared in the welter of conflicting claims imposed upon him following a long series of successive waves of one-dimensional analysis. Focusing their splintering techniques on ever more limited areas of investigation, such analyses operating in many disciplines have brilliantly illuminated obscure and sometimes central working parts of human existence and have immeasurably increased the sum of human knowledge. Yet when improperly understood and utilized, they seem also to have contributed to an enlargement of the surrounding area of darkness in which man fumbles toward a recovery of himself, each partial clarification all too often giving rise to intolerant ideological certitudes, each with pretensions to a holistic grasp of the human condition. . . .

Thus contemporary man seems perilously adrift, no longer aware of the boundary conditions which help him to define himself, so poorly attuned to his world that he seems almost to have forgotten the language of life, bereft of whatever is life-enhancing in the at least partial truth of autonomy. His individuality has been reduced to columns of figures in statistical tables, to the common ground of physics and chemistry and the infinitesimal workings of molecular mechanisms. His social existence has become a mere focal point of historical or economic "forces," his nature nothing more than clay to be modelled at will by the environment. Before him stretch inhospitable roads leading ultimately through a wilderness of abstraction to disintegration.

After the "death of God," will Man be next?

It quickly became clear that flawed approaches were being made to various institutions to determine the extent of their interest in co-operating with a regionalized Aspen program. It also became clear that under existing administrative arrangements the Institute could not control the quality of any regionalized programs offered in its name by other institutions. On these grounds, the trustees of the Aspen Institute, acting on Slater's advice, voted to suspend the feasibility study. It was understood that the grant would be reactivated when the manner of the approach to other institutions had been rethought and new provisions were made for quality control.

These events occurred after the spring of 1974 incident to a general change in the administrative structure of the Aspen Institute. At that time, Amos A. Jordan, who had made important contributions to the Institute since joining it in the fall of 1972 as executive vice-president, resigned to resume his career in government by becoming the principal Deputy Assistant Secretary of Defense for International Security Affairs. In a reshuffling of duties, John Hunt joined the Institute as a new vice-president, with responsibilities that covered a wide range of administrative and substantive functions. He was to co-ordinate the reinstated efforts to establish Aspen-related Executive Seminars, select humanists to participate in Institute activities, develop special humanistic conferences and workshops, and direct the Executive Seminars held in Aspen proper. But all this was overtopped by his responsibility for giving specific meaning to Slater's summons to the Institute: "Carefully and deliberately to nurture the humanistic element in all aspects of its work."

Still another example of the search for "wholeness" occurred in early July, 1972, when the Aspen Institute and the International Association for Cultural Freedom co-sponsored a conference on The Intellectual and Power: His Role and Responsibility.

Of the thirty-three participants, nineteen were Americans and the other fourteen were from Austria, England, France, Germany, Indonesia, and Portugal. An interesting aspect of their collective profile, visible to a tutored eye, was the high proportion of the participants who were members of the Aspen Institute's board of trustees—and who jointly underlined the unusual nature of the board itself as an *international* body of men and women who were not letterhead figures, but were personally and directly engaged in the substantive work of the Institute.

In addition to board chairman Robert O. Anderson and Institute president Joseph E. Slater, the participant-trustees included Paul H. Nitze, former U.S. Secretary of the Navy; Thornton A. Bradshaw, a Harvard Ph.D. and president of the Atlantic Richfield Company; Sir Alan Bullock, vice-chancellor of Oxford, who was both a Fellow of the Institute and a trustee; Walter Orr Roberts, also a Fellow and trustee; Ambassador Soedjamoko of Indonesia; Alexander A. Kwapong, vice-chancellor, University of Ghana; and Marion Countess Doenhoff, publisher, *Die Zeit*, of West Germany.

With Sir Alan Bullock in the chair, a question posed through force of contrast served as the take-off point for the conference discussions. It was observed that in a former day, the intellectual traditionally thought of himself as playing the role of an outsider. He stood removed from the process of production and administration, and was the permanent critic of these two realms and of the general culture of society. But given the realities of the modern post-industrial society—as analyzed by Daniel Bell, a participant in the seminar—was it not time for the intellectual to reconsider the traditional view of his role? Should he now see and accept a different view of his function?

The participants promptly ran into heavy weather, starting with a squall over the definition of the term "intellectual." Thus the challenging question which Walter Orr Roberts raised when he looked around the table and asked: "What am *I* doing *here*? I'm a scientist. I never knew that I was an 'intellectual.' " Or again, when the discussion turned to the political responsibilities of the intellectual, one participant was heard to say in a stage whisper to his neighbor: "What am I supposed to do when I first get up in the morning? Am I supposed to come to attention and salute my official political responsibilities? No, by God: The first thing I do —and will continue to do—is to wash, brush my teeth, and then have breakfast!"

"In the affairs of the Aspen Institute," so Joseph Slater once said, "Sir Alan Bullock fills an indispensable role as 'the general wise man.' " As chairman of the conference, he filled that role in his concluding statement. Bullock saw two comments as being particularly helpful. One was Don K. Price's observation that a wide spectrum of activities was open to the intellectual who wished to be politically engaged. The intellectual—at least in a free society —could move in and out of different points of the spectrum at different times. Doing so, admittedly, was full of moral and mental pitfalls. But the possibilities existed for him to be a political activist for a while, following which he could withdraw from the role and re-enter it later on.

The second helpful view was Paul Nitze's emphasis on the relationship between the factor of time and the development of a normative consensus concerning what should or should not be done in the political realm. Intellectuals who contributed the most to the conduct of politics, said Nitze, were those who could see further than the immediate problems facing a government—who did not allow themselves to be mesmerized by the instruments and the mechanics of power. The instruments and the mechanics of power were the politician's and not the intellectual's "natural" vocation. Secondly, said Nitze, the intellectual who was an adviser to men of political power would himself be well advised not to be impatient for quick results. It might take many years before his ideas gained wide acceptance and were put into effect. Yet if his ideas were right, if he lived in order to prepare others to perceive the truth about themselves, if he squarely confronted them with a range of choices that were true to a problem, the future could confirm him as a person whose voice was the voice of destiny.

As in all great questions, said Sir Alan Bullock in conclusion, the participants who rejected or who agreed with the starting hypothesis concerning the new role demanded by the intellectual, were both right. On the one hand, it would be disastrous if intellectuals became wholly politicized and were denied or denied themselves the independence and the time they need to pursue their proper vocation. On the other hand, it would be equally disastrous if the gap between intellectual and political leaders grew so wide that our society became wholly an adversary culture—if the educated classes, with their influence on education, became wholly alienated from politics and the conduct of government. It would be all the more disastrous if the intellectuals, as in the case of the German intellectuals during the time of the Weimar Republic, adhered to a bystander's role, yet continued to raise the expectations and the demands of what society and government can be asked to provide its constituent members.

Bullock capped his summary of the two salient positions which dominated the conference by referring to them as comprising a "magnetic field of tension" where two positions must be upheld even as they act and react on each other. There can be no fixed gravitational center in the relationship between intellectuals and the political order. The center will constantly shift its location. At times the independence of the intellectual must be stressed, while at other times they cannot and should not escape the claims of politics. It is right and proper to look for ways to facilitate the exchange between politicians and intellectuals. But in the end a continuing tension between the two is to be expected. A full reconstruction of the conference, prepared by John P. Mackintosh, a participant who is a member of England's Parliament, is awaiting publication.

III

Two more particular examples of the search for "wholeness" merit notice, and of these, one entailed the relationship of women to the work of the Institute. Prior to 1974, individual women, besides serving on the Institute's Board of Trustees, had participated in the core Executive Seminar, in the Seminar on Asian Thought, and in special conferences. Though their numbers were rapidly expanding, they were still inadequate in the aggregate. What is more, the participation by women in the programs of the Institute seemed due more to chance than to policy.

The case here was the subject of recurrent discussions between Slater, his associates at the Institute—and their wives. But at last, with Slater's backing, one of the wives—Libby A. Cater— secured a grant from the Rockefeller Foundation which enabled the Institute to make a down payment on its first order of priority where women were concerned. This was to provide financial support for fellowships that would enable a substantial number of qualified professional women to take part not only in the Executive Seminars, but to participate as full-fledged members of the year-around work of the Institute's "thought leading to action programs."

As a sub-aspect of the larger undertaking just mentioned, a grant from the Rockefeller Family Fund enabled Libby A. Cater to organize a seven-day Aspen workshop in August, 1975, on the subject of "Women and Men: Changing Roles, Relationships and Perceptions." This was not just another case of women talking only to women about unrequited grievances. With one-third of the thirty participants men, the immediate object of the workshop was to emancipate the subject of sex roles from the limited circle of intellectuals who had heretofore concentrated on it. Scholars who had thought systematically about the implications of changes in these roles in every enclave of American society were brought together with representatives from major institutions affected by those changes, for a joint consideration of their institutional implications. Further, the August seminar was not conceived of as a one-shot affair. It was meant to synthesize existing knowledge about the dynamics of sex differences in society, to formulate new lines of inquiry into the realities of the case, and to set the agenda for a large-scale conference on the subject in 1976.

The second of the two particular examples worth noting was symmetrical in form with the one just mentioned. What it entailed was the relationships between the artist and the Aspen Institute. Slater was the first to say that the Aspen Institute's right to the identifying term "humanistic" would be deeply flawed unless it had an Arts Program along with its other activities. He also recognized that any such program had to be congruous with the resources and capabilities of the Institute. The Institute, for example, could not afford to assemble in Aspen costly exhibitions of works of art. What, in fact, was it uniquely equipped to do? The search for an answer to the question led to a number of experiments and to protracted discussions that Slater had with equally concerned and knowledgeable people such as Julius Bloom, the director of Carnegie Hall.

All this bore fruit in 1974 when the two prongs of a long-range Aspen Arts Program were finally agreed to. The first prong entailed the direct involvement of artists in the Institute's activities straight across the board from the Executive Seminars to the "thought leading to action" programs. It was Slater's conviction that artists such as Isaac Stern and Robert Mann had a world of experiences and special perceptions which could enlarge the perceptions of other leaders of thought and action—just as they could, in turn, gain much by being fully integrated into all aspects of the Institute's work.

The second prong of the Institute's long-range Arts Program entails an effort to promote musical education—starting with the early learning of music in the family and in pre-school years, and extending from there to all levels of education and to society at large. As an aspect of this long-range effort, an Aspen workshop on "musical literacy" was held in August, 1975. Organized by Slater and Bloom and chaired by Isaac Stern, the workshop brought artists together with leaders in education, communications, and the foundations they might not otherwise have encountered. These included Sir Alan Bullock; Asa Briggs, Provost of Wooster College at Oxford; Thorsen Husen, the world-renowned Swedish educator who knows as much about educational developments in the United States and Japan as in Europe; Daniel Schorr, the broad-gauged television commentator; Lloyd Morrisett of the Markle Foundation; Douglass Cater of the Aspen Program on Communications and Society; and Frank Keppel of the Aspen Program on Education for a Changing Society.

The object of the workshop was to formulate the issues of "musical literacy" in various countries, to identify the obstacles in the way, and to formulate ways and means for overcoming them. As in other aspects of the search for "wholeness," the workshop gained in clarity and focus from the intense face-to-face discussions among diverse individuals who brought their special fund of knowledge to bear on a common interest.

20. INTERACTIONS

The larger examples of the movement to weave all things into a single humanistic whole have been reserved for this chapter. Prior to 1974, the only fully operational "thought leading to action" programs of the Aspen Institute were those on the Environment and the Quality of Life and Communications and Society, though a great deal of work had gone forward on the four additional programs envisioned in Slater's 1969 plan—Science, Technology, and Humanism; Justice, Society and the Individual; International Affairs; and Education for a Changing Society. By mid-1974, however, all of these were formally inaugurated with the appointment of their respective directors.

At the time of this writing, it is still too early to report on the substantial content of the four programs and on what they produced after each held a workshop in Aspen in the summer of 1975. But it is in point to indicate the planned direction for each of the four, along with the intersections among the "thought leading to action" programs now that a "critical mass" has been achieved with respect to all of them.

I

Science, Technology, and Humanism. An Aspen program under this heading came to official birth in 1974 when Slater followed through on his definition of good philanthropy as being a "marriage between good money and good people." In this instance, "good people," transposed from the plural to the singular, meant Walter Orr Roberts. To Roberts, the entwined issues of science, technology, and humanism represented a personal challenge of

353

the highest urgency and significance. So much so that he resigned as president of the University Corporation for Atmospheric Research he had formed and agreed to become the director of the new Aspen program, continuing at the same time with the many facets of his personal scientific investigations.

The point of departure for the Aspen program he designed is the recognition that throughout the world increasing numbers of people are voicing their hostility to an old vision—stemming from Francis Bacon—of science and technology as a liberating and ennobling force in human affairs. The particular grounds for this hostility may vary from one person to the next. But the common ground is the contention that scientific and humanistic thought are diametrically opposed in spirit; that science and technology have become autonomous ends in themselves; that they subject human beings to their own requirements instead of serving human needs; that they destroy human freedom, and are directly responsible for conditions where the world is becoming uninhabitable, a place shorn of hope, dignity, and beauty.

In Roberts' opinion, very serious consequences could follow if this hostile view led to "scientific and technological arrest" in various societies. For the solution to the world's cardinal problems —including those stemming from the new technologies—must include major scientific and technological components. He does not argue that the future should be entrusted solely to the care of the scientific and technological community. His argument is that in the equations of the contemporary world, humanistic purposes will not be advanced by the rejection of science and technology, no more than science and technology can assure human self-fulfillment without the integration of humanistic social purposes into their practices. To see only one side of the case and not the other is to invite distorted responses to public issues at a time when science and technology pierce the frame of human concerns everywhere. They have an impact on questions of war and peace; on freedom and justice; on energy, food, and natural resources; on transportation, shelter, and the environment; on health and the genetic future of man; on intellectual and aesthetic experiences; and so on.

In today's world, therefore, no nation-state and no region can ignore the imperative need to use the powers of science and technology in ways in which the controlling perception will be humanistic in cast.

It will be the purpose of the Aspen program on Science, Technology, and Humanism to mobilize humanists, leaders of public action, business leaders, and members of the scientific and engineering community for joint concentration on a series of concrete and conceptual problems which have a direct bearing on the humanistic uses of science. This will be done under two broad programmatic headings of which the first is Values and Decisions: Public Choices; the second is Humanistic Values and the Nature of Scientific Knowledge. Each of these in turn covers a number of specific projects which will entail co-operative efforts with other programs of the Aspen Institute or with other interested organizations.

Several examples, of the many that could be cited, must suffice here.

Take first a specific project titled Climate and Humanity to be pursued on a co-operative basis between Roberts' program and the International Federation of Institutes for Advanced Studies. While the impact of climate changes on the quality and character of human life has been recognized by reflective men back to the time of Plato, the changeability of climate and weather and a burgeoning world population have posed urgent questions of choice bearing on the human capacity to feed that population. Droughts, for example, which periodically ravage large areas of the earth cause great human suffering and dislocation, intensify the stress on the ecosystem, and pose major moral problems wrapped up in questions of emergency relief. A greatly improved understanding of climate and the climate-food equation is needed to provide both space and time scales for instituting in advance a range of measures that can moderate the effects of drought.

Accordingly, Roberts' program will focus on a dramatic case history of "drought and man"—namely the events stemming from the 1972 climate anomalies in the USSR, India, Latin America,

355

Australia, and the Sahel, with their attendant impact on agriculture—and, not least of all, on the price of food in the American supermarket. So many political, moral, and ecological components are present in the case history that the study, through the force of its internal logic, will be cross-linked to the Aspen programs on International Affairs, Justice, Society, and the Individual, and the Environment and the Quality of Life.

Take another example. Under the heading of Technology and the Educated Person, Roberts' program will study the implications of the application of new technologies to the education of men and women of diverse cultures. It will inquire into the kind of education that is suited to a post-industrial and post-traditional society, knowing that a multiplicity of models for education must co-exist in a modern world. But can and should a common education ideal be formulated for the latter part of the twentieth century in such a way that the development of an educated person—at home in the realm of technology—becomes an accepted individual and social goal around which educational philosophy may once again cohere? There are obvious cross-linkages between the inquiries into this question and the Aspen program on Education for a Changing Society.

Take a final example. Under the broad heading of Humanistic Values and the Nature of Scientific Knowledge, Roberts' program will seek ways and means to bridge the gap between scientific and humanistic thought, as well as the gulf between both of them and the public decision-making process. The specific questions posed in this connection are of the following order. What are the underlying similarities and differences between the fundamental operative values involved in the theory and practice of the physical and life sciences and the humanities? What are their common philosophical roots? Does the recognition and assumption of social responsibility impede the creative instincts of practitioners in these fields? Further: What have the advances in computers, data banks, jet planes, and instant global communications done to man's perception of the good life and to the moral responsibilities of one ethnic or national group for the welfare of another? How do the laymen in different societies view the mysteries of science and the miracles of technology? What values are indigenous to science and technology, and what values are lacking? What is the difference between factual and value judgments? The questions are endless, and being endless, interlock with those that impinge on the work of all the other Aspen programs.

The challenge of Roberts' enterprise is as clear as it is complex. It demands the best efforts that humanists, scientists, and political leaders can collectively muster. But the will is present to meet the challenge head-on. "In striving," said Goethe, "one may stray, but in striving, find the right way."

II

Justice, Society and the Individual. Robert O. Anderson had long stressed the centrality of issues of justice and law to the nature of contemporary society and to the life of the individuals in it. Moreover, the issues had been raised and discussed in all the core Executive Seminars, and in various workshops or special conferences held in Aspen or elsewhere.

In addition, a program full of promise had begun with yearly grants from the Joseph Hazen Foundation. Hazen, who had been admitted to the New York bar in 1922, had for many years served as legal counsel to the Warner brothers in the development of their motion picture interests, including talking pictures. He had subsequently joined with Hal Wallis to become a successful producer of films in his own right and had also prospered in oil ventures. But he had reached a point at the end of the 1960s when he decided he had had enough of business and it was time for him to retire. He had, in the intervening years, formed a foundation to serve as the vehicle through which he exhibited his collected works of art, generally in university communities. He would personally travel with the canvases to the place of exhibition. The high insurance rates on the shipments of the art, however, coupled with the tendency of curators to be careless in the handling of the works, made him doubt the worth of what he was doing. If, however, he

357

stopped the exhibits by giving some of his art collection to a museum, was there something else he could do with his time and resources?

In 1970, when he was in this questioning frame of mind, he came to the Aspen Institute for the first time to participate in an Aspen Executive Seminar and stayed on for a seminar on Asian thought. He later recalled:

> I found the participants—and what they said—to be of great interest to me. But then I asked myself a question. What happens to the businessmen when they go back to their corporations? What happens when they face problems of civil rights, human rights, and the like? Will they decide cases and controversies in the light of an Aspen vision, or in the light of their interests in having a balance sheet at the end of the year show greater profits? I assumed they would be under tremendous pressure to decide in favor of more profits. But then I thought some more about the matter. It seemed to me, as de Tocqueville recognized long ago, that most political, social and economic questions in the United States tend to come before the courts in the form of legal questions. If so, then how our controversies about justice and injustice were resolved would depend in large measure on the perceptions and values of our federal judiciary. The decisions by circuit court judges and courts of appeal judges would permeate the whole of our society.

On this line of reasoning, Hazen concluded that *these* judges were the very people who could benefit the most from exposure to the Aspen Executive Seminar. They could not only renew contact with the writings of leaders of Western thought over the millennia, but would be physically and intimately exposed to a cross-section of people from all walks of life as against the insularity and isolation of daily life on the bench. They would not be deferred to in the Executive Seminars. They would challenge and be challenged in turn, would be compelled to explain themselves, might be prodded to embark on new avenues of inquiry, study, and reflection. "Why is it," Hazen asked, "that many great books have been written by prisoners, and not one by a guard or warden?" It was his way of suggesting that judges, too, were in urgent need of education and re-education.

He subsequently talked with Slater about what he had in

mind. "I would," said he, "be glad to provide five fellowships for one year so that judges of the Circuit and District Courts could come to Aspen to participate in the Executive Seminars." The offer was accepted on an experimental basis. The first five who came out were enthusiastic about the experience. Word spread through the federal judiciary. The Chief Justice of the United States encouraged what had begun, and Hazen arranged to continue his grant of fellowships to federal judges so that a sizable percentage of all who comprise the national membership of the Circuit and District Courts may eventually participate in the Executive Seminars.

Still, while all this was being set in place, successive efforts to formulate a comprehensive Aspen program on Justice, Society, and the Individual encountered common difficulty. It was that the whole of moral and political philosophy was involved in an adequate treatment of the problem of justice. How, then, was one to limit the scope of the subject to the dimensions of a distinctive and manageable program?

Any such program, for example, would have to pay some attention to considerations that are *antecedent* to the theory of justice and on which it is dependent—considerations such as the dignity of man, man's aspiration to personal freedom and to happiness, the social character of man, and questions about human equality. In addition, there would be the need to consider a number of notions *internal* to the idea of justice itself, such as those of theory of justice—including questions about the necessity, authority, and limits of government; questions about the several kinds of liberty in political society and about the relation of freedom to authority, law, and government; questions about the resolution of conflicts concerning political, economic, and social equality. In addition, there would be the need to consider a number of notions *internal* to the idea of justice itself, such as those of right, due, obligation, claim, and status. There was also the fact that theories of justice differ and perhaps conflict, depending on how they formulate the criteria of the just and the unjust in terms of two other sets of considerations: those about the equality and

359

inequality of individuals and of the ways in which they should be treated; and those concerned with what is lawful and unlawful, constitutional and unconstitutional, and, in the broadest of views, right and wrong.

There was another difficulty, which surfaced first at a planning meeting held in New York in 1973, where the participants included Mortimer Adler, William Gorman, Charles Frankel of Columbia University, Chief Judge Irving Kaufman of the Second Circuit Court, and John Nields, a former Wall Street lawyer who has chosen a new career as a professor at Sarah Lawrence. The difficulty, to restate it in a single sentence, was this. Some of the participants insisted that an Aspen program on Justice, Society, and the Individual could begin with specific action-oriented projects without first going into theoretical issues; others insisted that before any action-oriented projects could be mounted, the lineaments of a "just society" must be clarified first.

Still, after intense and sometimes caustic debate in which the chief protagonists were Mortimer Adler and Judge Kaufman, the July meeting in Aspen produced in the end a compromise draft plan for a projected new program. There the matter rested for ten months, but not for loss of interest. It was Slater's conviction that any Aspen program depended for its success on the person chosen to head it, with a bare minimum of procedural rules and inhibitions. The search for a director was a protracted process, but at last, in July, 1974, a figure of the first rank in the legal profession was found to head the Aspen Program on Justice, Society, and the Individual.

That individual was Dean Robert B. McKay of the New York University School of Law. McKay had been deeply involved with problems related to equal educational opportunity, the one-man, one-vote principle in legislative districting, the criminal justice system, the administration of justice, and legal education. Among other things, he had served as chairman of the New York State Special Commission on Attica (1971–72), as chairman of the Mayor's Rent Control Committee (1968–69), and chairman of the New York City Board of Corrections (1973–74). He continues as chairman of Citizens Union, vice-chairman of the National News Council, and vice president of the Legal Aid Society.

When McKay studied the proposed program that had been formulated in July of the preceding year, he saw, as he said, that he was being "entrusted with a unique vehicle for the examination of almost any aspect of the contemporary world, using the lens of justice to consider whether proper standards of liberty, equality, and fairness have been applied." He also recognized that his main problem was to define and delimit the scope of inquiries to be pursued by the program. It was obviously necessary to catalogue all present institutions, programs, and organizations concerned with the infusion of justice into the social structure. It was also obviously necessary, in the light of the catalogue, to identify major social problems that require analysis in terms of the implications for justice as they arise in the context of a search for ends and means. McKay, however, thought that, without waiting for the full inventories of what other law-related agencies were doing, it would be possible to proceed with programs that would find their internal unity in the idea of justice and the rule of law.

At present, McKay's design contemplates action-oriented activities with respect to questions in four areas. They are first, the right of access to equal opportunity; second, punishment and responsibility—this, with a view toward catalytic action that can convert into actual policies an existing consensus about what needs to be done to reform the whole of the American correction system; third, training for professional responsibility—this with a view toward clarifying the system of licensing in the professions, along with questions of morality and justice which arise in the practice of the professions; and fourth, law training for non-lawyers.

In addition to directing the affairs of his own program, McKay is meant to be the "general counsel" for the Aspen Institute straight across the board. This is another way of saying that he and his program will be involved in far more than "bar-and-bench justice" since issues of justice crop up at every turn in the work of the Institute.

In the case of the program on Communications and Society, for example, they arise in connection with such matters as the right of access to the media, "fair comment" by the media, shield laws to protect reporters from being forced to disclose sources of information, electronic eavesdropping, the right of privacy, televising of trials, fair trials, and a free press, defamation and libel. In the case of the program on the Environment and the Quality of Life, critical issues of justice are posed by the need to balance the rival claims of environmental protection, the rights of private property, and the need for industrial development. They also arise under circumstances where resources are scarce, or are subject to monopolistic or quasi-monopolistic controls. Who, then, should get what, when, and how?

Still other questions of justice arise in the context of the Aspen program on Science, Technology, and Humanism. In our "information age," what are the bounds to governmental secrecy? In the computerization of knowledge, what shall be regarded as "proper" or "improper" data to be transposed on cards? What happens to the deposit of this data, as in the case of an arrest record but not a conviction in the case of credit information? Then there are the questions of justice which are indivisible with the concerns of the program on International Affairs. How can one foster the development of a world community held together by a network of common laws and common concepts of justice? How can such a community provide itself with better means for the resolution of disputes? How can one best proceed to outlaw "weather warfare," as in the case of an attempt to change the world's climate by deliberate interference with the world's ice-cap?

It will be the object of the "general counsel" to highlight the interconnections among the particular questions of justice that arise at diverse points in the work of the Institute. Beyond this "scanning" role, it will be his further object to bring new sources of perception and judgment to bear on the search for solutions to the questions noted.

III

International Affairs. The internationalization of the Aspen Institute pre-existed the formulation in 1974 of a specific program in International Affairs. The evidence on this head starts with the fact that the Aspen Institute was born out of the body of an international event—the Goethe Bicentennial Convocation. Secondly, the core Executive Seminar took into account the philosophical ideas of the ancient Judaeo-Christian world, the ideas of classical Greece and Rome, and the subsequent Great Conversation which led to further development of Western versions of concepts such as equality, liberty, justice, and property. Beyond that, the international perspective on human experience was further enlarged by adding Asian texts to the readings of the core Executive Seminar and by institutionalizing an Executive Seminar on Asian thought.

The "genetic urge" toward internationalization was also visible in the composition of the Institute's board of trustees. Starting with the symbolic election of Albert Schweitzer as the honorary chairman of the first board of trustees, by 1974 active members of the board included seven scholar-practitioners from Canada, Colombia, the Federal Republic of Germany, Ghana. Indonesia, Japan, and the United Kingdom. As a matching piece, the Institute's program for scholars-artists and special guests-in-residence and for exchange fellowships regularly included creative people from outside the United States. In addition, while participants in the early special conferences included non-American specialists, the number and variety of these were dramatically expanded after 1969, starting with the program on the Environment and the Quality of Life.

Still further, starting in 1969 with the co-operative arrangements between the Aspen Institute and the Asia Society, the Institute swiftly expanded its explicit partnerships with non-profit organizations having aims parallel to its own. By 1974 there were fourteen such co-operative partnerships, and many of these were international in nature. In the private sector, and aside from the Asia Society, they included linkages between the Aspen Institute and the International Council for Educational Development, the Overseas Development Council, and the Aspen Institute's own invention—the International Institute of Environment and Development. Also, the Institute had entered into a close working relationship with two major international organizations in the public sector. One was the United Nations Environment Program, whose director, Maurice Strong, is a trustee of the Aspen Institute. The other was the World Bank, whose president, Robert McNamara, is also an Institute trustee.

Yet another emblem of the Institute's internationalism was the creation in 1970 of its Statesman-Humanist Award. As indicated elsewhere, the first recipient was Jean Monnet, the "father" of the European Common Market. The second was West Germany's Chancellor Willy Brandt, who was honored in September of 1973 for his efforts to defuse the legacy of post–World War II tensions in German-Russian relations. Further, in late 1973, Aspen Institute Berlin was established as an integral part of the Aspen Institute, and began to function in the spring of 1974 with the active backing of the Berlin Senate. Aspen Institute Berlin will address major humanistic problems confronting societies and individuals everywhere—problems being worked on by all the Institute programs.

The Institute had effectively carried out a large number of continuing international activities, including an annual arms control workshop, a series of task groups leading to Karl Kaiser's widely used book on U.S.–European relations, an annual meeting of top leaders of the United Nations, and sessions on the international dimensions of the major issues with which the Institute has been concerned. The main difficulty, however, was to find a person qualified to make the design for an Aspen program on International Affairs his own business. In the words of a sympathetic but irreverent friend, "Joe Slater's search for the person he wanted had the complexity and high seriousness of a quest for a new Grand Lama of Tibet." At last he found what he was after in the figure of Harlan Cleveland. In years past, Cleveland had been a political executive with the United States foreign aid program, publisher of *The Reporter* magazine, dean of the Maxwell School of Public Administration at Syracuse University, Assistant Secretary of State for International Organization Affairs in the administration of President Kennedy, United States ambassador to NATO, and for six years after that the president of the University of Hawaii.

No nation [Cleveland observed] now controls even that central symbol of national independence, the value of its money: inflation and recession are both transnational. And so are most of the other problems we used to regard as primarily "domestic." Energy, pollution, human rights, racial tensions, education, science, technology, business, labor, food, transportation, population, culture, communications, terrorism, revolution, law enforcement, arms, drugs, religion, ideology—name a category, and its international aspects are likely to outweigh its "domestic" aspects, now or soon. A national government which handles overall "domestic" and "foreign" policy in separate compartments (the White House staff, for example, is still subdivided this way) will have chronic trouble matching its policies to the realities outside the office walls.

In Cleveland's view, during the next few years new factors in the environment for international affairs will perhaps provide "by a fusion of disenchantment with necessity, a new spasm of creativity in the history of transnational institutions." Even now, changing assumptions, aspirations, and attitudes make the world's people so much more interdependent than their institutions and their leaders' rhetoric yet expresses. Values once assumed to be "settled" are now invaded by doubts. Quality of life is challenging quantitative growth as the central goal of national development. Charity is seen to be too fragile and unjust a basis for aid from the rich to the poor. Doctrines such as freedom of the seas and national control of air space and communications are questioned as ethically and technologically obsolete.

Further, for the first time in history, barriers of prudence are seen as limiting what people can safely do to nature or to other people. Nuclear weapons are likewise setting an upper limit to warfare, but the "population bomb" is still ticking, while climatologists are now warning that weather changes in the decades ahead may be adverse to food production. Meanwhile, the revolutions in communications and transportation are connecting people, and especially their leaders, with each other in ways that are inherently revolutionary. No violence will be "local," no disruption one-of-a-kind, no fad or fashion limited by geography or culture if the mass media are looking on. No place need be "remote" that has a jet runway, direct-dial telephones, satellite radio and television, and terminals connected to a major computer. The technologies that shorten time and distance will also compromise national secrecy and individual privacy and make society more vulnerable to individual desperadoes or small groups of terrorists.

At the same time, however, Cleveland noted certain developments that could help mankind enhance control of its destiny. Systems thinking, for example, has created new ways to help an individual encompass in a single mind "the situation as a whole." Other developments, such as the fast computer and the complex simulations it makes possible, enable groups of human beings, drawn from different cultures and politics, to develop new comparative approaches to policy-choice analysis and make complex decisions in the more mindful knowledge of alternative futures. Further, the leaders of nations have a growing capacity to talk to each other directly. The fact that English is now a "second language" of most educated people around the world means that there now exists an international means of communication which *can*—depending on what is said and who is listening—lead to action together.

> The key resource in both the modernized and modernizing world [said Cleveland] is information. Unlike other resources, information is not subject to the law of conservation of energy: it can be disseminated without being dissipated. Satellite communication of data packages will make the information world rounder than the world of coal and steel could ever be.

Against the background of the foregoing analysis, Cleveland

would have the central aim of the Aspen program in International Affairs "to develop concepts, ideas, and action proposals for adapting old transnational institutes and inventing new ones, to enable individual human beings to cope with global problems." This continuing task will be approached by building outward from the Aspen Institute's existing web of contacts around the world—to create a continuously functioning multinational network of analytical minds whose collective product is ideas about international action.

Cleveland has recognized the difficulty of knowing where to begin a new program in International Affairs—since everything is related to everything else, and no person or program can presume to deal with all things all at once. In his view, however, it is worth while to mount an international consultation leading to the draft of a *general* strategy for "next steps"—perhaps during the next ten years—in the mutation of international institutions, "public" and private. At the same time, since "peace comes in parcels," his suggestions for a continuing inquiry into how the world can be managed for mankind falls naturally into four categories, and these he means to explore in a two-year work program extending from the fall of 1974 to the summer of 1976.

One of the four—*the international management of conflict*— entails inquiries into international institution-building. Major workshops will be organized in Aspen, in regions of the United States, at Aspen Institute Berlin, at a proposed Aspen-Hawaii and Aspen-Japan, and at other locations that may be convenient to Latin American, African, Pacific, and Asian participants. The object will be to consider procedures for the identification, prevention, and the resolution of conflict; to limit conventional and strategic arms; to revive international peace-keeping—a "consortium of the concerned"; to establish a Golden Rule of active and timely international consultation; to practice "preventive diplomacy"—as in the case of the conflicts about resources.

The second category for inquiry—*the management of global technologies*—will have linkages with the Aspen program on The Environment and the Quality of Life, and on Science, Technology, and Humanism. What this entails will be a search for ways in which the ambivalent technologies of destruction or development, of pollution or prosperity, of coercion or consent can be organized to work for rather than against individual human beings. The third category for inquiry—*the international management of money and commerce*—will consist of efforts to formulate suggested standards of behavior for multinational enterprises (with suggestions for action by governments covering both incentives and inhibitions on the development of international business); and to explore to what extent, if any, such private standards and national-government actions should be translated into international agreements and institutions.

The fourth category for inquiry—*the international management of development*—will focus on the new basis of the relationship between rich and poor nations. The coming struggles over resources, including energy, food, and metals, will require ways of thinking and institutional arrangements which get beyond the postwar concepts of national development planning aimed at economic growth and supported by aid-as-charity. A special urgency attaches to these issues: in the years just ahead, minimum human needs threaten dramatically to outdistance the world's capacity to supply them—at least under present assumptions and arrangements. This aspect of the Aspen program in International Affairs may be seen as a continuing international inquiry into the ethics, justice, and politics of development and the distribution of resources to serve human needs. It thus lends strength to, and draws strength from, the Aspen program on Justice, Society, and the Individual.

IV

Education for a Changing Society. The Aspen Institute since its inception had been a form of education for a changing society. Yet it was not until 1974, after many intervening probes, that it formally mounted an action-oriented program bearing that name. A leading reason for the intervening delay was symmetrical with the one noted in connection with the design of an Aspen program on Justice, Society, and the Individual. Specifically, education, like justice, cuts into and across a wide range of subject matters— ethics, politics, and economics; art and science; change and progress, virtue and truth, knowledge and opinion; desire, will, sense, memory, mind, and habit; family and state; man, nature, and God. Indeed, virtually everything at the focus of the Institute's own attention was shot through with educational aspects.

In 1974, however, with the appointment of Francis Keppel as the director of the Aspen program on Education for a Changing Society, the proposed structure and substance of a manageable venture began to take shape. Keppel had previously distinguished himself as the dean of the Harvard Graduate School of Education and had later served with equal distinction during the Johnson Administration, first as United States Commissioner of Education and then as Assistant Secretary for Education in the Department of Health, Education, and Welfare.

At its present stage of development, the programmatic content of the Aspen venture Keppel heads is based on two key assumptions. The first is that the impetus for change in educational institutions ranging from pre-school through the university is more likely to derive from changes in the wider society—such as judicial and political decisions involving the rights of children, civil rights, and equity financing—than from pedagogic initiatives taken within the institutions themselves. Hence to meet the problems of social change lying ahead, education will need allies, resources, and directional signals from other sectors of society that are now concerned with matters such as taxation, housing, urban development, industrial and governmental training, scientific research, pension programs, programs for senior citizens, and so on.

The second major assumption is that the present definition of education is in need of substantial change. Keppel does not subscribe to the popular view of education as something which goes on only in schools and colleges, and is confined to the years of an individual's life extending from childhood to early maturity. He shares a view central to Douglass Cater's Aspen program, that the revolution in communications has had a massive impact on human learning; television in particular has affected the way children learn about society and the way adults learn about public affairs and the arts. In the case of his own program, Keppel's working definition of education includes all lifelong learning of an institutionalized character directed toward the goal of human fulfillment and social benefit.

On the basis of these two assumptions, the Aspen program will begin by identifying and estimating the nature and the force of major societal factors likely to impinge on the lives of individuals and of educational institutions. How, for example, will education be affected by changing individual and societal goals and expectations—and by the imperative need to upgrade the capacity of the citizenry to grasp the scientific and technological aspects of political issues in a range from environmental balance to arms control? What values are developing and what promise do they hold, as in the case of the new insistence on equal opportunity and education rights? Do various external trends affecting American education—whether they take the form of changes in demographic patterns, in resources and the allocation of funds, in the nature of occupations and the demand for educated manpower—either reinforce or checkmate each other? What particular issues are they likely to raise for learning, as well as for educational institutions?

A parallel line of inquiry will focus on the nature of the internal or external factors that would enable—or prod—educational institutions actually to adapt themselves to the needs of a changing society. For example, if the cross-tensions between the rising rival demands for equal educational opportunities and for quality in education are to be eased, what kind of selection policies and institutional innovations are necessary? If the present incoherence in the governance of educational systems is to be remedied, how can one clearly define the roles that can best be played by governmental authorities, by educational administrators, and by leaders of unions and associations? What criteria for consultation and collaboration can be formulated for all these parties who impinge on the governance of educational institutions?

370

The interplay between the internal and external aspects of early learning at one end of the educational scale and lifelong learning at the other end perhaps afford the clearest illustrations of the inquiries the Aspen program will make into the factors that will enable educational institutions actually to adapt themselves to the needs of a changing society.

In the case of early learning, the Aspen program contemplates a careful study of the effects of extensive day care on family relationships, personality development, and social interaction. The object here will be to suggest criteria for those governmental policies which directly or indirectly impinge on the foregoing matters—policies, for example, related to welfare and employment, day care centers, medical care and nutrition, labor-management contracts and other industrial practices.

In the case of lifelong learning and work, the Aspen program will look at something more than special educational programs for the illiterate, the handicapped, the unemployed without skills, and the skilled but displaced professionals. It will also study the grounds for dissatisfaction with present working conditions, along with the nature of the demand for career changes in middle years; and still further, on-the-job advancement opportunities for women and minorities, or their access to professional careers. "If it seems sensible to take seriously the idea of lifelong learning," Keppel has observed, "change will be required not only in the schools and colleges, but in existing policies and practices in the private and public sector." To this end, the Aspen program will explore the impact on education of issues such as vested and portable pensions; the potential for American education of workers' "sabbaticals" as part of labor and government contracts; "sandwich courses" for employees; and tax policies to encourage private sector investment in employees' educational development.

It remains to be said that Keppel has subdivided his program into preparatory and follow-through phases. The object of the first phase, extending from the present to 1977, will be to formulate educational policies that can be proposed for adoption by the Congress and the federal administration, by state and local governments, and by private institutions. The object of the second, extending from 1977 to the 1990's will be to help prepare the ground for the actual adaptation of education to the needs of a changing society.

With the latter purpose in mind, a deliberate attempt will be made, starting right now, to make promising young figures in government, scholarship, and educational institutions active collaborators in shaping the Aspen program which Keppel heads. There are, of course, obvious difficulties in forecasting years in advance who in particular will hold leadership posts in the 1980's and beyond. Yet it is possible to identify the type of person between the ages of twenty-five and forty who might play such a role and who can be prepared in advance to fill it. A long lead time for advance preparation is necessary since the task ahead, enormous in itself, is complicated by the fact that all too many forces in society have a vested interest in bending their weight to the end that educational institutions will stand still—though the wide society around them is in oceanic flux.

V

Pluralism and the Commonweal. This major new "thought leading to action" program was launched in March, 1975, with the appointment of Waldemar A. Nielsen as its director, followed by the convening of a seminar on "Government and the Arts" at Aspen Institute Berlin. The new program was not part of the five-year plan Slater had formulated in 1969 for the Institute's development. Yet it was a logical extension of the Institute's commitment to a pluralistic society, hospitable to democratic and humanistic values. It was also a logical response to a need which had long been the subject of discussions among Robert O. Anderson, Thornton Bradshaw, a Trustee of the Institute and president of ARCO, Nielsen, and Slater.

The need was to preserve a healthy balance between two countervailing imperatives which confronted democratic societies the world over—without regard to differences in how they organized the economic functions of production and distribution. First, a democratic people, acting through their instruments of government must respond collectively to common challenges if they are to achieve common goals. Second, and conversely, if a monolithic order of life is to be avoided—if the humanistic values, outlets for individual talents, and freedom of expression are to be safeguarded—there must be multiple centers for social invention independent of the formal organs of government. That in turn implies the presence and survival of a wide range of cultural, educational, and scientific institutions comprising the "non-profit" sector of communal life.

In stating the conceptual basis for the Institute's new program, Nielsen has observed that "a variety of centers of thought and diverse sources of initiative and entrepreneurship are an important assurance of creativity, adaptability, and orderly progress in every sphere of human existence. In fundamental human terms, multiple centers of action, coupled with an active sense of private responsibilities for the general welfare, make for a richer, more humane, more open, and less callous society. Yet in the United States, and elsewhere in the world, the diverse centers of thought and action which are the instruments of pluralism, are fighting for survival in the face of developments that have brought them under siege."

Three American-based examples, cited by Nielsen, add point to his arguments. In education, "the parallel system of private and state-supported institutions is being undercut as private education faces severe financial difficulties." In science, the "growing weight and influence of federal research and development programs— many of them with a military cast—greatly complicate the task of maintaining a balance among three interests: institutional dependence, scientific freedom, and government guidance." In the electronic media, "the growth on the one side of commercial monopolies over communications in various locations, and the struggle of public broadcasting to survive on the other, poses a whole new range of issues of politicization, responsibility and freedom." In these and in other areas of concern to the Institute, it will be the purpose of the program on Pluralism and the Commonweal to assess in different societies the changing roles and responsibilities of the private and public sectors, and to formulate responses to new problems, new dangers, and new opportunities rising from these changing roles.

21. THE ROAD AHEAD

I

Any human institution worth writing about is a product of factors more complex than its public records ever make clear. There is a literature of reports, a continuing folklore that is passed from mouth to ear, along with the rounds of housekeeping chores which may be irrelevant to "greatness" but are essential to the business of mere survival. All these, together, serve to outline the history of an institution. The *significance* of that history, however, somehow rests on an alternation between the institution's aims and everyday frustrations, between its changes and continuity, between its hopes and fulfillments—as the achievements of one generation, and then of a second, became the prologue to the tasks awaiting the third.

By 1975, the Aspen Institute had come a long way not only since the hour of its birth out of the body of the Goethe Bicentennial a generation earlier. It had also come a long way since 1969 when Joseph Slater assumed its presidency. All the "thought leading to action" programs were in being. Some were more firmly established than the newer efforts, but with strong leadership in every program area, the Institute was in a position for the first time to address itself effectively to a wide range of interrelated human and social concerns.

For more than twenty years, Robert O. Anderson had supplied the vision, drive, and leadership that had transfigured the form and force of the Institute. He remained the single most important source of financial support for its activities. But the base of support had been widened by contributions of other individuals, most notably by contributions of foundations and cor-

375

porations.[1] The Institute's budget, though lean when compared to the budgets for most American institutions of higher learning, had increased ten-fold since 1969.

At the same time, with the establishment of the latest program—Pluralism and the Commonweal—the Institute completed a shift in both the locale and the emphasis of its activities. Today, it would be an abuse of language to refer to the Institute as a "summer-time mountain retreat." It is an integral part of the Aspen community and of the state of Colorado to whose cultural development it made a major contribution. But the headquarters of the Institute are not in Aspen proper. Its headquarters are in New York. Nor are its activities confined to the summer months in Aspen, which account for about one-third of its total efforts. Its activities, as noted at the outset of these pages, are a year-around affair. The action-oriented programs, for example, are directed from offices in Boulder, New York, Palo Alto, Princeton, and Washington, D.C.—while an international extension of all its full range of ventures is now operating in Europe at Aspen Institute Berlin. At the same time, a number of the Institute's programs are being conducted in collaboration with a network of other national and international institutions—an arrangement that enables the Institute to draw strength from and contribute strength to the network with a minimum administrative staff for its own specific purposes.

[1] Since 1971, the Institute has received substantial project and program grants from foundations such as the Atlantic Richfield Foundation; the Arca; Benton; Boettcher; Alvin and Peggy Brown; Carnegie Corporation of New York; Edna McConnell Clark; Marcus and Harryette Cohn; Commonwealth Fund; Danforth; Ford; General Service; German Marshall Fund; Joseph Hazen; Kresge; Charles F. Kettering; Lilly Endowment; Henry Luce; John and Mary R. Markle; Andrew Mellon; National Home Library; North Star; Rockefeller Brothers Fund; Rockefeller Family Fund; Russell Sage; Spencer Fund; Thomas J. Watson; and Marie C. and Joseph C. Wilson; as well as from the National Endowment for the Humanities and the City of Berlin. Corporate contributions were made by companies such as ABC, A. T. & T., Boise Cascade, Bristol Myers, Borg Warner, Chase Manhattan Bank, Coca Cola, CBS, Container Corporation of America, Deere & Company, Exxon, First National Bank of Chicago, Ford Motor Company, General Mills, General Telephone and Electronics, Goodyear Tire and Rubber, IBM, Motorola, NBC, Northern Natural Gas, Rose Associates, Sears Roebuck, Smith Barney, Sperry Rand, Weyerhaeuser, and others.

The facilities at Aspen, however, provide a superb setting for intensive summer workshops where the year-around preparatory efforts pursued elsewhere come to a head. So, too, the Executive Seminars, first launched in 1950, will continue to bring to Aspen— as well as to Japan and elsewhere—business and other leaders for two-week sessions on vital ideas central to Western and Asian thoughts. All this is another way of saying that the Institute will continue to maintain a base in the Colorado community where it was founded. But it is also another way of saying that the vision and reach of today's Institute extend far beyond its original roots in Aspen. Its vision and reach—carried forward in year-around programs—extend throughout the United States and, increasingly, throughout the world.

All this, in turn, has set the stage for a major structural task which the Institute began after 1973, but which must now be enlarged upon in the years ahead. It is the task, as Joseph Slater put it, of "building connective tissues" among the various activities of the Institute. In the "President's Letter" published in the Aspen Quarterly in early 1975, Slater put the whole of the case like this:

Increased co-operation among Institute activities is important not only because it may result in greater effectiveness or a broadened perspective on problems. It is important also because integrated approaches to specific issues are one way of integrating the Aspen Institute itself— an essential need at this stage of our development.

Our central theme in the period ahead must be to reinforce efforts to achieve a "soul" for the Institute—a common purpose, a common approach—so that our collective effort will have genuine national and international significance. As Thomas Wilson pointed out at a recent program directors' meeting, societies, concepts and institutions that flow mainly from compartmentalized disciplines and sections cannot succeed in mobilizing the intellectual and physical resources needed to confront global problems today.

Building connective links among our various programs will increasingly integrate the Aspen Institute. There are at least two other integrative tools we shall apply. The Institute's leaders will identify two or three tasks annually that can be carried out collectively by all or many of the different programs. This will involve developing an annual *Overview* of the human condition to which all programs will bring their special insights and perspectives. Additionally, it will involve joint planning of activities directed toward a commonly agreed goal, including the selection of integrative themes such as "Culture and Democracy in America," "Pluralism and the Commonweal" or "Choice and Implications."

With a common purpose and approach, the Aspen Institute can more effectively bring to bear its unique characteristics on the central problems of today. Among these unique characteristics are the active participation of Institute Trustees and Fellows in the full range of Institute activities, leadership that combines intellectual and managerial achievement with a record of effective social activism, and an international network of individuals and institutions motivated by a commitment to thought, instructive action and the maintenance and extension of humanistic values. Also characteristic of the Institute are its approach to problems based on an analysis of the situation as a whole, its orientation toward the development of policy alternatives, its consideration for the human past and present and its commitment to the human future, its emphasis on humanistic values as an essential guide to decision-making and its systematic efforts to achieve impact on public debate and policy-making with a view to developing national goals in its various areas of concern.

As we start a new stage, our efforts must be not to undertake more or different things—either because they are needed or merely to be active—but to realize more effectively our total commitment so that we may be faithful to our calling of humanism and reflective thought leading to constructive action.

II

A final word. Regardless of the programmatic directions the Aspen Institute takes in the years ahead—regardless of how its present work, plans, and affiliations are modified—it is hoped that the attitude which now informs the inner life of the Institute will somehow prove an exception to the law of surprise noted at the outset of these pages.

That attitude has a negative and a positive side. On the negative side, the Institute rejects an apocalyptic approach to human experience—an approach which envisions human experience as a thing of sudden endings and sudden beginnings, of sudden darkness or a flashing revelation. What the adherents to that approach acclaim at dawn, they denounce at dusk as being big with ruin.

What they decry at dawn, they hail at dusk as the arrival of the millenium. So, too, their belief that tomorrow will be better than today simply because twenty-four hours will have passed is displaced a moment later by a belief that the world will end within the next twenty-four hours.

When the apocalyptic-minded are in a majority, they are led by their absolutism to insist that the majority has a clear title of right to take all. When they are in the minority, they are led by their absolutism to insist that the majority has no right to anything except at the sufferance of the minority. They are unaware of a self-denying ordinance—"Conquer but spare"—that is vital to the constitutional morality of a democratic society. They are indifferent to the hard tasks of balancing the equities between equally strong claims of right, indifferent also to the problems posed when the arguments advanced on rival sides of a dispute are so evenly matched that reason deadlocks against itself.

While rejecting all this, the Institute, on the positive side of its governing attitude, has consistently tried to draw close to and take its bearing from a prophetic view of human experience. It has tried to understand far more than newspaper polls or what appears in the snippets of pictures which flash in and out of view on the six o'clock televised news—all divorced from context. It has understood that good fortune does not stand still in one place forever; that, in human affairs, the problems of success can be as difficult as the problems of failure; but the roots of politics are moral, and that the object of politics is justice and not the exercise of power merely for the sake of dominion itself.

It has understood other things as well. It has understood that the data of the political process are the variable wants and needs of real people; that real people cannot be programmed like robots, nor are they easily manipulated, at least for very long. Real people must be addressed in the language of choice, which is the language of "if." If we do *this*, the possible consequences might be thus and so, but if we do *that*, the possible consequences might be the other way around. Moreover, real people must not only be addressed from above. They must also be listened to from below, must be galvanized into acts of choice by appeals to their reason and will, must share in the acts of persuasion and in the decisions affecting their destiny.

All this explains why the leading architects of the Institute and the principal participants in its efforts over the years have been, at bottom, "teachers." They have lived in the world long enough to be conscious of all its ambushes, conscious of the darkness in which even the best of prudent intentions often flounder. Yet, knowing this, and knowing also that there are proper objects for anger as well as for love, they have been braced from within to withstand the corrosive bite of cynical knowledge. So braced, the architects of the Institute and their principal associates in diverse efforts have worked to perceive the truth about themselves and to help others to do so in their own cases. They have accepted full responsibility for their own lives and for the acts of choice they have made in concrete situations. If they have put the problems of political choice in terms that are true to the problems, they are entitled to the hope that they—and the many benefactors who have contributed to the financial support of the Institute's work—will be numbered among the people who have planted the seeds for a better, brighter, and braver future.

INDEX